THE BEST OF
PETER FINNEY
LEGENDARY NEW ORLEANS
SPORTSWRITER

THE BEST OF
PETER FINNEY
LEGENDARY NEW ORLEANS SPORTSWRITER

Introduction by
PETER FINNEY JR.

LOUISIANA STATE UNIVERSITY PRESS
Baton Rouge

Published by Louisiana State University Press
Copyright © 2016 by Louisiana State University Press
All rights reserved
Manufactured in the United States of America
First printing

DESIGNER: Mandy McDonald Scallan
TYPEFACE: Verb, display; Sentinel, text
PRINTER AND BINDER: Maple Press, Inc.

Library of Congress Cataloging-in-Publication Data

Names: Finney, Peter, author.
Title: The best of Peter Finney : legendary New Orleans sportswriter /
  introduction by Peter Finney Jr.
Description: Baton Rouge : Louisiana State University Press, 2016. | Includes
  index.
Identifiers: LCCN 2015035408| ISBN 978-0-8071-6306-1 (cloth : alk. paper) | ISBN
  978-0-8071-6307-8 (pdf) | ISBN 978-0-8071-6308-5 (epub) | ISBN 978-0-8071-6309-2 (mobi)
Subjects: LCSH: Sports—United States. | Newspapers—Sections, columns,
  etc. —Sports. | Sports journalism—United States.
Classification: LCC GV707 .F54 2016 | DDC 796.0973—dc23 LC record available at http://lccn.loc.
gov/2015035408

*To my wonderful family—my six children and their spouses,
my twenty grandchildren, and my five great-grandchildren—and in
memory of my wife and best friend, Deedy.*

CONTENTS

3. BOXING

4. COLLEGE FOOTBALL

5. PRO FOOTBALL

THE BEST OF
PETER FINNEY
LEGENDARY NEW ORLEANS
SPORTSWRITER

PETER FINNEY JR.

The second-floor balcony at 825 Chartres Street in New Orleans, where my dad grew up one block from St. Louis Cathedral, hasn't changed much since the mid-1830s. The French Quarter gallery has thin, white, wooden slats. It's nine feet wide and thirty feet long—a captivating, hidden oasis where someone can sit in the evening shade with a friend and a cool drink and eavesdrop on random conversations bubbling up from the street. Even today, hoofbeats reverberate off the macadam, usually accompanied by tall tales. Mule-drawn-carriage tour operators have been known to tell wild tales—"Did you know Napoleon actually came to New Orleans to sign the Louisiana Purchase before he was exiled to Elba?"—and they're not afraid to stick to them.

John Gabriel Finney, my dad's father, operated a Catholic church supply house at the corner of Pere Antoine Alley and Royal Street, literally in the shadow of St. Louis Cathedral and directly across from St. Anthony's Garden. Today, the church supply store is an art studio run by the family of the late George Rodrigue, who turned blue dogs into lots of green. John and his wife, Clara Giacomino Finney, had four children, but their substantial Catholic family was buffered from the worst effects of the Great Depression because churches still were being built in the 1930s—and every church worth its patron saint needed a marble main altar, a couple of side altars, and life-sized statues. Vestments and prayer cards never went out of vogue. Every evening after work, John would stop at the front-room bar at Tujague's restaurant on Decatur Street, a block away from home, hold up two fingers, and then, like magic, receive a pre-dinner cocktail, measured exactly to his liking. After supper, John would retreat to the comfort of his Chartres Street balcony. For my dad, born on October 17, 1927, the balcony at 825 Chartres doubled during his childhood as a wrought-iron playpen.

The tallest tale my dad ever heard on a French Quarter balcony came when he was eight. His maternal grandmother—Marie Montedonico Gia-comino—took him out to the nearby gallery at the intersection of Chartres and Dumaine streets, where she had grown up, and held out her right arm. Marie made a sweeping motion, starting at the cathedral and continuing in the direction of Faubourg Marigny, and regaled her wide-eyed grandson with memories of the French Quarter traffic jam one night in 1892. You haven't heard about the traffic jam? It occurred on the evening of September 7, 1892, when "Gentleman Jim" Corbett of San Francisco and John L. Sullivan of Boston squared off at the Olympic Club in the 2700 block of Royal Street for the world heavyweight championship, the first title fight in America governed by the Marquis of Queensbury rules, which dictated the use of gloves and standardized the length of rounds to three minutes, with a one-minute rest period (before that time, a knockdown determined the length of a round).

"Peter, you should have seen the line of carriages—it went on forever," Marie told her grandson. "Everyone was riding down Chartres Street to see the fight." Perhaps the seed of my father's legendary sixty-eight-year sportswriting career was planted at that moment. In 1957, when he wrote "Evolution of the New Orleans Sports Page," his thesis for a master's degree in journalism at Louisiana State University that he completed while on assignment covering LSU football and basketball, he remembered his grandmother Marie's eyewitness story. No, he didn't exactly cover Corbett-Sullivan, but in a way, he was there.

"The match between the Boston strong-boy, who trained on beer and pretzels, and the gentlemanly young bank clerk from San Francisco was a study in contrasts tailor-made for sportswriters," he wrote in his 1957 thesis. "Sullivan was a muscle-bound braggart who had told the Prince of Wales: 'I've heard a lot about you. Do you ever put up your dukes?' On the other hand, Corbett was a fashion plate and intelligent athlete, who took a scientific approach to boxing."

"Gentleman Jim" won in twenty-one rounds, and the international notoriety attached to that event ignited a press war among the city's four major daily newspapers. The *Times-Democrat,* a morning paper, chartered several trains to carry special fight editions as far as Meridian, Mississippi, and put thirty thousand copies into the hands of Jackson, Mississippi, readers by 8:00 a.m. the next day. The rush to tell a good story is the lifeblood of every journalist. My dad always says he loved his job so much he never worked a day in his life: "All I do is write."

· · ·

Beginning as a college freshman in 1945 at Loyola University in New Orleans and continuing through his retirement in 2013, Peter Finney Sr. entertained, informed, and inspired readers of the *States-Item* (1945–80) and the *Times-Picayune* (1980–2013) with his elegantly poetic take on sports celebrities and sports nobodies. My dad couldn't beat up your dad, but he surely could out-metaphor him. The man who simply loved to write earned lifetime achievement awards from the Pro Football Hall of Fame (the Dick McCann Memorial Award in 2010 from the Pro Football Writers of America for his coverage of the National Football League) and the U.S. Basketball Writers Association's Hall of Fame (2012). The National Sportscasters and Sportswriters Association named him Sportswriter of the Year for Louisiana seventeen times. In 2013 the Louisiana Sports Writers Association renamed the columnist-of-the-year award in his honor.

Scattered among his nearly fifteen thousand columns and 12 million words are gems that have delighted both hardcore sports fans who wanted inside information and casual sports fans who simply liked a good story, well told. This book presents just seventy-five columns, most of them selected because they chronicle iconic moments in Louisiana sports history: Billy Cannon's 89-yard punt return against Ole Miss in 1959; Tom Dempsey's then-NFL-record 63-yard field goal in 1970; the Saints' 31–17 victory over the Indianapolis Colts in Super Bowl XLIV in 2010, four and a half years after the levees and all hell broke loose. Other columns were chosen because they are shining examples of his measured craftsmanship and wit.

Except for some minor editing for length, the columns run exactly as they first appeared in the *States-Item* or the *Times-Picayune,* and they appear here courtesy of the NOLA Media Group (www.nola.com). My father sets the stage for each column with a brief scene-setter that provides context or additional information.

Over the course of seven decades, my father interviewed and wrote about nearly every major sports figure of his time: Ted Williams; Jesse

Owens; Joe DiMaggio; Muhammad Ali; Joe Namath; Jack Nicklaus; Tiger Woods; Arnold Palmer; Billy Cannon; Pete Maravich; Lee Trevino; Archie, Peyton, and Eli Manning; Eddie Robinson; Doug Williams; Dale Brown; Rusty Staub; Billy Martin; Brett Favre; Nick Saban; Shaquille O'Neal; Mike Ditka; Sean Payton; and Drew Brees. He didn't exactly interview Secretariat, but he summed up the Triple Crown winner's dominance in a thirty-one-length victory in the 1973 Belmont: "The Belmont wasn't a horse race. It was a horse, one of those once-in-a-lifetime superstars whose greatness perhaps was best reflected in the way jaded New Yorkers lost their composure and acted like little kids as Secretariat came screaming to Triple Crown glory."

Preference in selecting columns for this book was given to Louisiana events or celebrities who had a tie to New Orleans, but there are a few delicious surprises. One of my favorites is a classic 1963 take on the founding father of pro wrestling—"Gorgeous George" Wagner, who turned a backroads traveling circus into a multi-million-dollar entertainment spectacle. Wagner was in New Orleans for an exhibition, and the column lead said it all:

"You'll have to excuse my appearance," said the fellow whose well-scarred dome was flanked by two cauliflower ears and topped by wavy, white locks. "Today is Sunday, and all the beauty parlors are closed."

I had caught Gorgeous George with his hair down.

And this, on preparations for the 1972 global chess war between Russian-Armenian Boris Spassky and the quintessential ugly American, Bobby Fischer:

Brent Larsen, a grandmaster who doesn't hide his personal dislike for Brooklyn Bobby, calls Fischer "an arrogant young man who likes to see his opponents squirm." Once asked who he thought was the world's greatest player, Fischer replied: "It would be nice to be modest but it would be stupid if I did not tell the truth. I am."

• • •

Even a cursory reading of my dad's 178-page master's thesis delivers a clear message to the reader: Peter Finney did his homework, and he could relate a multilayered story in simple, direct language. Why was New Orleans such a vibrant sports town? Here's a quick answer, from his thesis introduction:

If there is anything that can surpass New Orleans' reputation as a gourmet's delight, it is her tradition as a sportsmen's mecca—a tradition as brilliant as that of any city in the United States.

Some evidence of this can be found in her claim to the country's oldest tennis club (New Orleans Lawn Tennis Club founded in 1876), the country's second oldest yacht club (Southern Yacht Club founded in 1849), and the country's third oldest race track (Fair Grounds founded in 1872).

But there is more when you consider New Orleans raced thoroughbreds and was a party to bare-knuckle fights, cock fights and dog fights at a time when the nation at large frowned on such things.

New Orleans, among other things, witnessed the introduction of fencing in America; witnessed the first use of boxing gloves; produced Paul Morphy, one of the greatest of all chess masters, and Pete Herman, the South's first boxing champion; watched Black Gold, a turf immortal, run his first race; and Earl Sande, the master jockey, ride his first winner.

It was in New Orleans that the longest fight in boxing history (110 rounds) was fought and that Ladies Day and the rain check were introduced to baseball. It was here also that the Cincinnati Red Stockings discovered five different amateur baseball teams capable of beating them; that Jack Dempsey knocked out Carl Morris in 14 seconds, one of the shortest kayos on record; that the great Bobby Jones lost to Nelson Whitney, 7-and-6, in the Southern Golf Championships; that Count Bernard Mandeville de Marigny introduced dice into this country.

All of this, of course, was in addition to the world-famous Sullivan-Corbett fistic epic, climaxing a boxing extravaganza in which New Orleans played host to three championship bouts on succeeding days.

His careful thesis research yielded this long-forgotten nugget on how New Orleans newspapers transmitted pictures from the LSU-Tulane game in Baton Rouge in the 1930s, before photos were transmitted by wire signal. Three photographers and their assistants would attend the game. After each major play early in the first quarter, an assistant would scribble a note to be placed in a box along with the photo negative, which then would be rushed back to New Orleans in time to make the morning paper. The *Times-Picayune* also employed an ingenious method to transport photographers' film quickly from Tulane Stadium to the newspaper's offices at Lafayette Square, about four miles away: photographers placed their film rolls in small pouches and attached the bags to carrier pigeons, kept at the ready in cages at the stadium, and the birds made the flight to the office in just a few minutes.

Take that, Steve Jobs.

• • •

Who knows what professional career my dad would have pursued had it not been for a chance encounter in June 1945—right after he had graduated from Jesuit High School—between his father and his friend Mr. Schaeffer, who owned Schaeffer's jewelry store on Carondelet Street downtown. A sports fanatic, Schaeffer had just returned from the offices of the *New Orleans States,* where he had taken out an ad and learned from his good friend, sports editor Harry Martinez, that the afternoon newspaper was searching for a reporter to cover high school sports, especially American Legion baseball.

"Didn't your son write for the school paper at Jesuit?" Mr. Schaeffer asked my grandfather. "He ought to go down and apply." My dad had played basketball at Jesuit and had served as the sports editor and editor in chief of the *Blue Jay,* the school newspaper, and he was looking for at least a part-time job to defray some of his college tuition expenses at Loyola. He walked in off the street, showed Martinez a few of his *Blue Jay* clips, and was hired on the spot at age eighteen.

The September 14, 1945, *Blue Jay*—three months after his high school graduation—ran a page 6 story carrying news of his landing a full-time job with the *States:*

Pete Finney, former sports editor and editor in chief of the *Blue Jay,* has taken another stride in the journalistic world. After being graduated from Jesuit with honors, Pete jumped right into a position as sports writer for the *New Orleans States.* His familiar "by-line" was flashed on the sports page consistently as the promising young scribe covered the American Legion baseball campaign and the city tennis tournament. The powers that be saw fit to send Finney to Austin, Texas, and Oklahoma City with the New Orleans baseball representatives, the Jays.

Versatility is Finney's middle name. In addition to his writing talents, Pete was a stellar guard on the runner-up Jay quintet, honor student and vice president of his class, and is very adept at other sports. Golf is one of his major hobbies, where he invariably shoots in the nineties. Ping pong and pool are the other sports in which he excels.

Getting back to his journalistic achievements, as a sophomore and junior Finney, as sports editor, paved the way for the "All American" and "All Catholic" honors that were bestowed on [the *Blue Jay*] under his editorship as a senior.

Since the *States* was an afternoon paper, he could cover prep games in the afternoon and evening, write his stories, work the copy desk in the morning, and then take most of his journalism classes at Loyola in the afternoon. He never wrote for the *Maroon,* the Loyola school newspaper, because he was already working full-time. "People always ask how I managed to work and go to college at the same time," he said, "but I just arranged my classes around it."

My dad played four years of basketball as a guard at Loyola, proudly pointing to his 37-point output—for an entire season—as a divine sign he should use his left hand for hunting-and-pecking a keyboard rather than taking set shots. Having played on basketball teams since his CYO days, he knew more about basketball than any other sport. In fact, after Loyola games, he would head down to the *States* and write a story about the game in which he had just played.

One story, at least, never made the *States.* After finally performing well enough to make the Wolfpack travel squad as a junior, he joined his teammates for a road game in Chattanooga, Tennessee. At the team hotel, Loyola head coach Jack Orsley assembled his players for their pregame meal, and they ordered off the menu. Not knowing the routine, my dad ordered a steak, medium rare. When Orsley saw the waiter rolling out the steak and pulling the silver lid off the plate with a theatrical flair—while everyone else was chowing down on chicken or hamburgers—he decided that would be the last time a backup guard with a limited shooting range would make a road trip.

All was forgiven, however, after my dad graduated from Loyola in 1949. Perhaps because the price was right, Loyola hired him to coach the "Wolfpups," Loyola's freshman basketball team, all while covering Loyola sports for the *States*. He later served in the late 1950s and 1960s as Loyola's part-time sports information director, sending out press releases to media outlets. Yes, it was a far different media world then.

My dad was an excellent student—he especially loved history—but even as a teenager, he had a strain of tunnel vision that often could be confused with absent-mindedness. One afternoon, he was scheduled to cover a baseball game at Audubon Park. Normally he would have taken the streetcar or bus from the French Quarter, but this time his dad had given him the keys to the family car. Everything went fine until after the game, when a reporter covering for the *Times-Picayune* graciously offered him a ride back to the office. My dad said, "Thanks, that would be great." The next morning, his father was down one car. "Peter, where's the car?" "Uh . . . it's in Audubon Park." My dad's younger sister, Patricia Finney Daniels, said the family considered having Tom, the youngest and most organized of the four Finney children, tag along with my dad on his future assignments just in case he needed to be straightened out on mundane details.

• • •

One day in late 1950, walking into an elevator at the *States,* my dad actually did have his head turned, this time for keeps. Doris (Deedy) Young, a light-haired, petite classified-ad telephone clerk, flashed her wide smile, compelling him to glance up from the stack of out-of-town newspapers he always seemed to be carrying under his arm. They were married on January 3, 1952, and in what became a repeating chord played softly throughout their sixty-one years of marriage, they seamlessly combined pleasure with business: their honeymoon was in Mobile, Alabama, where my dad covered a few expenses by filing stories on the Senior Bowl.

My parents had the kind of marriage my five siblings and I considered a movable feast. We knew we were loved because my parents loved each other. Their loving commitment and their unity created the foundation for an incredibly happy childhood. My dad attached a sports event to each child's birth to help him remember the year in which we were born.

In November 1974, when my sister Barbara Finney Weilbaecher was in heavy labor with my dad's first grandchild, the labor nurse kept trying to get the obstetrician into the delivery room. The problem was that the doctor was a huge Tulane fan, and he was peppering my dad with a million questions about the LSU-Tulane game that weekend. Finally, my mom walked up and got the doctor to concentrate on the human football—Peter Weilbaecher—about to be snapped.

My dad taught my little brother Michael, then in grade school, a lesson he had learned in his own youth. Michael was up late, as usual, finishing his homework, and he needed to sharpen his pencil. The only problem was, the electric pencil sharpener was located in a study right next to my parents' bedroom, and they were both sound asleep. Michael evaluated his options and decided to wake up my dad, who grabbed the pencil out of his hand and raced toward the kitchen. "I followed him because I wondered what he was doing," Michael recalled. "When I got to the kitchen, he took out a steak knife and started to whittle the pencil down." Michael said, "Dad, there's a sharpener in the back room!" My dad gave Michael "the stare"—and a hand-sharpened pencil—and went back to bed.

My parents were grounded in reality, and they handled crises as they arose. When my dad was a guest on a local radio show one evening, my mom was home alone with six children and an almost-empty refrigerator. So she picked up the telephone, got through the switchboard to my dad, and asked over the air, "Can you pick up two gallons of milk and a loaf of bread before you come home?"

When my mom passed away in 2013 after a lengthy illness, my dad, as always, summed up their relationship simply: "She was my best friend."

You could always tell when the Finney family was coming—all you had to do was close your eyes and listen. Somewhere around the corner, the blue-and-white Volkswagen bus, with its 57-horsepower rear engine, was chugging along, packed with two parents and six kids and equipped with no seat belts. In those dark, benighted days before Ralph Nader, life was good. With its three rows of utilitarian seating, plus a nice hatchback to store another kid or two, the VW bus was the weapon of choice for a large Catholic family. My dad once explained to his friend and former *States-Item* sportswriter Charlie Young why he had bought the van: "Charlie, it's important for every kid to have a window."

Vacations to the Trade Winds Motor Hotel on the Mississippi Gulf Coast for a week each summer ran like clockwork, depending on engine compression. My mom and dad would pack us and anything that didn't move into the van, and then set off on I-10. Approaching the high rise that led to New Orleans East, my dad would slam the accelerator to the floor to coax the van up to 60 mph—and then say a prayer. By the time we sputtered to the top of the high rise, we might have been doing 20 mph. Looking out from the rear window, I learned to read lips as drivers veered around us. But it didn't matter. Once we reached the top of the mountain, we took it on faith that we really would have a vacation that year. Next stop, the Trade Winds!

In any New Orleans family of eight—living on a newspaperman's salary—life is about sacrifice and red beans and rice. My mom fretted a lot over the years about how to pay that forty-four-dollar-a-month house note, but somehow she and my dad did. All those side jobs my dad gobbled up at every opportunity balanced the budget. And each of us went to Catholic school. Throw in our first cousins—the children of my dad's older brother John—and there was a Finney in every grade at St. Leo the Great School. You just weren't sure who belonged to whom.

In 1968 my dad wrote a book about LSU football—*The Fighting Tigers: Seventy-Five Years of LSU Football*—and he and my mom finally had something called disposable income. Instead of the Trade Winds, they took us to the Gulf Hills Dude Ranch in Ocean Springs, Mississippi, a gilded resort in our eyes, where there were rolling hills, golf, swimming, tennis, and horseback riding. The thing I remember the most about that vacation was my mom taking us to breakfast in the main dining hall. In the middle of the room was a silver fountain, with tiny holes strategically located. From each hole, fresh-squeezed orange juice poured out, and all you had to do was hold your cup steady and watch it fill up. The bacon was as thick as my index finger. We hadn't died, but we had gone to heaven.

Our mom almost never refused a task or sacrifice—although one day we did get on her last nerve and she got in the VW and drove a few blocks to get away from the craziness of six kids. Since word traveled fast on Hathaway Place—the horseshoe street where we grew up—one of the neighborhood moms came over to lay down the law to us: "Stop doing things to upset your mother!" Stay-at-home moms had each other's back in those days.

Sacrifice is never easy, but my mom embodied that. In addition to her six children, she had seven miscarriages. Her small body had been poured out as a libation. A charm bracelet she wore included small pendants representing all 13 of her children.

The day after her funeral, my dad, my two sons (Peter III, who is a Catholic priest, and Jonathan) and I spoke to about 350 men at St. Anthony of Padua Church on Canal Street about what it was like being the leader of and growing up in a large Catholic family. The event had been planned long before my mother's death, but my dad insisted on going as a way of celebrating my mom's life. The outpouring of support he received from friends and total strangers was an incredible blessing for all of us, especially my dad. He deflected any praise toward him to Deedy. "I have a great family, and a great wife," he said.

• • •

Bernard Saverio Diliberto—forever known to the Who Dat Nation as "Buddy D"—was another Jesuit graduate, four years younger than my dad. When people ask if Buddy D could have played in Peoria, I always give thanks that Peoria is in someone else's focus group. Buddy D died of a heart attack on January 7, 2005—eight months before Hurricane Katrina—and he probably was my dad's closest friend.

The two New Orleans sportswriters—Buddy D graduated to TV and radio in the 1960s—couldn't have been more dissimilar. Buddy didn't need a focus group to tell him what played in New Orleans because, in a very real way, he was New Orleans. His exotic speech patterns had potholes large enough to swallow a "Mitsubishi"—just the memory of Buddy D trying to squeeze that word past his lips in a commercial still triggers uncontrollable laughter—but we all understood what he said and where he stood. (What does that say about us? Actually, it makes me feel pretty good.) Buddy D's heart was bigger than his fifty-thousand-watt mouth.

As a sportswriter in New York during the 1980s, I had the good fortune to cover a series of Super Bowls, and on the Tuesday before the game, thousands of reporters and photographers would crowd around quarterbacks such as Joe Montana and Jim Plunkett to ask inane questions and then follow up by asking incredibly inane questions. On one occasion, someone asked Plunkett, whose parents were disabled: "Jim, let me get this straight. Is your mother blind and your father deaf, or is your mother deaf and your father blind?" From the back of the pack, waving his microphone like a drawn sword, Buddy D would cut to the chase, bellowing out a question of substance with an inflection only a Barq's-swigging, crawfish-sucking New Orleanian could truly appreciate. When Buddy D's voice rang out, I remember a reporter next to me asking: "Who is *that* guy?" That was Buddy D, the guy who asked the questions everyone wanted to ask but was waiting for someone else to ask.

When my dad was called up for active duty with the 122nd Light Bombardment Squadron of the Louisiana Air National Guard in March 1951—as part of the nation's military readiness for the Korean Conflict—Buddy was there at the Union Passenger Terminal in New Orleans, tearing up and waving my dad good-bye as he boarded his train for Langley Air Force Base in Hampton, Virginia, just south of Washington, DC. My dad served at Langley for eighteen months, but the closest he got to any conflict was taking out the base's garbage cans. On weekend furloughs, my dad relied on his knowledge of geography: Langley was close enough to Manhattan to hop a train and catch a few Broadway shows.

Buddy, meanwhile, enlisted in the army and actually shipped out to Korea, where he earned a Purple Heart after catching shrapnel in the backside from an exploding bomb. "There I was, taking shrapnel in a bunker in Korea, and there you were, in New York City, watching *The King and I* and Judy Garland on Broadway," Buddy used to kid my dad. A decade or so later, when Buddy and my dad were in Manhattan covering a Saints game, they finally took in a Broadway show together. As the theater darkened and the orchestra played the overture for three or four minutes, Buddy had seen enough. He leaned over to my dad. In his classic New Orleans stage whisper, Buddy shouted: "Pete, they can't get the curtain open!"

In 1980, when the Saints started 0–14, Buddy pulled a paper bag from beneath his chair during a live broadcast leading into Monday Night Football and placed it over his head—instantly creating the "Ain'ts." The gag caught on with Saints fans and created a nationwide fad. The only problem was that when Buddy D put the bag over his head, not many could understand his fractured English, which former *States-Item* columnist Angus Lind aptly described as "Dilibonics."

When the Bears came to New Orleans to play the Patriots in Super Bowl XX, Buddy D was doing television for WDSU-TV in New Orleans and got a telephone call at his broadcast desk just before the end of the 10:00 p.m. news. It was a friend from another radio station, "tipping him off" that Bears quarterback Jim McMahon had been overheard on Bourbon Street calling the women of New Orleans "sluts." Buddy went with the information as a teaser at the end of the broadcast. When the story didn't pan out, Diliberto was told by NBC network officials to leave town for the week. "They told me to get out of the area code," Buddy told my dad. Buddy wound up watching the Super Bowl from Pensacola, Florida.

Nevertheless, Saints fans loved him because he wore his emotions on his sleeve and never mouthed the company line. When Jim Mora was crashing and burning at the end of his career, Diliberto made a special trip to Baton Rouge to speak confidentially to Gov. Edwin Edwards, hoping the governor would pressure Saints owner Tom Benson to hire Mike Ditka back from the TV booth. My dad went with him, not knowing exactly what the meeting was all about. He was under the impression they would be interviewing Edwards, not lobbying for Ditka. After Ditka eventually got the job and went 15–33 in three train-wreck seasons, Buddy D admitted on the air: "That's going to be on my tombstone."

My dad and Buddy D shared that trait: Always admit it when you're wrong. Buddy also could poke fun at my dad. Even into the 1980s, Buddy would harangue him about getting his mug shot in the newspaper updated. "You're still using your confirmation picture!" Buddy would tell him.

• • •

After many years of covering prep leagues, the *States* assigned my dad in 1954 to cover LSU, the premier sports beat for a young, energetic sportswriter. He reported on the final year of head coach Gaynell Tinsley, who was fired after a 5–6 season and a ninth-place finish in the Southeastern Conference.

When Paul Dietzel was hired from Earl Blaik's Army staff in 1955, LSU endured three more nonwinning seasons before breaking through in 1958 with a perfect 11–0 record to win the national championship. My dad never forgot what Dietzel told him a few months later—it had nothing to do with college football—when the Green Bay Packers hired a relatively obscure New York Giants assistant, a man Dietzel had coached with on Blaik's staff, as their new head coach. "Watch out for Vince Lombardi," Dietzel told my dad in February 1959. "He's the best coach I've ever been around." Five NFL championships in seven years proved Dietzel correct.

After the thirty-four-year-old Dietzel won the national championship in 1958, my dad broke the news that LSU's board of administrators had decided to write him a new five-year contract calling for $16,500 a season—a $2,500 increase over his most recent salary. Nick Saban earned $7.16 million to coach Alabama in 2014.

One of the most intriguing LSU stories he covered was the furor triggered by Billy Cannon signing a contract with Bud Adams of the AFL's Houston Oilers under the goalposts after the Sugar Bowl on January 1, 1960. One month earlier, Cannon secretly had signed a contract with the NFL's Los Angeles Rams, whose general manager was future commissioner Pete Rozelle, after the Rams had selected Cannon in the first round of the NFL draft. The case wound up in court, and the judge ultimately ruled in Houston's favor, saying the Rams had taken advantage of "a naive country boy." Whenever Rozelle met my dad over the next thirty years, the commissioner would flash a wide smile and ask, "So how's that naive country boy doing?"

• • •

My earliest memories of my dad come from our Christmas home movies. Later, in the 1960s, I knew exactly when he was home. He'd walk into our house in Gentilly smelling like a cigar. My dad never smoked, a rarity for a journalist in those days. But during eight-hour shifts inside the old open newsroom of the *States-Item* on Lafayette Square—with redlined copy flying around to different editing stations on black conveyor belts and white glue pots providing a primitive form of "copy and paste"—the smog produced by cigars crowded out the oxygen and permeated his clothes.

My dad is a master storyteller who has had a profound impact on my life. My sister Beth Finney Donze and I are journalists because he was. It's that simple. He taught us some important lessons: The word "that"—when used after "said"—is the most overused word in the English language; be willing to admit it when you make a mistake; be fair; keep your writing short and snappy.

Once when Beth was in elementary school, she dictated a short-story assignment for him to key in on the typewriter. As she spoke, he mentally edited out some of her superfluous words, telling her like an English professor: "Just say it!" I type with four fingers because I learned to beat on his old Royal typewriter, fascinated by the mystery of carbon copies. I was unafraid to make mistakes—that's what the "X" key and red pencils were for. My spell-check was Webster's dictionary. I never crashed and completely lost a story unless someone took out the garbage.

My dad can say more in a couple of sentences than most people can say in a thousand. He once summed up the tactless criticism leveled by Mike Ditka that his wife Diana had to suffer living in New Orleans because of a limited supply of high-end shopping boutiques: "Keep one thing in mind. Mike and Diana, at the moment double-parked in New Orleans, will always be Chicago folks who can't wait to get back 'home.'"

Those life lessons still resonate and came into sharper focus in 2007 with an unusual convergence of circumstances. When LSU crushed Virginia Tech 48–7 at Tiger Stadium, my dad wrote a column for the *Times-Picayune;* I covered the game for my former newspaper, the *New York Post;* and my son Jonathan reported for the *Daily Reveille,* the LSU student newspaper. Jonathan was a nineteen-year-old sophomore at LSU at the time, and he was studying mass communications. In reflecting on three generations of Finneys covering a football game from the same press box, I wrestled with the image of the carbon paper winding through the roller of the manual typewriter. We are not carbon copies—I am not my father and my son is not me—but in so many ways we are blessed to share in a vocation that can bring joy and enlightenment to others. One of my prized possessions is a large poster in a gold frame—given to us by my son, Father Peter Finney III—that has all three of our stories in a purple matting. The headline reads: "A Three-Generation Press Box."

After more than a year of studying communications, Jonathan decided to switch majors to kinesiology and since then has graduated from LSU Medical School. After he made the decision to change his course of studies, Jonathan fretted over how he would tell my father, because he thought he might be disappointed. "Are you serious, Jonathan?" my dad told him, laughing, recalling his days of taking every freelance job to keep the family budget out of the red. "That's the best decision you've ever made in your life." Dr. Jonathan bleeds purple and gold. The grandfather he calls Poppa bleeds black ink.

. . .

Before the New Orleans Saints were born—on All Saints Day, November 1, 1966—my dad relied mostly on college football, college basketball, boxing, horse racing, golf, and major league baseball to provide the raw material for the five columns he did each week for the *States-Item*. His pro football focus ramped up when the Saints came to town with a cast of characters better suited to a Mel Brooks screenplay.

In reviewing the first ten years of Saints' sins on the field—both venial and mortal—my dad tried to keep his readers from wallowing in despair. The Saints had produced so many cheap laughs:

• The time linebacker Steve Stonebreaker threw an expensive punch during a Yankee Stadium free-for-all against the Giants, which triggered the creation of The Touchdown Club, a group of fans who tried to help Stonebreaker pay his NFL fine.

• The time ageless Doug Atkins, who at six foot eight, 280 pounds, and age thirty-seven, told his roommate at training camp at Cal Western, "I know how to stop this," and then fired a shot through the ceiling of his dorm room to quiet some noisy rookies in the room above.

• The time Archie Manning tried to dive for a touchdown near the goal line against Chicago only to have a Bears defender knock the ball loose and send it squirting backward like a greased pigskin until it wound up near midfield.

• The time the Falcons pounded the Saints 62–7 at Tulane Stadium in 1973.

• The time linebacker Johnny Brewer, checking in near the end of his career, made sure his good plays didn't go unnoticed. He sneaked into a meeting room of coaches after the lights had gone out and the game film was rolling, and when the film showed Brewer involved in a good play, he'd shout in a muffled voice from the back of the room, "Run it back. Who was that? Brewer?"

• The time Coach Tom Fears, upset by his team's repeated special-teams mistakes, decided to take charge in practice. Injuries had created confusion on special teams, so, Fears was explaining, special team- ers should be ready to fill in. "Dodd down," he offered as an example, "means Al Dodd's replacement should run onto the field and take Dodd's place." In practice, the kickoff team, one that included de- fensive lineman Richard Neal, went onto the field. Standing in his coaching tower, Fears shouted, "Neal down," hoping Neal's replace- ment on the kickoff team would take Neal's spot. Nothing happened. "Neal down!" Fears screamed again. Again, no movement. "Dammit, I said, 'Neal down!'" By this time, Doug Atkins got into the act. Hav- ing no idea what was going on, he yelled, "You heard coach. Every- body kneel down." Whereupon forty players did exactly that. They knelt down. In the tower, Fears was purple. "Everybody get up," he screamed. "I said, 'Neal down.'" Guys were kneeling, standing up, and then kneeling down again. It was like being in church.

That was the trouble with the Saints. People remembered them more for fights, follies, and misdirected cannon shots during Tommy Walker's halftime extravaganzas than for touchdowns and goal-line stands. By the time they had played ten seasons, they were already on their third canine mascot (a St. Bernard named "Gumbo"). Entering the 1977 sea- son, my dad wrote this about the Saints possibly running afoul of the Louisiana SPCA.

Gumbo I ate rocks and died.

Gumbo II escaped. Apparently, he couldn't take it any more. He's still at large. No kidding.

Gumbo III slept through a couple of games last fall, suggesting the Saints might be sued for cruelty to St. Bernards.

Question: Can the '77 Saints keep Gumbo III awake? Or will the torture (the victims, when you consider the 10-year record, have to be ranked among the most loyal fans in all of sport) continue into a second decade?

Of course, the torture did continue—and far beyond the second decade. One of his greatest lines about the Saints spending forty years wandering in the desert came in 1997, when the Saints and the Bears—two teams headed nowhere—locked horns in a game the Saints finally won, 20–17, on an 89-yard TD pass from Heath Shuler to Randal Hill. Throw out that play, and the Saints passed for just 96 yards that day. "You felt like you were looking at two coffins on wheels playing bumper cars," he wrote. The Saints finished 6–10 that year, the Bears 4–12.

• • •

One of my dad's staples was his annual New Year's Eve column, in which he would predict the winners and losers in all the major sporting competitions over the upcoming twelve months. He got the idea from Pete Baird, dean of the city's horse-racing writers, who would compile a complete Kentucky Derby order-of-finish chart before the race was even run. "You ought to do that for the entire year in sports," Baird suggested. The New Year's Eve prediction column, mostly light-hearted, started in the early 1960s. Readers would cut out the column, put checks on the "hits" and X's on the "misses," and then mail my dad the results from time to time. "I never knew so many grown people had crayons," he laughed.

His 1964 predictions were clairvoyant in one respect. He predicted that after the 1964 football season, LSU and Syracuse would be invited to the Sugar Bowl. It was an amazing prediction because not only did he get the teams right, but at the time the pairing would have been impossible: the Louisiana state law prohibited sports competition between whites and blacks, and Syracuse had several prominent black players, including running backs Floyd Little and Jim Nance. The law was overturned in early 1964, but my dad had no way of knowing that would happen. When his colleague Marty Mulé expounded on what a great insight he had and wondered if he had known for certain the state supreme court would overturn the law, he replied, "What, Louisiana had a law like that? I didn't know that."

Racial integration came late both to the sports fields and the press box, especially in the South. *States-Item* editor Walter Cowan, a progressive, was looking for ways to increase the coverage of predominantly black schools in the sports section. Cowan had heard of R. L. Stockard, who had worked part-time for the *Baton Rouge State-Times* while he was the sports information director at Southern University in Baton Rouge. When Stockard gave up that job to become a professor at Southern University in New Orleans, Cowan offered him a part-time job in 1960 to cover black high school and college sports for the *States-Item*. That decision did not sit too well with many of the *States-Item* staffers. Stockard recalls that when he walked into the paper's cavernous newsroom on Lafayette Square for the first time, no one even bothered to acknowledge his presence. "I learned how to deal with it by finding a desk as far away as possible and typing my stories," Stockard said. It was the ultimate freeze-out. Just then, my dad came into the office, approached Stockard's desk, and extended his hand, saying, "Hi, I'm Peter Finney, and I work in the sports department. I just want to let you know, if you need anything, just let me know." Stockard told me he never forgot that moment. "At that time, the only African Americans who worked in the building were janitors," Stockard said. "Your dad was the first non–African American at the paper who talked to me and made me feel welcome. He flashed that big smile. I can't tell you how that made me feel. I'll never forget it."

Darrell Williams was among several African American sportswriters who worked their way up at the *Times-Picayune,* covering the prep beat before being assigned to the college or pro beat. Williams covered the NBA Finals with my dad in 1994, and he marveled at the way my father could get information out of players and coaches by asking simple, direct questions. In the meantime, Williams was running around interviewing as many players and coaches as possible to put together a comprehensive story and notebook. "I was running on so much adrenaline," Williams said. "One day, when we were about to sit down and write, he told me, 'You make friends easily. That's a big deal in this business.'" Williams said he's never forgotten the encouraging words.

• • •

In third grade, I had a school picture taken in my St. Leo the Great school uniform. When we got the strip of thumbnail-size photos back a few weeks later, I remember cutting out one of the photos and scribbling a note to my dad on the back: "To my playful father." That pretty much sums up the essence of my father's personality. He can face even difficult situations with a playful heart. He's always believed humor is an essential ingredient for a long, happy life.

Sportswriter Bill Bumgarner was walking with my dad one day at Lakewood Country Club in the 1970s. They were following Jack Nicklaus, whose clubs were being toted by his cult-hero caddie, Angelo Argea, who sported a gray Afro that looked like a leftover wig from Mardi Gras. When Jack walked off the first green, my dad turned to Bumgarner and asked: "Is it a two-stroke penalty if your golf ball gets caught in Angelo's hair?"

Deadline pressure is something that never seemed to worry my dad, although he did appreciate having the freedom to think about what he wanted to write. Producing five good columns a week was a beast of a responsibility, and he was constantly mulling over ideas for his next column. Often he was oblivious to the real world, especially if that world had something to do with automobiles.

My brother Tim and I were with him one August day when he was driving the VW minivan across the Causeway bridge to get to St. Paul's School in Covington, where the Saints were training. As he approached the south Causeway toll booth, we expected him to slow down, but he zoomed right through. "Hey, stop!" the toll clerk yelled, leaning his body outside the booth. My dad slammed on the brakes of the VW, put the stick shift in reverse, and sheepishly rolled backwards to the booth. "I'm sorry," he told the attendant, reaching in his pocket for a dollar bill. "I was thinking about my next column."

Gil LeBreton, a sports columnist with the *Fort Worth Star-Telegram* and formerly a staff sportswriter with the *Times-Picayune,* covered the 1984 Los Angeles Olympics together with my dad. The main press center was the downtown Los Angeles Convention Center, and they decided to head out for lunch. For some reason, my dad was driving the rental car. He left the parking garage and turned left . . . then left at the corner . . . then left at the next corner. That's where an L.A. police officer pulled the car over. "Sir, do you realize you just turned the wrong way three times onto three successive streets?" the officer asked. This was not exactly a rhetorical question. Shrugging his shoulders, my dad, expecting the cop to understand, said: "I'm from New Orleans."

The ultimate happened one day when my dad locked his keys in the car—somehow with the engine still running. "Well, it'll turn off when we run out of gas," he told me. The American Automobile Association took a hit whenever it allowed my dad to sign up for yearly coverage. He is what emergency service professionals would call a loss leader. My sister Beth was in the car with him one day at a Popeye's fried chicken place, just after the fast-food industry had invented something called a drive-thru lane. My dad shouted his order—into a trash can.

But he always was able to keep his head in pressure situations, usually using humor as his shield. In Super Bowl XX, the Bears were beating the Patriots 23–3 at halftime on their way to what would be a 46–10 rout. But at halftime, theoretically at least, the game was not over, and there certainly was no need to choose a story angle just yet, even though the *Picayune* had about twenty people covering the game. My dad doesn't like to lock onto the ideal angle for his column until, well, the ideal angle hits him. The idea might come early in the game, but more often than not, the light bulb goes off after the postgame interviews. At halftime, *Picayune* sportswriter Les East said a nervous editor, with checklist in hand, was trying to pin down everyone's story angles. The editor asked my dad—probably four hours before deadline—what his column was going to be about. My father looked up at him with a straight face and replied, "The Preakness." The editor left him alone after that.

· · ·

My father's reporting and writing skills were tested under extreme pressure when he flew to New York on June 24, 1975, to cover local hero Tony Licata, who was battling Carlos Monzon for the WBA middleweight championship at Madison Square Garden. My dad took a nonstop Delta flight to JFK. He chose Delta because it was scheduled to get into JFK a little earlier than another nonstop from New Orleans, Eastern Flight 66.

When he arrived at JFK that afternoon, there was a thunderstorm brewing. A few minutes later, while he was still at the airport, Eastern Flight 66 crashed at 4:10 p.m. while attempting to land, killing 112 of the 124 people on board. The cause was severe wind shear. When the *States-Item* sports staff heard the news, George Sweeney, not knowing what flight my dad had taken, called my mom. "What airline did Peter take to New York?" George asked. Deedy replied: "Delta." "Are you sure?" "Yes."

At the horrific crash site, my dad collected whatever information he could. Eyewitnesses said the plane was coming in too low and hit a light tower before bursting into flames. The headline in the *States-Item* read, "Flash of Fire in the Sky Leaves 'Field of Bodies'":

By Peter Finney

New York—A "field of bodies" is the way a New York policeman, one of the first on the scene, described yesterday's crash of an Eastern Airlines 727 bound from New Orleans International Airport to New York.

"It was impossible to tell who was alive," he said. Unfortunately, there weren't many alive after the 4:10 p.m. crash not far from Kennedy International Airport—its destination....

Mo Friedman, an airport employee, described the crash scene as "a big flash of fire, like an atomic bomb. The flames went up in the air about 500 or 600 feet. She went right across the highway. The rain was coming down pretty heavy."...

"The bodies I picked up fell apart in my hands," said ambulance driver Gene Zerskey. "I saw one kid about 20 years old who was just wandering around in the bushes. He didn't know who he was. He was in a complete state of shock."

Two priests moved among the mass of bodies, administering last rites. Their somber faces told a story. As priests, they are used to death. Such massive death, they are not used to. Nobody is.

• • •

In August 2010, six months after the Saints beat the Colts in Super Bowl XLIV, my dad received the Dick McCann Memorial Award at the annual Pro Football Hall of Fame Enshrinees Dinner in Canton, Ohio, symbolic of his lifetime excellence in covering the NFL.

He doesn't really like public speaking—that's one of the reasons he never went into local TV when he could have made a lot more money than he did by writing for a living. My dad has always been great at knowing himself, discerning his strengths. But on this night he was a classic storyteller. He spoke from the heart—with no notes—and kept his stories, like his writing, short and to the point.

He was eighty-two at the time, and he was celebrating sixty-five years of sportswriting, so he decided to have some fun at his own expense with the twelve thousand fans assembled at the Canton Civic Center. "I understand I'm the first winner of this award to have actually seen the Canton Bulldogs play," he said, eliciting roars from the sellout crowd. "Off the record, Jim Thorpe was a fine player, but he was a terrible interview!"

He got serious, though, when he acknowledged what the Super Bowl victory meant to a city that Hurricane Katrina had almost wiped off the map four and a half years earlier. "Seriously, I'm coming from a city that has proven how important a pro football team is," he said. "It's incredible what the New Orleans Saints have done for the city of New Orleans, the state of Louisiana and the whole region.

"You've got this coach [Sean Payton] who won the Super Bowl—he's the first coach to win the Super Bowl and go to sleep with the Lombardi Trophy. Since that time, the trophy has been circulating throughout the state and the region. It's a pep rally, the Holy Grail. First, there was Hurricane Katrina, then the oil spill. It's been a beacon of hope; it's like the season never ended.

"I still can't believe the Saints won the Super Bowl," he added, drawing more laughter. "But if No. 9 [Drew Brees] stays healthy, they've got a chance to win it again."

That was it. Three minutes. Short and sweet.

When ESPN's Chris Berman was presented with the Pete Rozelle Radio-Television Award, an honor given to someone in the broadcasting field, Berman spoke for twenty-seven minutes. "I didn't realize ESPN invented the game of football," someone said.

Everyone needs an editor. But on this night, my dad did just fine without one.

"When I think of New Orleans, I think of Peter," said Jerry Izenberg, the veteran columnist of the *Newark Star-Ledger,* who has covered every Super Bowl. "That city needs Peter. I hope the people of New Orleans understand what they have in him."

"It's never been like work to me," my dad said. "It's something I enjoy doing. That's how I feel. I've just been lucky to hang around, I guess."

• • •

It was March of 1972, and the balcony at 825 Chartres Street hosted another big event in my dad's life.

New York–born Al McGuire, the curly-haired Irishman who coached Marquette's basketball team, was in town to play Tulane. My dad had phoned him to set up an interview. "The players are out seeing the sights—Bourbon Street and all that stuff," McGuire told my dad. "I told them there's more to this city than Bourbon Street, but I don't know if I succeeded. Meet me at the Café Du Monde, and we'll talk." Actually, what my dad mostly did was listen.

McGuire spoke about his own mother: "If my mother had a choice of a spot to live out her last days," he said, "it wouldn't be a rocking chair on a back porch looking out onto a Technicolored landscape. She'd pick a hotel on 42nd Street. Near Times Square. She'd watch people. That's the important thing. People."

McGuire had been born one story above a bar in Queens, a reality that gave him a healthy sense of perspective. "I admit it's important to have people call you 'Coach,'" he conceded, "but any coach who takes himself too seriously should have his head examined. Coaching is nothing more than a coffee break. A guy will come down to the coffee shop, check the scores, then go back to his own problems. If I could get all the kids who ever played for me to come back and give me one year of their lives, I'd have 'em drive a cab for six months and work as a bartender for the other six. Then they could say, 'OK, world, I'm ready.'"

In addition to his basketball job, McGuire had strung together a series of investments—three restaurants, real estate holdings in Wisconsin and North Carolina, clinic appearances. That's why, when one of his star players, forward Jim Chones, was offered $1.6 million to turn pro, McGuire didn't bat an eye. "I looked in my refrigerator, and I looked in Jim's refrigerator," McGuire said. "Having done that, there was no way I could tell Jim not to take the money."

My dad then led McGuire from Café Du Monde across Decatur Street into Jackson Square, and they took a right turn down Chartres Street, climbing the 140-year-old stairs to the second-floor balcony of his boyhood home. My dad introduced McGuire to his mother, Clara Giacomino Finney.

McGuire made a point of spending an hour talking with her, peppering her with questions and listening as she retold stories from her own childhood. McGuire never once talked about himself. He wanted to know about Clara.

She told McGuire the story her mother had told her—about the night in 1892 when a steady stream of carriages went past the house to watch John L. Sullivan lose the heavyweight championship to Jim Corbett. "Ah, Gentleman Jim," McGuire told my grandmother. "He made a lot of Irishmen happy. Just like, I'm sure, that statue of Andrew Jackson makes a lot of pigeons happy."

When Dick Enberg, McGuire's CBS colleague, asked his terminally ill sidekick in 2001 what he would like on his tombstone, McGuire responded: "Had a good time, see ya." That was pure McGuire. So were his parting words to the steady stream of friends who dropped by for a last visit: "Remember, cash bar at the wake."

After McGuire left the Chartres Street balcony that day in 1972, my grandmother asked my dad what the Irishman with the gift of gab did for a living. They had talked for an hour, but nothing much of their conversation had been about sports, much less about basketball.

"He's a philosopher," my dad replied.

A philosopher, telling stories on a French Quarter balcony.

Chapter 1
BASEBALL

Bats in the Parlor: Rusty and Chuck Staub Created Cleaning Problem
May 23, 1961

Rusty Staub was just a carrot-topped kid when I first met him at Jesuit High School in 1961. He was tearing up the prep leagues and had to wait until his 18th birthday on September 13 to sign his first professional contract with the Houston Colt .45s.

Twenty-three seasons later, Staub left an impact across the major leagues—a .279 career batting average, 2,716 hits, 292 home runs, and 2,915 games.

He captivated Montreal as a home-run king and as a French-speaking Le Grand Orange. He played just three seasons there, but he was so beloved the Expos retired his number in 1993.

Alma Staub, Rusty's mom, told me Rusty's father, Ray, honed his son's skills by tossing him assorted objects to hit—acorns, apple cores, tennis balls—with a miniature bat.

"He was hitting the ball a city block when he was 12," his playground coach Firmin Simms told me.

Rusty could hit in his sleep.

$\bullet \quad \bullet \quad \bullet$

Until the lady of the house issued her edict—no more batting practice in the parlor—the home of Alma and Ray Staub had cleat marks on the floor, bats on the chair, broken lamps, windows and—almost—a broken head.

"It was an accident," said Ray. "Rusty was taking a swing one day in the living room, and he didn't see his 11-year-old sister until the last moment."

The lump on Susan's noggin was merely another episode in the unsponsored serial "Life with Rusty and Chuck."

Carrot-topped Rusty is a 17-year-old Jesuit senior first baseman who has pro scouts ogling. Some say the price will go as high as $50,000.

Chuck, a year older, is a freshman outfielder at Loyola and he, too, may have a pro career ahead.

Last year both were members of Jesuit's national American Legion champions. This season Chuck was an outfielder on the most successful baseball team in Loyola history while Rusty's hitting sparked the Blue Jays to the city and state championships.

These accolades couldn't have come at a more opportune time. They've almost made Ray Staub forget he has a heart condition.

Because of it he has not seen either of his offspring play since last summer's city Legion series. Whether he does in the future depends on how well he follows his doctor's advice.

Still, it's difficult for Ray, himself a former pro catcher (a season-and-a-half in the Florida State league), to temper his enthusiasm.

When his sons play at home he provides his oldest daughter Sally, 13, with a flock of nickels for a telephone report every two innings—or else drives past the ball park with a neighbor to try to get a peek at the scoreboard.

When the Jays were on their march to the Legion championship, he had broadcasts relayed to him (he couldn't listen) by his wife.

"The proudest moment of my life was when I picked up the newspaper the morning after they won the Little World Series," said Ray. "I wasn't able to control my emotions."

Neither was Alma Staub, who suddenly forgot the many times supper went cold and house-cleaning was sabotaged.

"It has all been worth it," she says. "Not only the cold supper and the bats in the living room, but the string of summers without a vacation."

Rusty and Chuck are both products of the NORD leagues and Bunny Friend coach Firmin Simms.

"Firmin has been a wonderful influence on their lives," says Ray. "When it came down to a vacation or playing for Firmin, it was really no decision."

Rusty is considered the "Babe Ruth of Bunny Friend." Today youngsters at the playground will point out landmarks struck by some of his prodigious home runs.

He played on several NORD city championship clubs in baseball and was a member of the 1957 team which captured national Biddy Basketball honors.

The careers of both boys were launched when their dad made miniature bats for them to use as toddlers. "They began by hitting the ball off the ground like you would a golf shot," said Ray. "They'd hit it and then walk after it. It kept 'em pretty busy."

In their early days, both were fixtures at Nicholls High School practice sessions (Ray formerly coached the Reb basketball, football and baseball teams and has been a teacher since 1940).

From here, the normal steppingstones were Cub Scouts, CYO and NORD leagues.

This summer Chuck will play in the All-American League and Rusty for Jesuit in the American Legion. Because of a baseball rule, Rusty will not be eligible to sign a pro contract until Sept. 13, when he becomes 18.

Will he sign or go to college?

"I want both boys to get a college education," says Ray. "That's definite. I wouldn't rule out the possibility of Rusty signing, but whether he does or not, he'll go to college. You can lose your batting eye, but not an education."

Guidrys Raised a Yankee
October 18, 1978

How dominant was "Louisiana Lightning" Ron Guidry? Well, from August 1977 through the 1978 World Series, Guidry was 37–4. Guidry was throwing smoke when the Yankees captured their 21st and 22nd world championships over the Dodgers.

Guidry found himself in the eye of a Yankees' hurricane in 1978. A week after the All-Star Game, the Yankees trailed the first-place Red Sox by 13½ games. Manager Billy Martin suspended Reggie Jackson for defying his order to bunt. A week later, George Steinbrenner fired Martin.

Incredibly, five days after Martin's firing, it was announced before an

Old-Timers Day game in Yankee Stadium that Martin would be brought back to manage the Yankees in 1980—a Steinbrenner-endorsed, quasi-sabbatical.

The Yankees caught fire in September, beating the Red Sox six straight. Guidry pitched a two-hit shutout in Fenway, then followed it a week later with another two-hit shutout against the Red Sox in Yankee Stadium. In the World Series, after the Dodgers won the first two, Guidry won Game 3, triggering four straight Yankees victories.

• • •

It was a time when it was not difficult to become enamored with the New York Yankees.

Mickey and Roger were knocking every other fastball into the seats. Yogi was hitting bad pitches for home runs.

Remember the Roaring Fifties?

Grace Guidry does. She watched her son grow up in Lafayette, smallish but strong, a youngster wedded to a pitch-and-catch existence from his toddling days.

On weekends, Ron Guidry played ball in the backyard until his mother called out of the window: "Come in, son, the Yankees are on." Grace Guidry was a Yankee fan.

By this time, Grace had converted her husband, railroader Roland "Rags" Guidry. As for her son, selling the likes of Mantle, Maris and Berra to a wide-eyed 9-year-old was a piece of cake.

Over and over in front of the family TV set, Ron Guidry told his folks: "One day I'm going to play for the Yankees."

"All of this is like a dream," Grace Guidry was saying yesterday from the Guidry home in Carencro. "I never dreamed it would happen. But here it is. It's happening."

What is happening is this: The 27-year-old offspring of Grace and Roland Guidry is the toast of Manhattan. What odds would you have put on Ragin' Cajun Ron replacing Broadway Joe in the icy hearts of Gotham?

But here it is. If the Yankees beat the Dodgers tonight and end it all, Ron Guidry's Saturday masterpiece in Dodger Stadium, when his 94-mile-per-hour fastball froze LA's sluggers, will be picked over and analyzed by connoisseurs of the national sport.

If the Dodgers win, and push the Series into a seventh game, the southpaw Horatio, all of 158 pounds in soaking-wet pinstripes, probably will be handed the ball by Billy Martin tomorrow and asked to win the team's first world championship in 15 years.

"Ron just called," said his mother. "He and Bonnie had just picked up Jamie at the babysitter's. It was the first time they had been away from their 11-month-old daughter. Ron sounded great. He told us he'll be ready if they need him in the seventh game."

Left to a mother's instincts the Yankees might not now be on the threshold of another championship.

During Ron Guidry's formative years, years spent with the Half Pints in Lafayette's kiddie league, the man of the house had to soft-sell his wife on Ron becoming a pitcher.

"She didn't mind Ron playing baseball," Rags Guidry recalled. "But she didn't want him on the mound. She was afraid of him getting hurt. Getting hit by a line drive. So he started out at 8 and 9 playing the outfield and first base.

"The boys on the team kept putting the pressure on me. They saw what Ron could do in practice, so they got me to work on my wife. Finally, it happened. He started pitching. The Half Pints started winning. And his mother came to see him. She was amazed."

So was the University of Southwestern Louisiana when they caught a glimpse of Ron throwing for an American Legion team.

"He got a scholarship to USL on what he did in American Legion," said Rags. "Northside High didn't have a baseball team. All Ron did in high school was run track—the 100, 440, 880. He once ran the 100 in 9.8."

It must have been unnerving to Dodger fans Saturday to watch Guidry sprint from the mound after baffling their heroes with his Cajun fog ball. Steve Garvey looked like a Little Leaguer as he swung fruitlessly at balls in the dirt.

Down the stretch, the little lefty was awesome. He won a crucial game from the Red Sox in the pennant drive and an even bigger one in the play-off against Kansas City.

Ron's parents flew to New York for the first two Series games. "It was my wife's first plane trip," said Rags. "She was real nervous about flying, but now she's ready to go again. She liked everything about New York but the traffic. That kind of scared her. I wanted to show her Broadway but she backed off because of the traffic."

During the season the Guidrys kept their son well-stocked with crawfish, with Cajun coffee, with Louisiana rice.

"Ron took us out in New York and we tried the shrimp," said Rags. "It was nothing like home. They still haven't discovered seasoning up there."

When Guidry was pitching at USL, a scout made the observation: "I don't think he'll ever be a pro because he won't ever want to leave home."

The scout was half right. He's left home, but can't wait to return. "He's going to drive back through Carolina and do some hunting with Catfish Hunter," says Rags. "He asked me to set up a duck hunt for him and Catfish later in the year."

Rags Guidry should have no trouble lining one up. At the moment, Acadian country is fighting for claiming rights. Ron grew up in Lafayette, but his folks later moved to Carencro, a town of some 2,000 outside the Cajun capital.

When a story appeared in the *Lafayette Advertiser* saying "Lafayette's Ron Guidry," the mayor of Carencro protested.

That's what happens when you've got a live fast one that can hit the corners.

In southwest Louisiana, Ron Guidry is moving up fast on crawfish étouffée.

Fire-Eating Martin and Steinbrenner Meet Once Again
October 13, 1982

Billy Martin and George Steinbrenner were a chemistry experiment gone wild. Kept in separate vacuums, they were relatively harmless. Mixed together inside a Bronx lab, they were baseball's equivalent of nuclear fission.

Trying to make sense of it all was none other than New Orleans Judge Eddie Sapir, who became Billy's friend and legal adviser.

Billy learned baseball under Casey Stengel, who once famously said: "The secret of successful managing is to keep the five guys who hate you away from the four guys who haven't made up their minds."

For Billy, hate—what he would call motivational dynamite—had its place, and he always was ready to light the fuse.

• • •

Mickey Mantle introduced them at baseball's winter meetings in '69. "I'd like you to meet Eddie Sapir, a city councilman from New Orleans," Mantle told Billy Martin, rookie manager of the Minnesota Twins.

It was a friendship that quickly flourished, beginning when Martin brought the Twins to City Park Stadium for an exhibition game in 1970, warming as Sapir got Martin to discover the wonders of boiled crawfish, solidifying as Martin realized, with every controversial step down a thorny path sprinkled with championships, one-punch arguments and contract disputes, that valuable legal advice was only a phone call away.

"Billy Martin is a part of New Orleans," Municipal Court Judge Eddie Sapir was saying the other day, pointing to the filing cabinet at his Broad Street offices, cabinets filled with every aspect of Billy Martin Enterprises—representing his dealings with Minnesota, Detroit, Texas, the Yankees and Oakland, endorsements, correspondence on Lite Beer ("I didn't punch that doggie") commercials, correspondence on a prospective movie on the life of a combative, cerebral manager who is part of one of baseball's great success stories.

In a year torn apart by a strike, bloodied further by a split season, baseball has rallied with a glittering array of drama in the mini-playoffs that has made pro football, by comparison, so much cold mashed potatoes. Now it approaches a showdown that may overshadow the World Series: Billyball vs. George Steinbrenner, Reggie Jackson and other Damn Yankees.

No. 1 in pinstripes, whose genius was sharpened at the elbow of Casey Stengel, brings his Oakland A's into the Bronx Tuesday, the start of a best-of-five to determine the American League champion.

No one could have written a better script. On Saturday, the Yankees run the bases like a bunch of sandlotters that would have left Billy Martin aghast. They get chewed out by Boss Steinbrenner. Then they home-run Milwaukee out of it, a slumping Reggie Jackson providing the key wallop.

Oakland, meanwhile, wins in three straight, pitcher Mike Norris responding to Billy barbs with a brilliant performance, the A's reflecting the inspired leadership of their diminutive skipper.

To appreciate what Billy Martin has done in Oakland, you might compare it to a coach taking over the 1–15 Saints and getting to the playoffs in two years.

Martin assumed command of a team that was 54–108 in '79, the worst in the majors, the sad remains of a dynasty that had won three straight world championships, a reflection of Charlie Finley's pinch-penny budget. The A's averaged 3,900 fans, who discovered the players were not even worth booing.

Suddenly, under Martin, Oakland discovered the bunt, hit-and-run, cutoff plays, execution, all translated into 83 victories and a second-place finish behind Kansas City in the AL West.

Come 1981, and the A's jump out with a record-setting 11 straight, a record-tying 18 wins in April, winning the pre-strike AL West, then disposing of post-strike winner Kansas City in three games.

Now the Yankees welcome Billy, son of Stengel, battler of Steinbrenner, in one of those made-in-heaven matchups.

As Martin's confidant, agent and business guru, Eddie Sapir has listened for hours as Billy painted a picture on the shaping of a managerial philosophy.

He found that Martin's is more than one-dimensional, extending beyond his obvious tactical genius.

"Billy learned from Casey Stengel that members of a team have only two things in common—they're male and they play baseball," says Sapir. "By watching Casey handle the different personalities when the Yankees were winning everything in sight, he learned a valuable lesson.

"Billy said he always made sure that Yogi Berra never pouted. When Yogi had something to pout about, he was useless. As for Mantle, who would show up for some games after some heavy drinking, Billy said Casey would act as if nothing was wrong. He was sweet as pie around Mickey. More often than not, once the game began, Mickey would sober up and hit a home run or two.

"But Casey was always rough on Billy Martin. 'I'm not your daddy,' he'd tell Billy. He was always goading him, criticizing him, playing to his combative nature. 'That's no Red Cross on your cap,' Casey would say to Billy. 'We're not running a charity here. We are the New York Yankees.' It got so Billy would run through the wall for Casey."

Which reminded Sapir of Martin's public dressing down of Mike Norris after a temporary slump.

"When Norris went to Billy for an explanation, Billy asked him if his comments embarrassed him, made him feel small in the eyes of his teammates," Sapir said. "When Norris said they did, Billy said, 'Good.' Then Mike goes out and humbles the Royals."

The 52-year-old with the haunting eyes has been haunted by controversy ever since the Yankees traded him in 1957 after a brawl in the Copacabana. Since then, there has been a series of fights, with players, with a sportswriter, with a marshmallow salesman.

Every time, says Sapir, Martin was goaded, usually by much bigger men who wanted a "piece of him," who wanted to "get their names in the papers."

"I was with Billy in Scottsdale after he had settled with the Yankees and come to terms with Oakland," says Eddie. "What I'm telling you is the absolute truth. Three times in one night, guys wanted to pick fights. We're sitting at a table having a drink, minding our own business, and this guy who had to be 6-6 and weighed a ton, comes over and says, 'So you're Billy Martin. You don't look so tough.' With that he rips off his shirt and tells Billy he wants to fight. They took him away. Later, in a restaurant, another guy—he's also about 6-6—wants to do the same thing. Billy asks me, 'Why do all these guys have to be 6-6?'"

Sapir was with Martin for the opening of Joe Namath's Bachelors III in Fort Lauderdale. "I arrived with Billy, left with Billy. He shook hands, posed for pictures, answered questions, never raised his voice to anyone. The next day there's a story in the paper that Martin got in a fight. Time magazine picked it up. No one checked. It was absolutely false. But, reputations being what they are, it was a long time before George Steinbrenner believed the true story."

How is the Martin-Steinbrenner relationship?

"They're really good friends, especially now that Billy is away from him," Sapir explains. "George can't stop meddling. And you don't meddle with Billy when it comes to running a baseball team. I was with Billy when he told George he was benching Reggie and starting Paul Blair in the fifth game of the '79 playoffs. Reggie was something like .079 against Paul Splittorff, Blair was like .400. George told Billy, 'If you lose, you're gone.' Billy wins, then Reggie, angry at being benched, hits three homers to win that big game in the Series."

There was the day in Chicago when Steinbrenner called Martin in the dugout during a game. Graig Nettles handed the phone to Billy and said, "It's George."

"Don't be calling me during the game, you a—," said Martin, hanging up on the Boss.

Eddie Sapir cannot wait for events to unfold.

"Billy and George really have a deep mutual respect. When you take the Steinbrenner personality and the Martin personality, and put them in opposite corners, you realize what a tremendous test of willpower you have in this series."

This Tiger Has It All
February 22, 1989

LSU right-hander Ben McDonald was a tall drink of water—6-foot-7 with a 96 mph fastball—and part of the stable of Louisiana prep athletes recruited by Skip Bertman to turn the Tiger baseball program into a perennial powerhouse.

McDonald, who also played basketball for one season at LSU, was the first pick in the 1989 major league draft—going to the Baltimore Orioles for a $1 million, three-year deal. He played nine seasons in the majors and compiled a 78–70 record and a 3.91 career ERA. McDonald also led the 1988 U.S. Olympic team to the gold medal in Seoul, with complete-game victories over host South Korea and Puerto Rico.

• • •

Most of the time, a baseball scout will show up at a ballpark armed with one of two weapons:

A radar gun, which tells you the speed of a baseball as it crosses home plate.

Or a JUGGS gun, which clocks velocity from the time the ball leaves the pitcher's hand.

In the Superdome on Friday night, the guns will be especially active when LSU faces Oklahoma State in the Busch Challenge.

That's because Ben McDonald will be pitching for the Tigers, and when McDonald pitches, you forget all about gun control.

"I don't use a gun," said Pirates scout Lenny Yochim. "And, with Ben on the mound, I don't know whether you need one. He has got it all—the velocity, the complete line of pitches, the mechanics, the body control, the athletic ability, the overall awareness. He's an outstanding young prospect."

Outstanding enough, said LSU Coach Skip Bertman, to become the first player selected in June's college draft. Outstanding enough, said Bertman, to sign (with the Orioles, he predicts) for a bonus in excess of $235,000, the sum paid to last year's top pick.

Ben McDonald is a junior, from Denham Springs, 6-foot-7, 212 pounds. Ordinarily, pitchers of McDonald's height tend to be gangly, subject to all kinds of fundamental flaws.

Not in this case.

McDonald went to LSU on a basketball scholarship, something that spoke for his agility. Before he was smoking batters, he was contributing, as a freshman forward, to a Dale Brown ball club that reached the Final Eight in the NCAA Tournament. The day after the Tigers were eliminated, McDonald was at baseball practice.

"Playing that season for a guy like Dale was good for Ben," Bertman said. "Dale got him thinking positively. Made him tougher. Sharpened his competitive instincts. Prepared him for setbacks all athletes experience along the way."

A good thing because few college kids were asked to rebound from the kind of trauma that rocked McDonald two years ago in the College World Series.

With the Tigers leading Stanford by three runs in the bottom of the 10th, McDonald was called on to relieve and proceeded to serve up a bases-loaded, game-winning home run.

The picture of McDonald, head buried in his arms, was a classic. It spoke volumes, giving mute, but eloquent, testimony to the agony of defeat.

"Ben was devastated all right," Bertman said. "Anyone would be. But the way he came back said a lot for the young man. He told me, 'Coach, I'm going to learn from it. In the long run, I'm going to be better for it.' And he has."

Bertman got an inkling last summer when McDonald, pitching for the USA Olympians, faced a team of Cuban All-Stars in Tennessee.

"The weather was brutal, at least 105 degrees," Bertman said. "Ben not only went the distance to beat the Cubans for the first time, he was just as strong at the end, throwing it 92 miles per hour. It was as impressive a performance as I've ever seen."

Local observers have seen quite a few. UNO Coach Tom Schwaner was awed last year as he watched McDonald mow down his Privateers with a fastball that was a blur. Ron Maestri, who went from baseball coach to AD at UNO, said Ben McDonald is what you'd build if you were looking for the "prototype pitcher."

"He has the body lean, the leverage and the loose arm. A week ago, the JUGGS gun caught his fastball at 96 miles per hour. That would be about 93 on the radar gun. We're talking major league velocity. And, along with this, he has a bite to his breaking pitch. This kind of talent, and the international competition he faced as a member of the Olympic team, gives him the seasoning the pros look for in a player coming out of college."

Size-wise, McDonald reminds his coach of 6-6 Dick Radatz, who pitched for the Red Sox. Earlier, you had 6-8 Gene Conley, who mixed basketball and baseball. And now you have Rick Sutcliffe, who stands 6-7.

At the moment, record-wise, McDonald stands at 2–0, with 22 strikeouts, four walks and a 1.32 ERA.

Waiting are the bats of Oklahoma State, a strong preseason choice to make it to the College World Series.

Whatever happens, the observation of UCLA Coach Gary Adams seems apropos. After watching McDonald two-hit his team last year, Adams took the loss in stride, explaining: "In a couple of years, I'm going to be watching him pitch in the big leagues."

Gift from Team Was His Prized Possession
March 9, 1999

I met Joe DiMaggio twice, each time a classic New Orleans moment. In 1959, he and former Chicago Bears quarterback Sid Luckman made a promotional appearance at Kirsch-Rooney baseball stadium near City Park as part of a national whistle-stop tour for V. H. Monette & Company, manufacturer's reps for U.S. Army commissaries around the world.

The Yankee Clipper was a stunning figure in his dark blue, double-breasted silk suit. While he was watching the New Orleans Pelicans take batting practice, someone coaxed Joe into shedding his coat and climbing once more into the batter's box.

Our other meeting came in the 1970s when Joe somehow agreed to play in the Italian Open Golf Tournament at City Park, a charity fundraiser where Chianti, Bloody Marys, beer, and muffulettas were strategically placed at every tee box.

I always thought: Here's a guy who's played golf at Pebble Beach and Augusta National, and now he's trying to hammer his tee into the igneous rock formation that doubled as a City Park tee box. Joltin' Joe had power to all fields.

• • •

Reluctantly, he removed the double-breasted coat of his dark blue suit. He kept the cuff links on his white shirt fastened but moved the French cuffs up, away from his wrists. He did not loosen his dark blue tie.

And there stood 45-year-old Joe DiMaggio, a picture of fashion, bat in hand, at home plate in Kirsch-Rooney Park, one Saturday in March 1959.

In town for a public appearance, Joe had agreed to a request from Mayor Chep Morrison to make an appearance at a preseason workout of the minor league Pelicans and, cheered on by a knot of maybe 500 onlookers, Joe wound up taking a few cuts at the offerings of Jim Kite, a Pelican lefty.

On the first pitch, Joe sent a dribbler back to the mound. On the second, he hit a soft roller to short. His audience grew respectably quiet. Whereupon, Joe motioned to Kite: "One more, if you please."

Kite grooved one and Joltin' Joe swung from the heels of his black patent-leather shoes. He sent a shot over the fence in left field—337 feet away—and, one more time, Joe DiMaggio, eight years into retirement, was greeted by a sound that seemed to follow him forever: The roar of the crowd.

There was no home run trot. Joe simply stepped out of the batter's box, gave an appreciative wave, dusted off his shoes, put on his coat and began signing autographs.

"I was there," said Mel Parnell, who was managing the Pelicans at the time, "and, boy, did that home run bring back some memories."

A sad memory for the Boston Red Sox southpaw who had been poison for the Yankees. A great one for the man of legend who died Monday at age 84.

For Parnell, it was one more reminder of the '49 season, the one in which DiMaggio missed the first 65 games because of a bone spur in his right heel. It wasn't until mid-June when a blistered DiMaggio (he had developed blisters the size of half-dollars on both hands taking daily swings in the batting cage) joined the Yankees for a three-game series in Boston.

In those three games, as the Yankees swept the Sox at Fenway Park, Joe DiMaggio was a one-man colossus, hitting four home runs and driving in nine, which merely embossed the legend of someone who, eight years earlier, had hit safely in 56 consecutive games.

"I'll never forget it," recalled Parnell of his role in history. "We had a 3–2 lead in the seventh when Joe comes up with two on and two out. I figured this would be the last time I'd be seeing him. I had been beating him all day with my best pitch, a fastball."

Parnell throws a fastball and Joe hits a high foul outside the first base line. Which the first baseman drops. He throws another that Joe fouls into the dirt. Then Joe takes a curve for a ball.

"I felt I could get him with another fastball," said Parnell. "I threw a good one, I thought, but there it went, screaming high over the Green Monster in left. I think that sucker's still traveling."

Parnell likes to count his blessings. "Think how lucky I was," he says, "to have been around two of the all-time greats. I had Ted Williams for a teammate and, in the five years I had to face Joe, from '47 to '51, I'm proud to say he got only four homers off me. He was such a special man, such a dignified presence, on and off the field. I treasured the friendship we had after we left the game. To me, he was the ultimate Yankee."

In retirement, the bashful son of a California fisherman walked through two generations as the strong, silent, stylish hero. A hero of literature: He popped up in the pages of Hemingway's "Old Man and the Sea." He popped up in the movie "The Graduate," in the song, "Mrs. Robinson," that asked:

"Where have you gone, Joe DiMaggio, a nation turns its lonely eyes to you."

Joe never could figure out what the song meant. The man who wrote it, Paul Simon, said it simply had something to do with heroes, a hero better known to a later generation as "Mr. Coffee" and the ex-husband of Marilyn Monroe.

As the years rolled by, as he approached senior-citizen status, he began to overcome some of the shyness and reticence that gave distance to his celebrity. It wasn't like that in '84, when he showed up in the Superdome as a non-playing poster boy for something called the Cracker Jack Oldtimers Classic, an event that drew the likes of Willie Mays, Hank Aaron, Don Larsen and Billy Martin.

On a night of reminiscing, I'll never forget one thing Joe said: "As proud as I am of the hitting streak, I'm prouder of being part of teams that won 10 pennants and nine World Series in my 13-year career."

He talked of how his roommate, Lefty Gomez, made the daily grind of the historic 56-game roll in '41 easier by keeping him loose and protected. When the streak began in mid-May, the Yankees were five games out of first place. When it ended two months later, they were up by 17. Incredibly, after going hitless against the Indians, Joe hit safely in the next 17 games.

A month later, his teammates surprised him with a silver humidor, purchased at Tiffany's, engraved with the autograph of each player, carrying the inscription: "Presented to Joe DiMaggio by his fellow players on the New York Yankees to express their admiration for his consecutive-game hitting record, 1941."

"I was never one for saving things," Joe told me in that '84 chat. "I gave the bat I used in '41 to my friend, the comedian Lou Costello. But that humidor sits on my mantelpiece. It's my most prized possession."

I asked if he ever got a call from President Roosevelt congratulating him on the streak.

"I never did," said Joe, "but you have to remember, in those days, presidents weren't doing those things."

Five years earlier, he did recall a meeting of sorts with FDR. It was DiMaggio's rookie season of '36 and the Yankees were playing the Giants in the second game of the World Series at the Polo Grounds with the president in attendance.

"We had a big lead in the ninth inning," said Joe. "The stadium announcer requested that everyone remain in their seats until the president left the stadium. He would leave in his limousine, through the gate in center field."

As it happened, Joe caught a towering drive for the final out in deep center, right at the clubhouse steps.

"I could have walked right in," said Joe. "But I waited, with the ball still in my glove, until the limousine drove through the gate. The president went right past where I was standing. He had that long cigarette holder in one hand. He winked and put up two fingers in that 'V' for victory sign. I tipped my cap. And the president, looking right at me, tipped his fedora."

A salute: One legend to another.

Bertman's Vision Led to Dynasty
May 23, 2001

Besides his five NCAA baseball championships, LSU coach Skip Bertman had a patriot's love of the Olympics. As the head coach of the U.S. team in the 1996 Atlanta Games, Bertman brought with him two Tigers: Warren Morris, whose dramatic, walk-off homer in Omaha had won the NCAA title a month earlier, and shortstop Jayson Williams.

"I just wish Warren and Jayson would have had time to enjoy that championship," Skip said. "We win the NCAA on Saturday, and two days later Warren and Jayson and me are in Tennessee getting ready for another season [the Olympics]."

Although the U.S. finished with the bronze medal in 1996 after losing to Japan in the semifinals, Bertman called the Olympic experience transformative.

"For me, watching Muhammad Ali light the torch was the thrill of a lifetime," Skip said.

· · ·

Skip Bertman likes to tell stories. Always has.

Like how he spent Halloween night in 1959, when he was a student at the University of Miami, a member of Zeta Beta Tau.

"I remember walking into the fraternity house that night, and all of the guys were betting on the LSU–Ole Miss game," he said. "Everyone was familiar with the Chinese Bandits. LSU football was in the papers and the national magazines. Everyone was huddled around the radio listening to the game."

When Skip arrived in Baton Rouge 25 years later, he said he relived that night upon being introduced to J.C. Politz, the man who called Billy Cannon's immortal punt return.

Cannon had sparked the Tigers to a national championship in '58, and Bertman realized football would always be king. LSU baseball was different, a minor sport played before tiny audiences, with a tradition based largely on the fact that major-leaguers such as Alvin Dark and Joe Adcock once wore purple-and-gold baseball uniforms.

So it came as no surprise to LSU's new baseball coach that his first proposal after he arrived in 1984 was met with a chorus of laughter.

"I remember telling the maintenance staff we were going to build some bleachers down the third-base line," Bertman said. "I remember saying we'd have to turn the bleachers in a little bit so the fans would have a good view. I could already see packed stands at Alex Box Stadium."

For many, Skip Bertman sounded like the guy in "The Music Man," a hustler "right here in River City."

"I've always believed," he said, "that anything you vividly imagine, ardently desire, sincerely believe, and enthusiastically act upon, absolutely must come to pass."

With five NCAA skins on the wall, who can argue?

But first things first.

There were no skins on the wall when Bertman planned his first baseball banquet in 1990.

The big draw would be Ben McDonald, the All-American pitcher, College Player of the Year, and the nation's No. 1 draft pick.

"I thought we could draw 500," Bertman said. "We finally decided the Pete Maravich Assembly Center was the best place for that kind of crowd. But when the only available date was Dec. 6, some began to wonder if it would work because it was close to Christmas and it was basketball season."

The approach was to eliminate the negatives. There would be a silent auction. A raffle. Bertman called around, collecting baseball cards, jerseys, memorabilia, winding up with more than 50 items to auction off.

The banquet drew 650, just about matching some crowds for an entire LSU baseball season in the distant past.

Entering the '91 season, Bertman had made nine trips to the College World Series, five as a Miami assistant, four as LSU coach.

"I not only had a vision that we'd win a national championship," he said, "I had rehearsed my speech, and I knew how I'd react."

Bertman had watched Dean Smith after his North Carolina basketball team won Smith's first NCAA title in the Superdome in 1982, and he had watched Jim Valvano when North Carolina State won the following year.

"Smith calmly stood up, smoothed out the lapels of his jacket, straightened his tie, and walked over to shake the other coach's hand," Bertman said. "Valvano jumped out of his seat and ran around the basketball court. I thought to myself, 'There are two ways to do it.' When the time came, I figured the Dean Smith method was right for me."

It was. Five times.

Hitting Was Ted's Favorite Subject
July 6, 2002

I'll never forget the meal.

Ted's meal—not mine.

I've eaten with some emotive people over the years, but I was anxious before my April 1961 lunch with Ted Williams, in town to scout Jesuit High phenom Rusty Staub for the Boston Red Sox.

I knew of Ted's reputation—he was taciturn and leery of the Boston media, with whom he had developed a "hate-hate" relationship over 20 years of scrutiny—and I thought I might have to carry the conversation or pull out quotes from him like, well, splinters.

But The Splendid Splinter proved to be engaging and dynamic, full of nonstop chatter. He talked with his hands. His fork became a baseball bat.

The tragedy of what took place after his death—Ted's body was placed upside down in a cryonics tank—is difficult to fathom.

• • •

The breaded veal cutlet disappeared under a mountain of red.

At that moment, the first thing I learned about Ted Williams became obvious: The man loved ketchup. Lots of it.

It was the early 1960s and Williams, a personnel evaluator for the Boston Red Sox, was in town to look over a hot prospect, Jesuit High slugger Rusty Staub.

Red Sox scout George Digby had arranged an interview at Turci's, an

Italian restaurant on Poydras Street, and there we sat, the three of us, as the Hall of Famer expounded on the subject closest to his heart: Hitting a baseball.

A bite of cutlet and ketchup and then: "Guys today lose power because they put their feet in a way that cuts down on the arc of their swing."

Another bite and a stat: "The year I hit .388 I got only nine infield hits and (Mickey) Mantle got 49. If I had just gotten a few of those, I mighta hit .425."

The clinic went on.

Every now and then Williams was out of his chair, holding an imaginary bat, flexing his wrists, addressing the art of placing wood on horsehide, doing it in a manner in which Werner Von Braun might discuss sending a rocket to the moon.

It was a fascinating 90 minutes, after which Williams and Digby headed off to watch Staub, a teenager Williams would call "as good a high school hitter as I've ever seen."

As they both eased into retirement there is nothing pitcher Mel Parnell enjoyed more than talking hitting with his one-time Red Sox teammate. And idol.

"Ted was a truly amazing person and athlete," Parnell said. "Here was a guy who had his career interrupted not once, but twice. First by World War II, then Korea. This alone would be enough to wreck anyone."

When he entered the service in 1943 as a Marine pilot Williams was at the height of his career. He had hit .406 to lead the league in '41, then led the league again the following year, hitting .356 and winning the triple crown.

Williams returned to the Red Sox in '46, carried them to the pennant and, six years later, was recalled by the Marines.

"In Korea," Parnell said, "Ted flies 40 missions. One time he's flying a fighter plane that's all shot up, they want him to bail out, but he lands it anyway. He gets out and the plane explodes. He comes back from Korea toward the end of the '53 season, plays in 37 games, hits .407. When he's 39 he hits .388 to lead the league. The next year he hits .328 to lead the league again. In his last season—he's 42—he hits .316. Can there be any argument who the best hitter was?"

Ted Williams was a hitter never reluctant to speak his mind. When the Red Sox were in town for an exhibition game in '57, Williams was at a bar with an ex-Marine who also happened to be a sportswriter. Under the impression he was involved in "Marine talk," he unloaded on "phony politicians" and he included Harry Truman. The story made national news.

Williams didn't deny his remarks. His only comment: "I will never talk to a drinking writer again." A week later, it turned out, the writer was flagged for DWI.

"Ted always spoke his mind," Parnell said. "And he was always refreshing."

When Parnell joined the Red Sox one of his first memories of Williams was not with a bat in his hands. But a rifle.

"Fenway Park had become a huge resting place for pigeons," said Parnell. "One time during an off-day practice, Ted must have taken 200 shots at pigeons flying over the field. Tom Yawkey, our owner, felt Ted was doing a service for the team. But when some of the churches in the neighborhood raised a fuss, Ted had to give it up. He was as good a shot as he was a hitter."

Parnell loved telling the story of the time his son, Mel Parnell Jr., was being interviewed on TV.

"I'm sure," Parnell Jr. was asked, "you'd like to become a great pitcher like your dad?"

Mel Jr. thought for a second.

"No sir," he said. "I want to be a great hitter like Ted Williams."

Mel Sr. understood.

Schott Thinks Inside the Box: Happy Birthday, Mr. Baseball
July 9, 2007

You could look it up, especially if it was about baseball in New Orleans, because Arthur Schott had the source material.

New Orleans' premier baseball historian could tell you, almost from memory, that about 125 years before the New Orleans Pelicans played basketball in 2013, the New Orleans Pelicans of 1887 began playing baseball in a regularly scheduled league. Pelicans manager Abner Powell invented the raincheck and came up with the idea of covering the infield with a tarpaulin to prevent flooding. Powell oversaw baseball's first "Ladies Day."

Schott could tell you the first team to bear the Pelicans label in public print came in 1870, when the Pelicans lost by a score of 51–1 to the major-league Cincinnati Red Stockings, who were making New Orleans one of their stops during a nationwide tour.

Said the *Daily Picayune* of that rout: "The famed Red Stockings played their finest game with the Pelicans of this city. Several of the Pelicans made some beautiful fly-ball catches."

Arthur Schott seems to have a record of every one.

• • •

On the eve of the Major League Baseball All-Star game, Arthur Schott celebrates his 89th birthday, this one two weeks after the country's oldest living baseball historian was honored with a Distinguished Service Award by the Louisiana Sports Hall of Fame.

Schott's seven sons were on hand for the occasion in Natchitoches, having grown up in a home that contains one of the finest private collections of baseball lore guides, programs, newspaper clippings, photographs, and microfilm dating to 1871.

It all began when Schott tagged along with his dad to watch the New Orleans Pelicans play the Little Rock Travelers in 1929, and he remembers being immediately fascinated by the baseball box scores, and the stories behind them, something he would use to inform and delight local fans in hundreds of columns, "A Schott From the Bleachers," many of which appeared in this newspaper.

Years ago, I asked Schott to come up with a personal list of records that will "last forever" and, sure enough, it included one of the magic numbers of the time: 714, Babe Ruth's home run total.

"I never thought it would be broken," Schott said. "All of which proves you should never say 'never.'"

Now that 714 has given way to Hank Aaron's 755, now that Barry Bonds is still swinging away at 751, what does historian Schott have to say?

"My feeling is," said Schott, "whatever number Barry Bonds winds up with, someone will come along and beat it. I used to feel no one would ever get close to Lou Gehrig playing in 2,130 straight games. Then along comes Cal Ripkin. That's one of the great things about the game. Baseball and records. They'll always go hand and hand."

If you're wondering what topped Schott's list of achievements that would stand the test of time, he came up with a doozy: Ty Cobb batting .320, or better, in 23 consecutive seasons. In this day and age, that seems safe.

Schott also gave a nod to Cy Young winning 511 games, to Cobb stealing 892 bases, to Joe DiMaggio hitting safely in 56 consecutive games, to Johnny Vander Meer pitching back-to-back no-hit games, to Walter Johnson pitching 113 career shutouts.

"What people forget about DiMaggio's 56-game streak," Schott said, "is, after it ended, he got a hit in the next 17 games. The closest anyone has come to 56 is Pete Rose, who made it to 44."

Leading Schott's list of amazing footnotes is Shoeless Joe Jackson, the Chicago White Sox star who received a lifetime ban for being implicated in the "Black Sox Scandal" of 1919, the year heavily favored Chicago laid down, and lost, to Cincinnati.

"Jackson wound up with 12 hits, a World Series record," Schott said. "He hit .375. He had 8 singles, 3 doubles, a home run. He had 18 total bases, and a slugging average of .563. In the outfield, he handled 17 chances without making an error. An incredible performance. And he's out of the game."

For Schott, it always has been there.

In the box score.

He remembers the smile on the face of Yogi Berra when he handed the Yankee star a copy of the box score of the game in which Berra hit his first major-league home run.

He also remembers the reaction of Ralph Caballero, who graduated from Jesuit in 1944 and three months later was playing third base for the Philadelphia Phillies at the age of 16, the youngest third baseman in major league history.

"When Arthur wrote about me playing with the Phillies in the 1950 World Series against the Yankees, he came up with the box score of my only at-bat. I was 0-for-1," said Caballero. "That was all right. But, in the story, he wrote that Whitey Ford struck me out. I used to kid Arthur. I told him he should have just said I got to bat in a World Series. I'd tell him I wasn't the only guy Whitey struck out in a World Series."

As for Berra, Caballero recalled another box score that had nothing to do with Schott.

"The Phillies and Yankees were playing exhibition games and, the day before, Yogi had gone 3-for-4," said Caballero. "Yogi reads the box and it says he went 2-for-4. He's mad as hell. He goes up to a New York writer and asks him for an explanation. The writer tells him it was a typographical error. Berra screams: 'That was no error. It was a clean hit.'"

CHAPTER 2

BASKETBALL

The Sad-Eyed Serbians
January 10, 1968

I received the following letter after my column on Pete Maravich appeared in the *States-Item:*

> Dear Mr. Finney:
> As one of the more than 5,000 fans who attended the Tulane-LSU game, I was completely captivated by the performance of Pete Maravich ... but I wonder if the people who say Maravich could play in the pro league right now aren't going a bit too far. He's still a sophomore.
> J.F. Bergeron, New Orleans

My reply:

It's easy to go overboard on Pete Maravich. However, I go along with those people who say Pete could play with the pros right now. He's a basketball prodigy—the equivalent of a seventh grader who should be in college. He's probably spent more time on a basketball court than many of the pros playing today. While Pete is not the percentage shooter that Princeton's Bill Bradley was, he's far more of a scoring weapon and a far better ball handler. Pete's chief asset stems from his ability to get shooting room, something he does with quick moves and deft dribbling. Once he gets to the pros, he'll simply have to buckle down for more contact—sharper elbows, bigger hips, etc.

• • •

"Wait until you see my boy," said Press Maravich to the press after he became basketball coach at LSU.

It sounded strange for a father to put the hat on his son this way, especially since he intended to coach him.

But one look at that sad-eyed Serbian entry of Press and Pete, and you realized they had learned to live with pressure.

Crew cut and graying at the temples, Press has a melancholy face created by worry lines, put there by bad passes, missed free throws and double overtimes.

At 6-foot-5 and 180, Pete Maravich strikes you as a commercial for malnutrition, a fellow who could tread water in a test tube, someone who gives you the impression he will fall asleep any second.

Tomorrow night the Maravich combo checks into Tulane gym at a time when Press' LSU Tigers hold second place in the Southeastern Conference and Pete owns the highest collegiate scoring average—44.3—in the nation.

Obviously, the LSU coach was wise in keeping Pete at home. Before the season, he told me why.

"When I saw him develop in high school," Press explained, "I felt I couldn't pass up the opportunity. I realized the extraordinary amount of pressure on both of us. He could be booed for having an off night, and I could be booed for leaving him in too long. But I'm willing to take that chance.

"Pete thrives on pressure. That's one reason I'm not too concerned. The thing that does worry me is that he can't shake off a defeat. Defeat stings him."

Last season Tennessee ruined a perfect year for the LSU frosh with a 75–74 victory in the final game at Knoxville. Trailing by two with eight seconds left, Pete got the rebound, drew a one-and-one foul and stepped confidently to the free throw line.

He made the first—but missed the second.

"I was worried when I couldn't find him after the game," said Press, occupied, at the time, with the varsity. He learned later that Pete had left the Tennessee field house and walked two miles to the hotel.

Young Maravich's deep wounds stem from the fanatical hold the game has on him. Pete once played with a heavily taped ankle that required him to wear a size 16 shoe (he ordinarily takes a 12½). Scored 42 that night.

Another time he played with a temperature of 104. Scored 47.

Last season against Southern Mississippi, nine stitches were required to close a cut near Pete's eye in the first half. He returned to rally his team with 42 points.

Press Maravich feels, if you're going to shed blood, the place to do it is on the basketball court. Growing up in the tough steel town of Aliquippa, Pennsylvania, Press shed some in street fights.

"I was christened 'Peter' and the guys in the block gave me a bad time," he says. "They said Peter was a sissy name. I was throwing papers at the time—the Pittsburgh Press—so, when they started calling me Press, I forgot about the 'Pete.' I christened my boy 'Peter Press.'"

While attending high school, Press worked in the steel mills from midnight until eight in the morning, not unusual in the 1930s. Because of his ability, he had his pick of several colleges but chose Davis-Elkins because a friend was going to the West Virginia school.

After scoring more than 1,600 points in four seasons, he returned as head coach in 1950. "When I got there," he says, "they had no gym. So I went to the president, and he told me they had only $35 in the athletic kitty. So I got some of the boys together and we went out and got a tractor and sawed down some trees. We got the local paper to take a picture—'Ground Cleared For Gymnasium,' the headline said. The publicity was a start.

"I went out and hustled retired carpenters. I promised one I'd build him a monument if he'd get volunteer help. With the students pitching in and some more scrounging, we had a gym with a tin roof within a year. It's still standing today—with 5,000 seats."

After four head coaching jobs, Press landed at Clemson, and it was during this tour of duty that Pete began to blossom into something special.

"We usually ate late during basketball season," says Press. "When Pete got home we'd go into the yard and work on a certain phase of the game. One day it would be dribbling, one day passing, one day shooting."

To pry 50 cents movie fare from his dad, he had to make his quota of baskets, and when the game moved indoors, he had to dump balls of crumpled paper into a small trashcan.

After making the starting varsity team as an eighth grader, Pete came home in tears from the opening game when the other four starters—two juniors and two seniors—wouldn't pass him the ball. In the second game, he got the ball—in time to win it with a long one-hander.

Today, getting the ball from his Tiger teammates is no problem for Pete. Monday night at Georgia, LSU led, 77–76, with four seconds left, and Pete had a one-and-one free throw. LSU called time.

"Pete," said Press, "we really need these points."

"Don't worry, coach," said young Maravich, a remark that got Press thinking. "You know," Press told a friend after the 79–76 win, "that's the first time he ever called me coach."

Billy Graham in Sneakers
January 25, 1973

The first time I met Dale Brown in 1973, I thought he was a little crazy. Highly intelligent, but crazy.

When he retired from LSU 25 seasons and two Final Four appearances later, he asked me: "Did you ever think I'd accomplish what I did at LSU?"

"No," I replied, "I didn't."

And we both laughed. I was just being honest.

No one could dislike Dale Brown, unless you happen to be Bobby Knight, who has issues with the man in the mirror.

But there's one thing I'll never understand: Dale's "freak defense." He tried to explain it to me one day—it's a mixture of man-to-man and zone principles. He could sell it, but not even he understood it.

• • •

A cynic in the presence of Dale Brown for more than 10 minutes might interrupt the LSU basketball coach in the midst of one of his homilies and ask: "Where are the stained-glass windows?"

To some, Dale Brown has come on like a Billy Graham in sneakers, his beady brown eyes zeroing in on you as he expounds on the old-fashioned ideals, ideals he maintains college athletics has left behind as they go tramp, tramp, tramping down a highway that says "Winning Is The Only Thing."

Coach Brown is not soft-pedaling winning because his LSU Tigers happen to be 6–6 at the moment. And are favored to be 6–8 Monday evening following visits by Kentucky and Tennessee.

"You have two won-loss columns," he was saying yesterday, sitting behind a desk in the LSU Assembly Center, one crowded with poems, slogans and souvenirs he passes out freely to anyone who will hold still for a second.

"The first column has to do with the score. The second has to do with the athlete himself. Has your team won? Sure, that's important. But more important is: Have I done my best? I say, if your team wins, and you can't honestly say you've done your best, then you're 0–1 for the night."

At this stage, Dale Brown feels his ball club is 6–6 and 12–0, and he has plenty of support around the SEC from friend and foe. Said one observer the other day: "You've heard of the saying about what you can't make chicken salad out of? Well, I've looked at the LSU personnel and I've seen them play, and you know what? I've stopped eating chicken salad."

Before the season, the SEC coaches' poll tabbed Alabama, Vandy, Tennessee and Kentucky as the title contenders, and tabbed Ole Miss, Mississippi State, Florida, Auburn and Georgia as outsiders. The only thing they could agree on was that LSU would finish in the cellar.

The Tigers still might. But they've already won twice as many games as most experts predicted, including an opening night upset of Memphis State. They've only been out of one game, a 104–83 loss to Utah State. They dropped a five-pointer to Vandy at home and, in Tuscaloosa, against the still-unbeaten Crimson Tide, they were down by only six points with three minutes left, and lost by 11.

Pumped up by their coach's evangelical zeal, the Tigers have taken to his rigorous training program ("We are the best-conditioned team in our conference," says senior forward Bill Whittle) and have zone-pressed and fast-broken their way to victories in games they had no business winning.

"When coach first came on with his poems and his inspirational messages," says Whittle, "I said to myself: 'Hey, what's with this guy? This is pure corn.' Now I believe all of us are getting the message. Everything he says is meaning more and more to me as the year goes on. I particularly like the one about 'one day at a time.'"

In Dale Brown's mind, there are two days in every week that should be kept free of fear and apprehension. By now, his varsity can quote the four paragraphs which, boiled down, tell you the only way to handle today is not to fret over yesterday or fear tomorrow.

When Brown was tapped as Press Maravich's successor last March, he went at it on a day-to-day basis.

"It was too late to do any serious recruiting," he says. "So my first goal was to sell basketball—LSU basketball—statewide. I knew I was coming to a school where football is overpowering. But I never looked on basketball being in a footrace with football. I simply wanted to build pride in basketball."

First off, Brown motored around Louisiana passing out more than 1,000 basketball nets, stopping every time he spotted a goal in a backyard and fast-breaking from barking dogs.

Then came the souvenirs—calendars, pendants, coin purses, coasters, potholders—all getting one message across: basketball was breathing at LSU.

All of this meant nothing to the LSU fans who hopped aboard the bandwagon for "Showtime with Pistol Pete," then quickly hopped off again. Only 6,500 turned out in the plush 14,000-seat Assembly Center for Dale Brown's home debut.

When the Tigers pulled their 94–81 shocker over Memphis State, however, and the word spread ("I've never seen any LSU team hustle like this one"), LSU sold 1,000 season tickets in six days.

Dale Brown is hoping the magic name of Kentucky, and his hustling Tigers, will pull 14,000 Saturday night, which would be the largest crowd ever for a basketball game in Louisiana.

It's significant that Brown will have as his guests 1,300 players and coaches from high schools throughout the state. "On my first swing through Louisiana," says Dale, "I found many of the high school coaches cool toward LSU. I have done everything to change this feeling. Look around and you'll find that most all of the solid college basketball programs in this country—not fly-by-night programs but solid programs—have been largely built on homegrown talent."

Brown dotes on the hungry athlete. Ed Palubinskas, his top scorer who wound up at LSU via the Australian Olympic team and a junior college in Idaho, hitchhiked from Canberra, the Australian capital, to Melbourne just to try out for the Olympics.

"Kids today are crying for discipline," says Brown. "They'll challenge you at first but, believe me, they want to be led."

Brown recalled a visit to San Francisco's Haight-Ashbury district when the phenomenon was at its peak. "You had these people who were supposed to be searching for freedom and what did you have? You had conformity. They all dressed alike, looked alike and smelled alike. It was a false search. They were looking for freedom and, when you saw those glazed expressions, you realized they were slaves to narcotics.

"I want to see the old-fashioned ideals return. Recruiting today brings out the worst character defects in coaches, in athletes, in people. I sometimes feel what college athletics needs is a Ralph Nader."

Indications are that, after a dozen games, LSU basketball needed a Dale Brown who keeps telling his players to look in the mirror each morning . . . and say:

"You may fool the whole world down the pathway of years

"And get pats on the back as you pass

"But your final reward will be heartaches and tears

"If you've cheated the man in the glass."

"You Have to Be a Little Crazy"
November 20, 1974

When the New Orleans Jazz made the switch in 1975 to the Superdome—after playing their first season in the Loyola Field House and the Municipal Auditorium—they were haunted by chronic problems with the Superdome's scoreboards. At the most inopportune moments, it seemed, the dome's shot clock or big boards would go haywire, sometimes stopping the action in mid-fast-break.

One night after the shot clock went dark—yet again—coach Butch van Breda Kolff finally decided to weigh in. Butch was highly intelligent. It took him just a few minutes every morning to zip through the *New York Times* crossword puzzle. His vocabulary was not exclusively four-letter words.

But the Dutchman's furnace had been lit one too many times.

"We've got the worst public education system in the country," Butch said, "but there's one word every kid in this town can spell: 'Malfunction.'"

• • •

"You can see I dressed for breakfast," said the new coach of the New Orleans Jazz.

Bill van Breda Kolff was getting some second glances from early morning patrons in the Braniff Place Coffee Shop, attired as he was in gold-and-purple warm-up togs. His clothes were somewhere between here and New Jersey.

"And our furniture's still in Memphis," said the 52-year-old Dutchman, onetime Knick pivot who has done a bit of hopscotching in a profession he terms "great but hazardous."

He has one of those National Geographic backgrounds, starting out at Lafayette College and then moving to Hofstra, Princeton, the Los Angeles Lakers, the Detroit Pistons, the Phoenix Suns, and finally to the ABA Memphis Tams and Charlie Finley.

When the Jazz called, he was in New Jersey trying to enjoy life as an ex-coach of the Tams, tending to his business, but twice a week driving 35 miles down the road to help a friend coach Stockton State College.

"I would handle the A's and T's," says Bill. "That stands for attitudes and turkeys." Translated, it means bad attitudes and bad players.

But it kept the Dutchman in touch.

"You know you have to be crazy to be a coach," he says. "If you weren't a little crazy, you'd be doing something else. It's like hearing someone say, 'You have to have good judgment to be an official.' Hell, if a guy had good judgment, he wouldn't be an official."

Van Breda Kolff has the looks of a mad genius, someone who goes down to his basement to experiment with bubbling test tubes. He is famous for his temper. In fact, one New York sportscaster, learning of his return to the game, remarked, "They better nail down the water cooler in New Orleans."

Puffing on a post-breakfast smoke, Bill looked as calm as still water. "I'm not what you'd call very calm, but I am calmer than in the past," he says. However, he is going to close practices for a while because, as he says, "My language is not the best and I don't like to chew out players in front of outsiders."

A realist with an unwavering philosophy on how basketball should be played, van Breda Kolff has strong likes and dislikes. He liked the way Bill Bradley played the game, unselfishly, but he did not like the style of Wilt Chamberlain and was bounced by the Lakers because fans paid to see Wilt play, not van Breda Kolff coach. In the long run, Bill feels fans pay only to see the team do one thing: win.

He went to LA after the team had gone 36–45 and took it to the finals the next two seasons. He lost the '69 championship to the Celtics on a shot by one of his assistants, Sam Jones.

"Sam shot the ball thinking Bill Russell was in the game and would tip it in," says Bill. "Only Sam forgot Bill was on the bench. It didn't matter, though. The shot rattled around the rim and went in to beat us."

So much for strategy.

His first order of business is a matter of selection. He'll listen to Sam Jones and Elgin Baylor and he'll eyeball practice, then he'll make some decisions.

"You've got to pick your team and go with it," he says. "Not for three or four games. Longer. A guy can't be looking over his shoulder thinking he'll be on the bench if he misses a couple of shots.

"Elgin may like something in a player I don't. But the decision will be mine. It's my job to get the club moving, to win games. But don't ask me what you can expect. One year at LA we were 22–22. And we finished 52–30. Everything clicked. But there was no forecasting it. If I could predict, I'd be on Wall Street making a million."

The Jazz' 1–15 start suggests comparisons with the Philadelphia 76ers of 1972–73, a club that finished 9–73, the poorest record in NBA history. Philly finished 59 games out of first place and lost 21 games by 20 points or more. So, by morbid comparison, the Jazz are ahead of the 76ers' pace, and remember, Philly was no expansion club.

Van Breda Kolff embarks on his newest venture tonight against Bill Russell's Supersonics. Crowd noise will be music to the Dutchman's ears. In-season, he never quite got accustomed to the peace and quiet of his home on a Jersey island.

"I like enthusiastic fans," he says. "The Lakers had what I call 'a theater crowd.' Polite applause. In my one year at Memphis, the crowds were small but plenty vocal."

It was like that at Princeton, too, except for one memorable occasion. When Bill Bradley had the Tigers on the championship map, every game in the 3,200-seat gym was SRO, filled almost exclusively with students.

"Before one game," says Bill, "our team was introduced and I didn't hear any roar. I had to look around to see where we were. Come to find out, practically all of the students sold their tickets, which brought quite a price. Everyone in the area wanted to see Bradley. That's one practice I stopped."

The Title Match: A Sparkling Gem
March 30, 1982

What I recall most about the classic North Carolina–Georgetown NCAA Championship Game in 1982 at the Superdome was the wall-to-wall action for 40 minutes.

Dean Smith had athletes. John Thompson had athletes.

There were fantastic plays and full-speed mistakes.

But Dean Smith had a freshman named Michael Jordan, whose 16-foot jumper from the left wing was an early glimpse of his greatness.

I remember keeping my eyes on Smith most of the game, seeing how he would react. With everything going crazy, Smith kept his sanity.

My lasting memory: Jordan wasn't even brought to the postgame press conference. You had to go to the Carolina locker room to talk to him. Michael sat quietly at his locker, talking to about five reporters.

• • •

It was a gem, a national treasure, the kind you want to place in a time capsule and, every now and then, take out and examine.

It had all the elements of high drama, joy and pain, down to an incredibly tense finish.

North Carolina 63, Georgetown 62 carved more than a niche in college basketball's hall of honors. It carved an alcove.

On Oscar night in the Superdome, sky-walking James Worthy won for production (28 points), best performance in a leading role (playing himself into exhaustion), best special effects (practicing the art of levitation).

Six-foot-3 Sleepy Floyd won for the best short subject. And 7-foot Pat Ewing won for the best performance by a rookie.

James Worthy was no tar heel. He was a hawk that seemed to trot the sky, dunking and quick-stepping the finest college defense in the country.

And Eric Floyd was no Sleepy. He was an alert ball of fire burning the nets from the outside, committing daylight robbery up and down the 94-foot battleground.

In the midst of a tempo that was intense, playing styles that were artistic, the winner shot 53 percent, the loser 52 percent. And, in the midst of savage defense, there were only 25 turnovers, 13 by North Carolina.

When it was history, when the final two seconds ticked away, James Worthy shared the hero's mantle with freshman Michael Jordan, while Fred Brown wore the clothing of the goat.

The script called for Worthy to carry Dean Smith's team most of the way, for Jordan to rescue his team in the final 15 seconds with a soft jumper from 16 feet. And it called for Fred Brown to commit the fatal error, the Hoyas' coup de grace, a pass he threw into the surprised clutches of James Worthy.

It was seconds after Brown's miscue snuffed out Georgetown's final chance, a turnover that came as the Hoyas probed for a final shot, when Georgetown showed the colors of a basketball family that had come so far.

With Worthy at the foul line, with only two seconds showing on the clock, with hopes dashed, John Thompson called Fred Brown over to the Hoya bench and said, "Keep your head up."

It wasn't easy. Then, as the Tar Heels began cutting down the nets at both ends of the court, as the trophies were handed out, every member of the Georgetown team saved a special consoling pat for sophomore Fred Brown.

What happened in those final seconds is easy to explain. Brown, thinking Sleepy Floyd was near the circle to take a pass, had a momentary lapse. Instead, Floyd had cut to the corner looking for an open spot, and a possible last shot, when Brown turned and released the ball.

Worthy was all alone and, so shocked for the moment, he hesitated on going to the basket. When he did, he was fouled by Eric Smith with two seconds showing on the clock.

Such an obvious fundamental mistake could not erase the artistry that went before it.

"I can't remember a more thrilling, a better-played championship game," Frank McGuire was saying outside the Carolina locker room.

It was McGuire who coached the last Tar Heel team to win the NCAA, 25 years ago, and it was McGuire who recommended Dean Smith as his successor.

"I'm glad he got this monkey off his back," said McGuire. "Now he can freewheel it the rest of his life. He's got that championship. And what a championship it was."

There was a sustained brilliance to this one that elevated it above other one-point finishes.

Worthy, seemingly, was on another planet, holing everything in sight—at least the ones Pat Ewing did not slap away. On the other side, you had Pat Ewing playing more like a senior than a freshman. From the moment he sank his first try, a seven-foot shot from the baseline, Ewing was off to a 23-point evening, to 11 rebounds, to two blocks and, get this, three steals.

He was absolutely superb. The five goal-tending calls against him in the first half did not detract from an epic performance.

The last moments were a memorable showcase to such a special game.

With Carolina leading, 59–58, and five minutes left, the Tar Heels went into their delay, looking for the easy basket.

Ninety seconds later, they got their basket, a layup by Jordan, but it was anything but easy. Driving the baseline, Jordan laid it up softly, high on the glass, beyond the reach of Ewing and, somehow, the ball fell neatly through the net.

Down by three, the Hoyas kept their poise. They worked it for almost a minute before Ewing let go with a 13-footer near the foul line that took a slow, bouncing route home.

When Carolina's Matt Doherty missed the front end of a one-and-one, there came the Hoyas, with Sleepy Floyd hitting a nine-foot jumper, a leaping leaner, that circled in through the back door.

Then the question arose: Would Dean Smith soon be zero-for-seven in the Final Four?

Michael Jordan said no. Carolina worked the clock from 32 seconds to 15 seconds, against a tightly packed Hoya zone, when Jordan found daylight on the left side, enough to drill a 16-footer.

Moments later, came Fred Brown's fatal pass.

"That pass," observed Frank McGuire, "illustrates better than anything what I've always said. You have to be good to get to the Final Four but, sometimes, you have to be lucky to win. A play like this is out of the hands of the coach."

As it turns out, James Worthy got Dean Smith over the "Big One" hump.

There was nothing John Thompson could do about it, not that he didn't try.

He said he went into the game like a student who wanted to show the teacher he knew something about the game.

"So many things were taught to me by the man sitting on the other bench," said Thompson. "I owe him a great deal, but I wanted to beat him as bad as I could."

When you keep score, that's what the game is all about.

Pistol Lived as He Played—Relentlessly, Full-Court
January 6, 1988

Pete Maravich never did anything halfway. You don't become one of the greatest basketball players of all time employing half-measures.

After he retired from the NBA, Pete went full bore into his Christian faith. His wife Jackie was a very religious person, and Pete embraced that faith at some point in his life.

In our last meeting, Pete handed me a little prayer book that he thought I might want to read.

Hearing about his death in 1988—on a basketball court—knocked me for a loop.

"Wait until you see my boy," Press told me the year before Pete arrived at LSU.

For me, Pete forever will remain the skinny, teenage prodigy who could produce basketball art with a no-look pass or a 30-foot hook shot.

Pete Maravich never dipped his toe in the water. He was all in.

• • •

And so, it happened he died playing basketball.

"Well," Press Maravich would say, "Why not? Can you think of a better way?"

Press Maravich died of cancer last April at age 71. He died in Pete's arms. Press was fortunate. He saw Pete Maravich of Aliquippa, Pa., grow into Pistol Pete of the LSU Tigers, the Atlanta Hawks, the New Orleans/ Utah Jazz, the Boston Celtics.

He saw Pistol Pete play basketball. It was a pleasure Jaeson and Joshua Maravich, ages 8 and 5, never enjoyed. In time, however, these sons of college basketball's most exciting player will have pictures painted for them by legions of fans who long ago isolated special moments from an ongoing magic show.

While film remains, everyone took away special images, many lost forever, of the kid in floppy socks, with the pipe-cleaner physique and those large, soulful eyes.

For Adolph Rupp, the coaching legend at the University of Kentucky, the image came on the evening Wildcat fans packed Memorial Coliseum to honor Pistol at his final game in Lexington. Pete responded with a shot from the corner, one launched as he was trapped by a Wildcat defender and most of his torso was beyond the end line. When the shot swished, it may have been the only time a field goal by an opposing player triggered a standing ovation in Big Blue country.

But that was Pistol Pete. Instinctive. Inventive. Incredible.

Like many geniuses, he also was intense and irascible.

During the father-son, coach-player days at LSU, Pete and Press were a love-hate team of hotheaded Serbians whose verbal clashes could make timeouts a hair-raising adventure.

How many times did you hear, "Dammit, you little SOB, I'm the coach and don't you forget it."

Pete did, of course.

With the Jazz, Pete and a short-fused Butch van Breda Kolff waged some classic off-court wars. While Butch had his own ideas about how the game should be played, his admiration for the Pistol's skills was boundless. "I see him do things with the basketball," Butch used to say, "and I still don't believe what I saw."

The game had a fanatical, almost eerie hold on him. When he was 12, he jumped out of the window of his house with a basketball under his arm and spent the night sleeping in the woods, cradling the ball. At the time, he was winning movie money playing "horse" with the varsity players at Clemson. At the movies, Pete always took an aisle seat—so he could dribble as he watched.

Time mellowed Pete. He and Jackie and the boys enjoyed their home in Covington, a white-frame house, circled by a picket fence, shaded by tall oaks, a cozy porch out front.

"This place is 100 years old," Pete told me on my last visit. He talked of how his unrewarded goal of a championship ring had become a "vain obsession." He talked of how he decided to "become a witness for Jesus Christ" after waking up in a cold sweat, crying and shaking.

He attacked his mission with the same zeal he attacked basketball— with a relentless, full-court press.

For a while after his NBA career was over, Pete became a recluse. He explored the Hindu religion, yoga, transcendental meditation.

Drinking had been a problem in college. "Even after I accepted Christ," said Pete, "the urge to drink was still there." He told of succumbing to peer pressure one night. One beer led to 10.

"It was December 13, 1983," said Pete. "I haven't had a drop since. I know now it was Christ telling me I had finally convinced myself to give up drinking."

Pete was happiest over his dad's last days. He and Press flew to Europe searching for a miracle cure for Press' cancer.

They spent their days reading the Bible. "His dreams for me, and for LSU, were bigger than anything I could have imagined," said Pete.

Moments before Press died in his arms, he told Pete, "It wasn't that long ago I was sitting where you are holding my father's hand."

Press was buried in Aliquippa as he wished—with a basketball.

On Tuesday, when Pete joined him, Jackie Maravich saw to it that Jaeson and Joshua were kept occupied doing something they enjoyed.

They went out and played basketball.

Coaching Was Labor of Love for Valvano
April 2, 1993

Jim Valvano talked machine-gun fast. Like so many born-and-bred New York basketball coaches—Al McGuire and Lou Carnesecca come to mind—Valvano could mesmerize any crowd, from reporters to 17-year-old high school recruits, with his wild storytelling.

McGuire once famously remarked to Billy Packer, his TV sidekick during March Madness, that he had just seen the first sign of spring in Milwaukee.

"Oh yeah, what was that?" Packer asked.

"The curbs."

Before Valvano won the national championship at North Carolina State in 1983, he had revived the hoops program at tiny Iona College in New Rochelle, New York.

Valvano said his recruiting pitch was easy.

"Hi," he would introduce himself to a hotshot prep player, "I'm Jim Valvano, Iona College."

"Oh, yeah? Which one?"

• • •

It's 10 years ago. You've just arrived in Albuquerque. It's late in the day. You need a column. You need it now. And, suddenly, there it is, in the lobby of the Ramada Inn.

James T. Valvano, coach of the North Carolina State Wolfpack, is interviewing himself as a favor for a local TV station. The sports anchor, you see, could not make it. So the cameraman asked Valvano, who at 37 is the youngest coach in the Final Four, if he'd talk for a few minutes.

Are you kidding? Of course, Valvano said.

Suddenly, holding a hand microphone, moving from one side to another, Valvano, in the manner of a hyper Dustin Hoffman, is playing dual roles, doing all the talking in a 20-minute question-and-answer session.

Q: Are you nervous?

A: Are you crazy? I've been coaching 16 years just for this. I'm having a ball.

Q: How did your team get this far?

A: It's kind of a love story. Basketball is a game for kids, and we hug and kiss a lot, and sometimes we cry. I believe in dreams.

Q: What did you do today?

A: We had a team meeting to discuss what we will talk about at our next team meeting. Tonight we're going to watch film of ourselves eating lunch.

Q: Do you think the altitude will affect your team?

A: I don't think so. If the players get tired, I'll just tell them to crouch down a little bit.

Q: As a New Yorker, how were you accepted in North Carolina?

A: As best as an Italian married to a Jewish broad can be accepted in North Carolina.

Q: What's the big difference between New York and North Carolina?

A: In New York, they say "youse guys." In North Carolina, they say, "y'all." Also, you can fish in North Carolina. In New York, I did most of my fly-casting at a fire hydrant.

On and on it went, until the cameraman exhausted his tape. But Jimmy V. didn't stop. By this time, he was surrounded by notebooks, which he quickly filled.

He talked about his coaching days at Johns Hopkins, where he also was baseball coach and wide receiver coach for the football team, where his most important job, he said, "was selling lacrosse tickets."

He talked about how he wanted to be a basketball coach since he was in the third grade, how he came to be a competitor growing up in Queens, fighting his older brother for baseball cards, playing stickball, playing hockey with a tin can.

He talked about how it was being the third of three brothers to play basketball for your father, who was a high school coach. He talked about how the teams would come to the Valvano home, dressed in coat and tie, for spaghetti dinners, "with flowers for mom."

"I learned as a kid of 7," he said, "that there can be a lot of love on a basketball team."

At the time, apparently, no team had hugged or kissed more than Valvano's Wolfpack. A team that had been 9–7 at one stage of the season had made a specialty of cardiac finishes.

"It seems we do our best when we're down by five with 30 seconds left," Valvano said. In the ACC tournament, State trailed Wake Forest by seven, North Carolina by six, Virginia by eight, all late in the game, and pulled every one out to win a ticket to the NCAAs with a 15–10 record.

The beat went on. In the NCAA Tournament, the Pack trailed Pepperdine by five with 24 seconds left in regulation, tied it, then won in overtime after trailing by six with a minute to go. The Pack beat UNLV on a last-second tip after trailing by 12.

Against Virginia, State overcame a 10-point deficit, winning on a surprise pass by shooting guard Dereck Whittenburg.

Whittenburg, who had made 11 of 16 shots, drove for the basket in the final second, drew a crowd, dished to Lorenzo Charles, who was fouled by Ralph Sampson as he attempted a game winner. With his team trailing by one, the poorest foul shooter on the team made both.

"That's destiny," Valvano said. "As for Whittenburg, I was shocked when he passed the ball. I didn't know he wanted someone else to be the hero. Boy, that's love."

It also was fate. Four nights later, Whittenburg and Charles were joined forever in Final Four lore. With five seconds remaining in a tie game against heavily favored Houston, Whittenburg made another pass to Charles, this one on an air ball, which Charles caught and converted into a championship slam against college basketball's famous Phi Slamma Jamma, a group of dunkers featuring Akeem Olajuwon and Clyde Drexler.

Valvano's Wolfpack had slain the giant. And there was Jimmy V., making a beeline toward Rocco Valvano, giving his father a Hall of Fame embrace.

Later, a proud son was explaining it all. "Dad," he said, "taught me all about the heritage of love."

Reed Laments Lost Basics
November 3, 2004

When Willis Reed was a senior at Grambling in 1964, he averaged 26.6 points and 21.3 rebounds a game, enticing enough to spark the interest of the New York Knicks, who selected him in the second round of the NBA draft.

The 1969–70 season was Reed's crowning achievement. Reed became the first player in NBA history to be selected All-Star Game MVP, the league MVP, and NBA Finals MVP in the same season.

He is one of the few Louisiana natives—Mel Ott of the New York Giants and southpaw Ron Guidry of the New York Yankees also come to mind—to become a New York sports icon. In Game 7 of the 1970 NBA finals, Reed limped out of the tunnel at Madison Square Garden and ignited the Knicks to their first of two NBA championships.

No one in the Big Apple has ever forgotten it.

• • •

As a ninth-grader, he was the tallest boy in high school, on his way to becoming a full-bodied 6-foot-10 NBA star.

Sure, young Willis Reed could dunk a basketball, but that's about all. The day came when he was asked by a couple of students practicing on an outdoor court to demonstrate the eye-opening art of Slamma Jamma.

"As I was dunking," Reed recalled, "my high school coach walked by. 'Look at him,' he said. 'There's a clumsy kid who can't even catch the ball.' He bawled me out, called me a showoff. And you know what? He was right."

The next day, to improve what little coordination he had, Reed was jumping rope. He spent hours practicing shooting, working on fundamentals, catching and passing the ball in his backyard, in the high school gym.

"I got a key from the coach," he said.

In many cases, that's how stars are born.

In the case of Reed, it was the birth of a classic overachiever. He was born in Hico, La. ("no red lights, two stop signs"), and grew up in nearby Bernice ("two red lights"), became a Hall of Famer with the New York Knicks and was chosen one of the NBA's 50 greatest players when the league celebrated its 50th anniversary in 1996.

Reed will be watching the Hornets open their season at home Wednesday night, watching as the franchise's vice president of basketball operations, silently applauding the kind of basketball fundamentals that do not wind up on highlight films.

The elder statesman says, "Michael Jordan and Julius Erving have ruined more basketball players than you can count." He explains it by saying, before any young man can hope to "be like Mike," he should work feverishly on the fundamentals that helped separate a legend, along with the kind of God-given talent precious few are blessed with.

"The goal of kids today is to make SportsCenter," said Reed. "Usually you make it with the flying dunk, with moves that defy gravity. Cable TV has been good in popularizing the game. But it can push fundamentals into the background."

When Reed made P.J. Brown a second-round pick of the New Jersey Nets in 1992, his advice to P.J. was to spend a year in Europe.

"P.J. came out of Louisiana Tech short on fundamentals," Reed said.

"A season in Greece worked wonders. He returned a far more complete player and went on to prove it."

If this year's Olympics proved anything to the U.S. basketball fan, it proved the Europeans are better shooters.

"I know we didn't have our best shooters in Athens," said Reed. "But as a group, the Europeans are better outside shooters at the world-class level. Why? Practice. Fundamentals. Over there, you have two-a-days. In the morning, you work on fundamentals. In the evening, you scrimmage."

As a rule, said Reed, the best shooters come out of rural areas, as did Larry Bird of French Lick, Ind., who spent a lot more time working on the art of the jump shot and all the fundamentals involved, than the "big-city kids," who grew up playing one-on-one.

With college practices now limited to 20 hours per week, Reed said players determined to become better shooters will have to spend more time working on their own, at odd hours, as Reed did in high school and later at Grambling State.

He went to Grambling as an all-state end in football and an all-state center in basketball, with only basketball in mind.

"I was a long-shot to make it in the NBA," said Reed. "When I was drafted by the Knicks in the second round, there were only nine teams in the league. But I had a backup. I had three offers from high schools to become a teacher-coach."

When he signed his rookie contract for $10,000, Reed had a unique request, keeping a possible coaching job in mind: "I asked the general manager for a rule book."

He didn't need it immediately. Instead, along the way, he found himself going one-on-one against three of the all-time greats: Wilt Chamberlain, Bill Russell, Lew Alcindor.

The highlight, of course, was sparking the 1970 Knicks to their first NBA championship, playing against the Lakers, limping on one leg, full of pain-killers.

He didn't do it with scoring—he had four points. He did it by limiting Wilt to 16 shots, forcing him out, cutting off his path to the basket.

While New Yorkers fittingly praised his courage that night in Madison Square Garden, Reed remembers he had something else going for him.

"Fundamentals helped," he said, talking of a sometimes-buried treasure.

When Dale Met Shaq
June 3, 2011

I first saw—well, looked up at—Shaquille O'Neal in 1989, just after he arrived at LSU as a 17-year-old, 7-foot-1 freshman, out of San Antonio by way of Newark, New Jersey, and a U.S. Army base in West Germany.

It was a Dale Brown meet-and-greet, and Shaq was standing with a bunch of tall guys. Stanley Roberts was another 7-footer, but I was immediately impressed with Shaq's intelligence, physical build, and rare mix of seriousness and playfulness, which worked well with Dale.

The crazy thing about that LSU team was that Shaq probably was its second-best player. I haven't seen a guard shoot the ball better than Chris Jackson, and that includes Pistol Pete, who was a wonderful scorer and shooter but stood out to me for his passing.

LSU never won a national championship with Shaq, but he's got four NBA championship rings and a 900-pound bronze statue of himself dunking the ball on the LSU campus. And he fulfilled a promise he made to his mom that he would get his LSU degree.

"It took eight years; it should have taken six or seven," Shaq said. "I had some other engagements. . . . I feel very secure now. I can get a real job."

• • •

Dale Brown never will forget the day in 1985, the day Shaquille O'Neal walked into the life of the man coaching basketball at LSU.

"He was carrying a duffle bag," Brown recalled. "He was wearing a white polo shirt, khaki pants, tennis shoes. I'm winding up a European tour, giving clinics, and I couldn't wait to get back to Baton Rouge. I'm at an Army base in West Germany, in a city named Wildflecken, and I find myself looking up at a young man, about 6 feet 8, smiling down at me."

Not only that. He's also wearing what Brown later learned was a size-17 shoe. The coach realized the young man's growing days were far from over.

"How long you been in the service, son?" Brown asked.

"I'm too young for the service, sir," came the reply. "I'm only 13."

This was almost too much.

It was enough to strike speechless, at least for a few seconds, a basketball ambassador already famous for some non-stop homilies, in the company of some future slam-dunk dynamo.

"So you're 13," said the coach. "I'd sure like to meet your dad."

Moments later, he did. He was shaking hands with a man named Phillip Harrison, a convert to Islam, someone Brown would call "The Sergeant," who oversaw a family of four—two sons, two daughters.

"The Sergeant" was a 6-5, 280-pound drill instructor from Newark, N.J., who played junior college basketball, joined the Army, was posted overseas and settled the family in San Antonio, where Shaquille (Arabic for "little one") Rashaun ("warrior") O'Neal (maiden name of his mother Lucille) wound up as schoolboy superstar at Cole High.

"From our first conversation," Brown said, "I realized Sarge had Shaquille pointed in the right direction. He never talked basketball. All he talked was education, education, education. I don't want my son to be a sergeant, I want him to be a general. I want him to be the best, and the only way to be the best at anything is through education. I don't want him being misled by white coaches making a lot of promises."

For a coach, this was kismet, a disciplined "yes-sir," "no-sir" youngster who appeared fully prepared to take on life at age 13.

But there was an immediate bump in the road.

"Can you believe," said Brown, "Shaquille was cut early on by his high school, suggesting he'd have a better chance making it playing soccer as a goalie? Thanks to Sarge, Shaq was plenty tough enough to fight through it. I kept in touch with him, kept giving him pep talks. He did the rest. Right from the get-go, he knew he had plenty to learn. He never stopped working. He had a passion to succeed, and he had the kind of personality that made him a joy to coach. He had plenty of talent, but no ego. He was embraced by teammates."

The day Brown landed the nation's top blue-chip recruit, Shaq made his feelings known to his coach.

"He told me he didn't want everything to revolve around him," Brown said. "He said he wanted to get rebounds and block shots a lot more than take shots. I told him he'd be doing all three, which he did. In his freshman season, he had foul problems. He fouled out of nine games. But what more could you ask? He was 'The Man.' He had grown up, to 7-1, close to 300 pounds, and he was leading the conference in scoring, rebounds, blocked shots and field-goal percentage."

Not only that. He was already into Show Biz.

After a 29-point, 14-rebound game in an upset of No. 2 Arizona, highlighted by a breakaway jam, Shaq broke into a hip-hop step he named the "Shaq-de-Shaq."

He began wearing a black baseball cap with the words: "I am the Shaqnificent."

When Kentucky freshman Jamal Mashburn, before a game in Baton Rouge, said Shaq was "all right but could be stopped," Shaq came up with a 28-point, 17-rebound performance against the Wildcats in a Tigers victory, despite being defended, at times, by four men.

All of which forced Mashburn to admit that Shaq "belonged in a higher league."

To Dale Brown, he always will.

I remember asking Shaq how it was playing for Dale during those three seasons in Tigertown. The memory was pure Shaq.

"I loved being around the preacher," he said. "It was like being in church. You could hear the choir singing and see the stained-glass windows. It was so much more than basketball. It was about life."

These are feelings shared by his college coach.

"More than the three years as his coach," Brown said, "I'll cherish the memories he left me as a fan of his for the next 19 years. Shaq once told me he was embarrassed by 'all the money they pay me for playing a game I love.' He meant it. There's no way of telling how much money he passed on because he didn't want to make a show of it, like he did in the wake of those two hurricanes, Katrina and Rita. He didn't want credit, he just wanted to do it. That's always been his way."

Brown recalled a request from a fan, the mother of someone dying of a brain tumor.

"Would Shaq make a call? It was game day. He not only made a call. He spent an hour at her bedside."

Brown recalled another fan, who was raising a 4-year-old dwarf.

"The picture of that tiny child, laughing, a toy in Shaq's arms, took your breath away. Watching the interplay, I look back on such a moment as Shaq at his best."

So how will Dale Brown remember Shaquille O'Neal?

"Many will remember him as basketball's King Kong. I'll remember him as Bambi."

CHAPTER 3
BOXING

Joe Beat U.S. to Germany
April 18, 1962

The second Joe Louis–Max Schmeling fight in 1938 was much more than a heavyweight prize fight. It was a battle of cultures and countries.

After being outclassed by Schmeling in their 1936 fight, Louis trained seriously and felled the German boxer in their rematch in the first round. It was a stunning blow to Chancellor Hitler's pride.

• • •

At a White House meeting in the summer of 1937, President Roosevelt grabbed Joe Louis by the arm, felt his biceps, and told the heavyweight champion of the world: "That's the kind of muscle we need to beat Germany."

The funny part about it was Louis, who fought himself out of humble diggings in Lexington, Ala., with an icy stare and granite fists, beat the United States to the punch.

The U.S. celebrated its victory over Hitler in 1945, several months after Roosevelt passed away.

Louis demolished Germany, symbolized by snarling Max Schmeling, less than a year after he exchanged small talk with FDR.

Joe reminisced about Max yesterday on a trip here to beat the drums for Monday night's all-star show that will feature Ralph Dupas, Eddie

Machen and Cassius Clay and be close-circuited into the Loyola Field House.

In 1936, a year before he took the title from Jim Braddock, the up-and-coming Louis was upset by Schmeling in 12 rounds.

Max knocked him groggy with an avalanche of right hands, leaving Louis helpless on the canvas with a foggy noodle and distorted features.

"I saw those movies so many times it made me sick," said Joe. "Schmeling hit me 54 times with his right. I made the mistake of jabbing with a left in the second round and dropping my hand. He crossed with a right, I went down and was never myself after that."

Overnight, Schmeling became a bigger hero in his native land than he had been as champion in the early 1930s. Hitler went into ecstasy.

"I've always felt that defeat helped make me," said Louis. "If I had beaten Schmeling, I might have gotten too cocky and never amounted to much. The whipping made me work all the harder."

Two years later, when the two antagonists came to grips under the lights at Yankee Stadium, newspaper ballyhoo built the fight into a match between Nazi-U.S. ideologies.

Hitler was chewing up Europe piece by piece and many Americans saw a second world war on the horizon.

"I went into the fight determined to keep my left up and to carry the action to him," explained Joe. "Max was a great counter-puncher and you had to crowd him all the time. I found that out looking at the movies."

Schmeling, who later joined the Nazi paratroopers and was wounded in the invasion of Crete, never had a chance.

After they sparred cautiously for a few moments, Louis staggered Max with a left to the head and dropped him with a right to the jaw.

Schmeling was up at the count of three but went down after a flurry of lefts and rights to the body and the head. The coup de grace was a right cross to the face that sent Max toppling forward on his face . . . and made Adolf cringe.

Ref Art Donovan stopped it after two minutes and four seconds when Max's seconds tossed in the towel. On a smaller scale, Louis' win was a vitamin shot in somewhat the same way as Col. John Glenn's supersonic transcontinental flight in 1957.

Did he have more of a thirst for the kill against Schmeling than he did at any other time?

"I can't say I did," Joe said. "I know I wanted to win it awful bad. I figured myself somewhere between a 'mean' fighter and a 'kind' one.

"This is one of the biggest advantages Liston has over Patterson. He's got that killer instinct. I believe I had it until I got the other guy in trouble—then I kinda slacked off."

As Louis sees it, the big difference between current fighters and those of his day is what happens outside the gym.

"They still train the same," he says, "but I never stopped once I left the gym. I never smoked or took a drink in my life.

"A couple of weeks ago a young fighter was telling me how far he was going to go. I took a look at the cigarette in his hand and shook my head. I thought to myself, he'll never be as good as he could be if he cut out smoking."

Aside from his monastic tendencies, Louis had a couple of idiosyncrasies.

"I always put on my left shoe and my left glove first," he said. "And I always had black-eyed peas the day of a fight . . . one spoonful for every round the fight was supposed to go."

Joe didn't have any trouble with his weight until he left the ring.

"It went up to 269," he said. "I've been dieting lately and have managed to stay around 234."

During his reign, Louis fought anywhere from 197 to 207.

"I think it was weight that hurt Billy Conn in our second fight," said Joe. "He was around 172 for the first one and over 190 for the second. He couldn't move like he did in the first one."

After Conn, Joe had only three fights before he retired as champion.

Does he have any regrets about making a comeback?

"None at all," he said, "except that maybe I came back too soon. I should have waited until I was in better shape."

Louis said he always tried to follow his mother's advice: "Do the best you can and then don't worry."

"Even when Schmeling beat me," he said, "I gave it all I had. I made mistakes. He was just a better fighter than I was that night."

The encore helped blot the earlier loss from his memory. He rates it, and his meeting with FDR, as the high spots of his career.

"I'll never forget," said Louis, going back to his White House audience, "the President talking about beating Germany. He knew it was coming, and I'll never forget who followed me into his office. It was two diplomats—from Japan."

A Day in the Life of Muhammad Ali
August 15, 1978

After Leon Spinks embarrassed him in February 1978 in Las Vegas, Muhammad Ali, at 36, figured if he were to regain his heavyweight title a third time, he would have to employ a new strategy: Something called training.

In the months leading up to the September 15, 1978, rematch in the Superdome, Ali ran daily before dawn in the Pennsylvania woods and sparred nonstop. His camp became a tourist attraction.

Inside his rustic cabin in the woods, Ali gathered us around. These were campfire moments for the little kid in each of us.

Ali told stories of his Louisville childhood, recited doggerel verse, rejoined the cut ends of a severed rope, made the ace of spades squirt from the middle of a deck of cards.

Now, how did he do that?

Somewhere deep inside Muhammad Ali lived a Louisville slugger who was born old. He loved to entertain. He was always on. His hands were faster than his tongue.

The hands, the hands.

This was a decade before Parkinson's laid claim to their dexterity and power.

People won't ever forget the rope-a-dope. I remember the rope.

• • •

DEER LAKE, Pa.—It was 20 minutes past four o'clock in the morning.

During the night, the fog had rolled in and the series of boulders bearing famous names—Willie Pep, Gene Tunney, Joe Frazier, Rocky Marciano, Jack Dempsey, Tony Zale, Sugar Ray, Rocky Graziano, Jack Johnson—left you with the eerie feeling of being in some kind of fistic cemetery, a feeling that would soon vanish.

The only thing stirring were four black mutts, rolling playfully in the dirt.

Muhammad Ali paid them no mind as he stepped from a log cabin and began walking toward a small, white-framed building. He was wearing running boots and he was dressed in a dark blue warmup.

"I'm going to the mosque to pray," he said. For 30 minutes, he remained inside, reading Islam scripture, asking Allah for the strength to become the first man to win the heavyweight title three times.

By 5 a.m., he had driven in a tattered tan Plymouth, across Highway 61, to his favorite running place, a paved road that took him up and down, past white fences, small homes, lush corn fields.

On this trip, Ali had the company of television cameras from New Orleans.

He was running and he was talking.

"He ain't pretty enough to be champion." Huff. "Whoever heard of a man drinking water from a little bottle with a small hole? That wasn't water." Puff.

Occasionally, he would pause to shadow box, peppering the morning mist with left jabs and uppercuts.

"Take that, you ugly thing."

A minute later, having dispatched the invisible Leon Spinks into an adjacent cluster of trees, he is saying, "Goodbye. Gotta run some more."

Ali ran for four miles. When he peeled off a heavy rubber corset around his waist, the sweat poured in Niagara quantities.

"This is our best part of training," said Bundini Brown, looking on in his gray sweat suit. "This is his gas station. This is where you tank up. It's more important than the gym. When you're up early, it means you been to bed early. Means you thinking clear."

Bundini has been Ali's longtime guru, coiner of the phrase, "Float like a butterfly, sting like a bee."

He was absent for most of Ali's preparation for his February fight with Spinks and, although he wasn't particularly apprehensive going into the fight, he soon realized his man was doomed.

"If you talk the same way to every woman, you're in trouble. What worked against George Foreman wasn't going to work against Spinks. You gotta keep hitting him in the head. You can't lay on the ropes. He ain't gonna wear out. You know, he's a nut. I knew he was a nut when I saw him in Vegas. He comes into his hotel lobby boogalooing up to the desk asking for his mail with the radio on, held up to his ear. That's a nut all right."

Ali has disappeared into his main headquarters, a huge log cabin that dominates the rustic setting. Gene Kilroy, one of Ali's many advisors, suggested this hideaway in the woods seven years ago. Muhammad came up with the cash, and today it represents an investment of $670,000.

Many felt it would be too restrictive for the inexhaustible playboy. The boondocks was no place for anyone who thrived on public exposure.

As it turned out, the 36-year-old fighter who loves to eat, loves to party, and now does not relish training, finds the camp a gift from Allah.

To avoid distraction, he entertains himself and anyone who'll watch, with a daily magic show—rope tricks, card tricks.

The camp has become the biggest tourist attraction in the state. And no wonder. Anyone is welcome—free of charge.

By the time Ali reappeared after his morning nap, a small crowd had begun to arrive, three of the curious a family from Belle Chasse that just happened to be driving by.

In this instance, the show included Ali eating watermelon ("I know why the colored like it so much; it's good"). Ali swatting flies ("Damn, I missed him"). Ali doing a card trick (after cutting the deck many times, he looks at the deck and says, "your card is the sixth from the top").

Finding the nine of hearts, time after time, brought a smile to the manchild's face. Thinking of Leon Spinks produced the put-on smirk and periodic monologues.

"I created the monster, and I will destroy him."

"He was so ugly as a baby, when he cried, the tears would come out of his eyes and go down the back of his head."

"He is so ugly he has to sneak up on a glass of water to drink it."

"Imagine this black man. He goes out and buys a white limousine. He wears a white hat, a white suit. A little boy sees him driving and he screams: 'Mama, mama, I saw a ghost. I saw a man driving a car without no head.'

"He's a vampire. All I gotta do is keep him from biting me on the neck.

"Here I am, the best-known man in all the world, and anyone can walk in here. You can't do that with John Wayne, you can't do that with Robert Redford. You can do it with Muhammad Ali."

By this time, the room has filled. Ali turns poetic. He is standing and punctuating his verse with choppy movement of the arms:

"Ali comes out to meet Spinks,

"But Spinks starts to retreat.

"If Spinks goes back any further,
"He'll wind up in a ringside seat.
"Now Ali lands a right,
"What a beautiful swing.
"The punch knocks Spinks,
"Clear out of the ring.
"Spinks is still rising,
"But the ref wears a frown.
"He can't start counting,
"Till Spinks comes down.
"Now Spinks disappears from view,
"The fans are getting frantic.
"But our radar has picked him up,
"He's somewhere over the Atlantic.
"Who would have dreamed,
"When they came to the fight,
"That they'd witness the launching,
"Of a black satellite."

He announces he's ready to eat. In minutes, he's polishing off three lamb chops and scrambled eggs.

"I'll see you in the gym at two o'clock. Be there. I'm in such good shape, I'm starting to get scared of myself."

Swan Song: Ali's Symphony Not Bad for an Aging Maestro
September 16, 1978

September 15, 1978: The day of the rematch. When Ali bared his midsection in New Orleans, the extra padding above his waist had vanished.

"I want you to know I'm real serious for this fight," Ali said. "Put your money on me. I cannot get no better."

• • •

The entrance had the trappings of a religious procession, two acolytes holding up the image of the man wearing a crown—"The Greatest," it said—while the man himself, in a white robe, followed with his escort.

Once in the ring, to the roar of "Ali, Ali, Ali," he looked more confident—shadow-boxing in his corner, preparing to win the title a third time—than Joe Frazier, mike in hand, preparing to lip-sync the National Anthem.

When Frazier finished his song, Ali began his, a 45-minute farewell symphony, sprinkled with some off-key notes, but, on the whole, an impressive show for an aging maestro.

The 36-year-old challenger brought out the amateur in the 25-year-old champion with a 15-round boxing lesson that reduced Leon Spinks to a confused street fighter.

Since his courageous night in Manila, Muhammad Ali had fought 85 rounds, most of them as some stumbling stumble-bum that tarnished what had gone before.

Not last night. Before the biggest live gate of all time—a Superdome crowd of 70,000 paid a whopping $6 million for viewing privileges—Muhammad Ali fought with wide-eyed intensity. He allowed Spinks to press forward, seemingly to chase him around the ring, but, for the most part it was Ali left hooks, countering off-target right hands by Spinks, that made for a lopsided evening.

My card had Ali ahead 13–2. Referee Lucien Joubert took away the fifth, which I had Ali winning, from the challenger for repeated holding. I gave Spinks the sixth on the strength of more effective punching, chiefly left hooks. But that's all. The rest went to Ali.

Although the Ali of diminishing skills was again obvious—he missed badly with right hand chops and there were repeated openings left by a bobbing Leon which he did not have the quickness to explore—there was a textbook quality to the performance of the one-time master.

He was never out of control. There was some periodic wrestling on the ropes between the two, but the closest Ali came to vaudeville were a few shuffle steps when he knew he had a champion of seven months in the bag.

It is difficult to predict just what the future holds for Leon Spinks. He was never in any danger of going down, and there were times when he replied to Ali's combinations with some of his own, displaying a ghetto instinct, a grim toughness.

But, as the evening wore on, as Ali's self-assurance crested, Leon resembled a man he always said he was, a man fighting an idol.

After it was history, he seemed relieved to be an ex-champion, to have a burden he found impossible to handle lifted from his broad shoulders.

"I can't let the world bother me anymore," was his post-mortem. "I had a lot of problems and I could not deal with it." That was $3.75 million saying his body was ready—but not his mind. He had no answer to the mystery, coming out of a corner that was a confused babble of strategy.

"Wiggle, Leon, wiggle," screamed Sam Solomon during the fourth round. "Hold on to your gusto, baby," shouted bodyguard, Mr. T, in the 12th, by which time Leon's gusto had evaporated. "You're the champ," implored Solomon at the start of the 13th.

At that time, the reign would be over in nine minutes.

Quo vadis, Ali?

"I'll think about it for six or eight months," he was saying, "and then I'll let you know. If I retire, I'll throw a party."

Those closest to the man feel this is it. "I don't think he'll ever fight again," said Gene Kilroy. "The more he thinks about it, the more I think he'll convince himself to retire. What more can he accomplish? He's done it all. Done something no one else ever did."

Ali punished himself for this date with destiny, rising at four in the morning to run miles down lonely roads in combat boots in the mist of Deer Lake, Pennsylvania. He was preparing all along for what he felt would be a 15-round fight, realizing his punch had deserted him, realizing, too, Leon was not likely to cave in lightly.

Yesterday he walked three miles before breakfast, watched television, had a long conversation with Kris Kristofferson. He gave his boxing lesson before a ringside that included Sylvester Stallone, Liza Minelli, Jerry Lewis, Lillian Carter, John Travolta, Lorne Greene.

After his victory, he had a telephone call from Camp David—from President Carter.

In two weeks, he'll begin filming another movie, "Freedom Road," in Mississippi.

Meanwhile, he'll rest and contemplate a retirement which, this time, appears certain. As usual, Shakespeare has already prepared the stage for the exit. From Julius Caesar, we heard:

"Forever, and forever, farewell, Cassius.

"If we do meet again, why, we shall smile.

"If not, why then, this parting was well made."

Curtain.

Quitter: It Had to Be One of Sport's Most Confounding Moments
November 26, 1980

The paparazzi were all there. Even Christie Brinkley, herself the frequent target of paparazzi throughout her modeling and film career, was ringside at the Superdome, taking photos.

I don't know if Christie got the shot, but I've never been more shocked by the outcome of a sporting event. When Roberto Duran raised his right hand in the eighth round of his welterweight title defense against Sugar Ray Leonard and said, infamously, "No mas," it was unilateral surrender.

• • •

He quit.

Roberto Duran quit.

What kind of odds would you have given?

The man who built a legend on stone hands and big heart handed the welterweight crown back to Sugar Ray Leonard last night more like a coward than the hero of Panama.

In the long history of boxing, it had to be one of sport's most confounding moments, a gladiator folding his tent like some preliminary boy who had taken too much.

What happened to the lion who had been beaten only once in 72 fights?

The official report: cramps throughout his body, making it impossible for him to continue.

Referee Octavio Meyrah of Mexico looked as perplexed as the veterans in Duran's corner, Ray Arcel and Freddie Brown.

"Fight, fight," shouted Meyrah when Duran broke off contact late in the eighth round.

But the Panamanian held up his right hand, as if to say "no."

He went back to his corner. Arcel stepped onto the ring apron, asking his fighter to explain. Duran shook his head.

When it finally dawned on Leonard that the champion had thrown in the towel, he leaped onto the ropes in a neutral corner and let out a whoop.

The surprising end came with 2:44 gone in the eighth, coming after Leonard, setting the tempo with side-to-side movement, repeatedly lured the champion into traps, peppering him with left hands, scoring with several left-right combinations, scoring well inside.

Unlike the first meeting, when Leonard seemed awed and tentative, Sugar Ray went out and gave a boxing clinic.

From the opening moments of the first round, when he got home a good jab and two excellent combos, the challenger oozed confidence.

Wearing black trunks with yellow trim, he kept a forward-moving Duran puzzled with lateral moves and, most significantly, made vital use of his incredible hand speed.

I gave Leonard all but two rounds, scoring the fifth for Duran, calling the sixth even.

In the seventh, obviously in control, Leonard did something most ringsiders would consider suicidal: he taunted Duran in the manner of Muhammad Ali, putting his hands down, sticking his chin out, going into a stutter step.

You could sense the rise in Roberto's temperature from the look behind the beard. He came forward. He swung. But he could not score.

Leonard countered once, twice, making use of the ropes as the befuddled champion took on the look of someone whose primal dignity had been damaged,

Sugar Ray opened the eighth confidently, jabbing effectively, moving back, moving laterally. When Duran caught up, Leonard retaliated on the inside, scoring to the body.

At no time was Duran in trouble. But this time the Panamanian was clearly outscored by a master boxer who more than held his own in the clinches, chiefly because of his bewildering hands.

The boos that greeted the surprising ending were not surprising at all.

In the minds of many, despite Duran's announcement he would retire, there lurked the likelihood of a third meeting—for more millions.

Whatever happens, for proud Panamanians who idolized this man as champion of two divisions, the moment can never be erased.

Roberto Duran had quit while still on his feet.

It was too much for one woman who sat in a $1,000 seat with the flag of her country in her lap.

She put her head in her hands and cried. "What happened? I cannot understand."

Neither could most of the estimated 25,000 in the Superdome.

A national hero had been disgraced. Like Sonny Liston against Muhammad Ali, he surrendered his title on his stool.

This could happen to any fighter. But not to Roberto Duran.

It did.

Today the flag of Panama flies at half-mast.

There wasn't much in the way of green space when I was growing up in the French Quarter in the 1930s, but St. Anthony's Garden behind St. Louis Cathedral doubled occasionally as a baseball diamond. I am at the far left, my older brother John is sitting next to me, and my younger sister Patricia is on the tricycle. (Photo courtesy of the Finney family)

Father Postert, an Oblate priest, was the rector of St. Louis Cathedral when I joined the Cathedral Knights—the altar boys—in the 1930s. When we became official altar servers, we received a black jacket with the "CK" letters in orange. I am in the second row on the far right, just in front of Father Postert. (Photo courtesy of the Finney family)

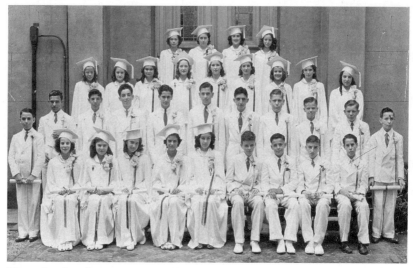

My graduation photo in May 1941 from St. Louis Cathedral School. I am the first boy seated next to the girls in the front row. We received our diplomas at Mass and then walked behind the cathedral to take the picture in St. Anthony's Garden. (Photo courtesy of the Finney family)

I graduated from Jesuit High School in 1945. This picture was taken on Jesuit's front steps, which haven't changed much since the 1920s. I'm in the back row, second from the right. Harold Cohen, far left in the front row, went on to become a Jesuit priest. (Photo courtesy of Jesuit High School)

I wasn't a great basketball player at Loyola University in New Orleans, but somehow Coach Jim McCafferty asked me to help coach the freshman team—the Wolfpups—in 1950. To my right is Johnny Hultberg (No. 8), a future dentist who was the uncle of LSU guard Jordy Hultberg. (Photo courtesy of Loyola University New Orleans)

Deedy and I were married on January 3, 1952, and since I was in the Louisiana Air National Guard, I had to report to Langley Air Force Base in Virginia. On one of our breaks, we got to visit Washington, DC. (Photo courtesy of the Finney family)

Before the computer age, there was something magical about ripping and running with an AP wire story as it fed off the teletype machine in the wire room of the old *New Orleans States*. (Photo courtesy of NOLA.com/*The Times-Picayune*)

This is what passed for a Sugar Bowl media day in 1954. I was able to engage in some light-hearted banter with West Virginia coach Art "Pappy" Lewis (*left*) and Georgia Tech coach Bobby Dodd (*right*). Tech won 42–19, and quarterback Pepper Rodgers was the game's MVP. (Photo courtesy of NOLA.com/*The Times-Picayune*)

A column mug shot in the 1960s. (Photo courtesy of NOLA.com/*The Times-Picayune*)

In 1970, Tommy Walker, the man responsible for the halftime shows during the early days of the Saints, decided to stage an ostrich race with members of the New Orleans media as jockeys. A day before the game, I went through my paces with one of Walker's assistants. (Photo courtesy of NOLA.com/*The Times-Picayune*)

The thing I remember most about riding the ostrich chariot was that the crazy animal had a mind of its own. My chariot veered to the left and nearly ran PA announcer Wayne Mack into the cutout bench area at Tulane Stadium. (Photo courtesy of NOLA.com/*The Times-Picayune*)

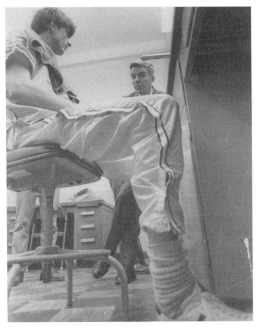

Wearing his trademark floppy socks, Pete Maravich talks after a game. Pete was the best athlete I ever covered but sometimes a reluctant interview. He could do things with a basketball that never had been done before and have not been done since. Everyone knew he was an unstoppable scorer, but I will remember him most for his passing. No one did it better. (Photo courtesy of NOLA .com/*The Times-Picayune*)

In 1971, the *States-Item* sent me to Oxford, Mississippi, to do a five-part series on the Saints' No. 1 draft pick, Archie Manning. It was called "The Making of a Saint." Archie turned out to be the best ambassador the city of New Orleans ever had. (Photo courtesy of NOLA.com/*The Times-Picayune*)

The Italian Open, the brainchild of New Orleans promoter Joe Gemelli, was one-fifth golf and four-fifths bourbon, wine, and beer. I am second from the left, joined in the murderer's row from the 1975 *States-Item* staff by Bill Bumgarner, Nat Belloni, Ron Brocato, and Bob Marshall. (Photo courtesy of NOLA.com/*The Times-Picayune*)

In 1978, Gary Player came to New Orleans having won three consecutive tournaments— the Masters, the Tournament of Champions, and the Houston Open. He famously told Buddy Diliberto before the New Orleans tournament that he would bet against himself because the odds of winning four in a row were astronomical. Player was right—he finished tied for fifth. It looks like he's handing me a sleeve of golf balls. I guess that's considered payola. (Photo courtesy of NOLA.com/*The Times-Picayune*)

The second-floor balcony above 602 Dumaine Street in New Orleans—a block away from St. Louis Cathedral—is a great place to watch the world pass by. From an adjacent gallery, my grandmother recalled watching the line of carriages stream down Chartres Street to attend the 1892 Corbett-Sullivan heavyweight championship fight. (Photo courtesy of the Finney family)

A Buddy D roast was special because there were so many easy Buddy D stories to tell. Buddy (*seated right*) and former WWL sports director Jim Henderson (*left*) were two of the best in the business, even though they were polar opposites in the Diction Derby. (Photo courtesy of NOLA.com/*The Times-Picayune*)

Take One: New Orleans Hornets owner George Shinn (*right*) talks about life after Hurricane Katrina. (Photo courtesy of NOLA.com/*The Times-Picayune*)

Take Two: Then again, maybe I've heard this story before. (Photo courtesy of NOLA.com/*The Times-Picayune*)

Paul Dietzel (*right*), looking serious here, never lost his "Pepsodent Paul" smile or his optimistic outlook on life. It was wonderful that he came back to LSU long after fans accused him of desertion for bolting LSU a few years after the 1958 national championship to take the head coaching job at Army. (Photo courtesy of NOLA.com/*The Times-Picayune*)

Enjoying the company of the love of my life, Doris (Deedy) Young Finney. She was the mother of our six children and kept the family circus on track. (Photo courtesy of NOLA.com/*The Times-Picayune*)

My kids always poke fun at me about my skinny legs, shorts, and choice of shoes. But at least they kept me cool talking in training camp to Saints backup quarterback Mark Brunell. (Photo courtesy of NOLA.com/*The Times-Picayune*)

Like I always say, if you hang around long enough . . . (Photo courtesy of NOLA .com/*The Times-Picayune*)

60 YEARS

The instruments have changed over the years, but good stories never change. The heart of any good story is conflict, passion, humor, and love. (Photo courtesy of NOLA.com/*The Times-Picayune*)

At Super Bowl XLIV in February 2010, I was joined by my son, Peter Finney Jr., who was covering for the *New York Post,* and my grandson, Peter Finney III, who got a credential to cover the "Saints" in the Super Bowl for the magazine published by the North American College, his seminary in Rome. (Photo courtesy of the Finney family)

In August 2010, I had a chance to travel to Canton, Ohio, to cover the Pro Football Hall of Fame enshrinees, including Dallas Cowboys running back Emmitt Smith (*right foreground*). (Photo courtesy of the Finney family)

I received the Dick McCann Memorial Award at the Pro Football Hall of Fame in 2010, and I decided to have some fun with the Canton crowd, who in the 1920s cheered for the professional Canton Bulldogs. I said: "Off the record, Jim Thorpe was a fine player, but he was a terrible interview!" (Photo courtesy of the Finney family)

Like I said, if you stick around long enough ... (Photo courtesy of the Finney family)

Covering the 2012 Final Four championship game between Kentucky and Kansas from courtside at the Mercedes-Benz Superdome. (Photo courtesy of NOLA.com/ *The Times-Picayune*)

In 2013, a week after my wife Deedy passed away, I joined my son Peter and his two sons, Father Peter III and Jonathan, at St. Anthony of Padua Church in New Orleans. We talked about family and faith. (Photo courtesy of the Finney family)

Counting my days at Jesuit High School, I've been connected to a keyboard for more than 75 years. (Photo courtesy of Frank H. Methe III)

CHAPTER 4

COLLEGE FOOTBALL

"Bounced Right into My Arms": Cannon Planned to Let It Roll
November 2, 1959

One of the built-in advantages of writing for an afternoon newspaper like
the *States-Item*—you remember afternoon newspapers, right?—was having
the luxury of a late deadline. At no time was that more of a blessing than on
Halloween night in 1959, when Billy Cannon ran 89 yards toward the north end
zone of Tiger Stadium and into LSU folklore.

Cannon might still be running.

I was able to spend Saturday night in Baton Rouge, and I got up early
Sunday morning to meet Bud Johnson, the LSU sports information director.
Bud drove me to a house in Baton Rouge that had a towering antenna capable
of picking up the TV signal of Channel 4 in New Orleans, which was the first
station to air a replay of the run.

What Bud and I saw was almost as amazing as seeing the play live. The
producers of the highlight show had the sense to replay the punt return over
and over, so it was easy to see every tackle Cannon slipped and then broke,
every wiggle, every zig, every zag. After the show, Bud drove me to meet with
Cannon and his wife at their apartment.

Cannon's punt return remains the most iconic sports play I have ever
witnessed.

• • •

BATON ROUGE—Let's just start by saying that's the way the ball bounces.

There was a moment of excruciating suspense when 67,500 souls fixed their eyes on the red handkerchief after Billy Cannon's classic 89-yard touchdown rumble Saturday night.

But then the referee's arms went up, and a thunderous cheer split the heavens. . . . Ole Miss was in motion . . . and the score would be OK: the Tigers 7 and the Rebels 3.

That was enough to shake strong hearts . . . but think of the outbreak of seizures had Cannon announced to the multitude his thoughts as Jake Gibbs' 47-yard fourth-quarter kick fell out of the skies.

"Until the last second, I wasn't going to play that punt," said Cannon. "I was going to let it roll. . . . Gibbs didn't kick this one as long as the others, and it was sort of dribbling toward me.

"Ole Miss was covering well, and I didn't feel like taking chances. . . . I had fumbled already and given 'em three points."

"But then, right at the end, the ball took a high bounce and fell right into my arms. . . . I took two steps forward and started running."

Movies of perhaps the finest clutch run in SEC history give the lie to Cannon's postgame modesty that "all the credit should go to the blockers."

True to some extent, Billy received two vital blocks—one from Lynn LeBlanc and one from Ed McCreedy.

But the film clearly shows Cannon being hit a half-dozen times along his treacherous route down the sideline past the Ole Miss bench.

The first tackler cracked at the 20-yard line, the second at the 23 and two more at the 25.

At the 30, end Jerry Daniels made contact and Cannon carried him 5 yards, where he was hit once again.

A heroic figure in defeat, Gibbs made a valiant try at a shoestring job at midfield . . . Cannon shook him off.

"I knew I had it around the Ole Miss 30," he said. "When I saw Johnny Robinson looking back for someone to block, I felt this was it . . . just don't stub your toe. . . ."

Cannon claimed he was oblivious to the tremendous roar accompanying his journey.

"But once I crossed the goal line, I kinda got tuned in all of a sudden and seemed to hear everyone at once. . . . I got hit hard in the game, but not much harder than by those guys who jumped me in the end zone. . . . I was lucky to get out alive."

"It was the finest run I've ever seen since I've been in football," said a breathless Paul Dietzel, LSU's coach. "No back in the country could have made that run except Billy Cannon."

That, of course, was the salient part of 1959's "game of the year."

The concluding chapter of this "made in Hollywood" spectacular was LSU's third goal-line stand of the evening.

In the first quarter, Cannon fumbled after a 15-yard thrust, and Ole Miss recovered on the LSU 31. The Rebs could get no farther than the 3 and, on fourth down, Bob Khayat booted a field goal from the 12.

A bobble shortly before halftime by fullback Earl Gros at the LSU 29 opened the door for a march to the 7, which was frustrated by the Chinese Bandits.

After Cannon's touchdown and Wendell Harris' extra point, Johnny Vaught called sophomore quarterback Doug Elmore from the bullpen, and starting on the Reb 32, he began making like an accomplished field general.

When Ole Miss pushed to the 23, Dietzel removed the Bandits and sent in the White team, which had a five-minute rest.

But the Rebs made them retreat to the 7, where they played a first-and-goal—a carbon copy of last year's situation in the second quarter.

Three plays carried Vaught's red-shirted marauders to the 2, but on fourth down, Elmore tried left end, where he was greeted first by Warren Rabb and then by Cannon.

The run died a yard short of immortality.

"I thought he'd try that rollout," said Rabb. "He ran the same play a few moments earlier and got a first down. . . . I moved over a little and was waiting."

Thirty-three seconds later, the game ended with LSU's goal-line still uncrossed after 38 quarters.

The Tigers' dressing room was a cross between a Turkish bath and the tunnel of love.

Dietzel's perspiring athletes were like a bunch of delirious schoolboys, planting kisses with reckless abandon and embracing one another with bear hugs.

The most eloquent quote of the night came from Go team guard Mike Stupka, who came over and put his arm around the most exhausted Tiger of them all.

"Thank you Billy," he whispered . . . and then went his way.

Don Purvis, clutching the game ball, said, "I wouldn't take a million dollars for this football. I mean it."

Archie: The Making of a Saint: From Toughest Year to Super-Manning
May 6, 1971

I've always appreciated class, and Archie Manning displayed that virtue regularly under difficult conditions.

Win or lose—mostly lose or lose with the Saints—Archie never took stage door left after a game. He stood at his locker, usually beaten down or hunched over, and answered every question.

For an athlete who could have had a strong sense of entitlement, Archie possessed rare maturity. Perhaps that was a by-product of the family tragedy—his father Buddy's suicide—just before Archie's junior season at Ole Miss.

Archie was just 20 at the time, but he handled the inscrutable death in a way that protected his mother and his sister. He always thought of others first, a lesson he and his wife Olivia passed on to their children.

• • •

In the summer of 1967, Buddy Manning, who operated a tractor dealership in Drew, Miss., drove over to Oxford to check on his favorite Ole Miss quarterback.

"I was watching the freshmen work when someone introduced me to Mr. Manning," Ole Miss publicist Billy Gates was saying recently. "I'll never forget what he said as he watched Archie: 'He's so skinny. I hope they don't kill him before he gets out.'"

Gates remembers Archie giving his weight for the program as 178 when, said Billy, "You knew he couldn't weigh more than 160."

Ask Manning today to name his toughest ordeal since he picked up a ball of any kind and he'll tell you quickly: "My freshman year at Ole Miss."

In that season, Ole Miss signed eight quarterbacks, and it got to be, more or less, a matter of survival. Some were moved to other positions, some were injured and never played.

Archie Manning played safety as well as quarterback, and listening to him relate some of his experiences, you conjure up a kind of Parris Island atmosphere.

"LSU's freshmen came to Oxford and killed us, 28-0," says Archie. "What followed will never be out of my mind. Wobble Davidson was our coach, and when the team got back to practice the next Monday, he had a little surprise for us. There were no footballs on the field. For 10 days—we had two weeks before a game with Alabama—we worked on fundamentals and we hit. Wobble wanted to find out who the hitters were. And he did. I remember Skipper Jernigan, an offensive guard, went from 220 to 190. I know there were some days when I went under 160."

The boot camp tactics paid off. The Baby Rebels bounced back to whip the Alabama frosh, with Archie tossing for two TDs. They then blitzed Vandy, 80-8, and beat the Mississippi State frosh to finish 3-1.

By this time, Archie had beaten out Shug Chumbler and Don Farrar, finishing not only with 30 completions in 55 attempts for seven touchdowns, but also leading the team with four interceptions, two of them against LSU.

His rural innocence was also winning him friends among the more worldly Rebels. Says Skip Jernigan, who prepped at Jackson, "I'll never forget be-bopping down the hall of the athletic dorm in my underwear and running into Mrs. Manning on the second floor. She was walking along yelling, 'Archie, Archie.' She had come to pick up his laundry. Everyone kidded him about it, but he never let it get him."

If Sis Manning was concerned with her son's laundry, Buddy Manning was still worried with weight. When Archie was in high school, Buddy bought him a set of barbells, which Archie used religiously.

"I never tried to see how much I could lift," he says. "I was interested in building myself up in the chest, arms and legs. By the time spring practice began, I was approaching 180 pounds."

An impressive spring, followed by a buildup in the fall, made Manning a marked man in his varsity debut against Memphis State. At halftime, he was hardly burning down the barn. With him at the controls, Ole Miss had picked up a grand total of two first downs.

"The defense, which had to play most of the way, was whipped to a frazzle, and the offense was hardly blowing hard," says Archie. "Coach Vaught lit into us pretty good, and we came back and won 21–7."

They came back because Manning, chasing his butterflies, threw for two scores and ran for another.

Everyone agrees Archie reached his sophomore heights with an unforgettable performance against LSU in Baton Rouge. The Rebels went there with a 4–2 record, on the heels of a 29–7 drubbing at the hands of Houston, a nightmare for Manning.

"Anyone who doesn't get pumped up playing in Baton Rouge just isn't human," says Archie. "The great thing about the '68 game is we had seven sophomores starting on offense. Maybe we were too young to get scared with all that noise."

That night Manning kept rallying his club, first with a 65-yard pass to Floyd Franks in the second quarter and lastly on a 74-yard drive that snatched victory from what looked like almost certain defeat.

With a little more than three minutes left, LSU had taken the lead, 24–20, meaning a field goal would do Ole Miss no good. Starting on his 24, Archie crossed up the Tigers by running his fullback on a draw to the 41. Seconds later, however, he faced a third-and-16 at his 35. Rolling right and then left, in and out of the arms of at least four Tigers, Archie found Franks on the LSU 21—a gain of 44 yards.

From there, a 13-yard completion got the Rebels to the 8, and then, with 55 seconds left and everyone in Tiger Stadium on their feet, Manning made a speech in the huddle, spelling out what each receiver should do on the next play. He rolled left and drilled the ball through two LSU defenders (one got his hands on the ball) into the arms of tailback Steve Hindman. Hindman stumbled backward into the end zone, clutching the ball to his shoulder.

Super-Manning was born right there. The 19-year-old had gone into Death Valley and, playing with ribs heavily taped because of an injury against Houston, completed 24 of 40 passes for 345 yards.

Said a beaten Charlie McClendon: "That boy has as good a delivery as any quarterback I've ever seen." Said Henry Lee Parker, scout for the Saints: "I'd like to have him right now."

By the time they did get him, it was one tragedy and many heroics later.

In August 1969, a despondent Buddy Manning took his life with a shotgun. His son, already matured beyond his 20 years, matured some more.

Says his Ole Miss roommate, linebacker Billy Van Devender: "After it happened, Archie seemed to sit down and think everything out before making a decision. He was more deliberate."

Archie had come upon the body and cleaned things up to spare his mother and sister the sight. "The fact he was able to go right into football helped occupy his mind," says Johnny Vaught.

Sis Manning credits football and also Archie's fiancée, Olivia Williams, a dark-eyed, dark-haired beauty from Philadelphia, Miss. "She was a big source of consolation to him," Sis said. "And so was her family."

Statistically, Archie responded with his finest season, completing 58 percent of his passes for 1,762 yards and nine TDs, running for 502 yards and 14 TDs.

There was his unforgettable performance in Ole Miss' 33–32 loss to Alabama, a nationally televised spectacular in which Archie wound up with 540 yards in total offense. He also blew holes in three proud defenses—LSU's, Tennessee's and Arkansas'—on their way to an 8–3 season.

St. Stanislaus, Doc, and Company
March 14, 1972

When I think of City Park Stadium in New Orleans, I think of one man, Felix "Doc" Blanchard, who went from playing five games there during three high school seasons with St. Stanislaus of Bay St. Louis, Miss., to becoming a West Point legend during those unbeaten wartime championship years of 1944–46.

Those were the days fullback Blanchard was "Mr. Inside" and halfback Glenn Davis "Mr. Outside" on teams that posted near-perfect numbers: 9–0, 9–0, 9–0–1. At West Point, Blanchard was a one-man terror—runner, passer, kicker, blocker, tackler.

"He could have won the Olympic decathlon," said Earl Blaik, his coach at West Point. A three-time All-American, Blanchard in '45 became the first junior to win the Heisman Trophy.

After the Cadets defeated Navy, Gen. Douglas MacArthur, busy in the South Pacific, fired off a telegram to Coach Blaik: THE GREATEST OF ALL ARMY TEAMS. WE HAVE STOPPED THE WAR TO CELEBRATE YOUR MAGNIFICENT SUCCESS.

In 1991, Doc presented his Heisman Trophy and his red-and-black St. Stanislaus jersey, No. 61, to his alma mater. They remained there, in a lighted showcase, until Hurricane Katrina arrived and washed them away.

· · ·

Talk about nostalgia.

There was Doc Blanchard, out of uniform—in a tux—sitting at the head table Saturday night at the Fontainebleau, along with Marchy Schwartz and Zeke Bonura, class of '27, Wop Glover and John "Baby Grand" Scaffidi, class of '28.

Doc was the youngster, class of '42—St. Stanislaus class of '42.

Just the thought that a high school in Bay St. Louis, Miss., run by Brothers of the Sacred Heart, could turn out such a cast of athletes for its inaugural Hall of Fame was enough to boggle the mind.

An All-American guard, Schwartz played on Knute Rockne's last Notre Dame team, the unbeaten, untied national champions of 1930.

Seven years out of St. Stanislaus, Zeke Bonura was playing first base for the White Sox, and going on to hit .307 in his major league career.

Scaffidi and Glover moved on to Tulane. "Baby Grand" was a guard on Bernie Bierman's 1932 Rose Bowl team and Glover the scatback whose zig-zag run against Southern Cal still occupies an alcove in Pasadena lore.

And then there was Blanchard.

His first impression on this writer, in the fall of 1941, was lasting. Jesuit was playing St. Stanislaus in City Park Stadium, and the Blue Jays were nursing along an unbeaten string stretching back to the start of the 1940 season.

But that afternoon, Doc was too much for a Jesuit team that would go on to win a second state championship. With the Jays leading 6–0, Blanchard faked a run up the middle and circled end for a touchdown. Then he kicked the extra point: Blanchard 7, Jesuit 6.

Two months later—Pearl Harbor.

The next thing you knew there was Doc Blanchard in West Point's black-and-gold, part of one of the most destructive forces unleashed in World War II, Army's football teams of 1944 and '45.

In a conversation I had with Earl Blaik years ago, the old coach would wander off into never-never land just thinking about his fullback.

"He was the best-built athlete I ever saw," said the colonel. "Six feet, 206 pounds and not an ounce of fat. I'll never forget those Atlas shoulders, those legs, that quick start."

Nor will the Army opponents who were steamrolled. Especially the Navy.

While the country was shoulder-to-shoulder in beating back the Axis threat, here at home the Army-Navy rivalry was never keener. Because of the war, both institutions had their finest teams ever, and both went into the 1944 game with perfect records.

It was in that one that Blanchard left Blaik with his most potent memory—carrying the football seven of the nine times and gaining 48 of 52 yards in a clutch scoring drive vital to a 23–7 victory.

"The Navy knew Doc was coming," said Blaik, "but they couldn't do a thing about it."

Today the coach's most prized possession is a telegram from Gen. Douglas MacArthur: THE GREATEST OF ALL ARMY TEAMS. WE HAVE STOPPED THE WAR TO CELEBRATE YOUR MAGNIFICENT SUCCESS.

Now we move ahead almost three decades, past Doc's Heisman Trophy season of '45 when he also won the Maxwell Cup, the Walter Camp Trophy as player of the year and became the first football player ever to win the Sullivan Award as the outstanding amateur athlete in America; and past a 25-year career in the Air Force as a jet pilot.

The Blanchard of today is a little thicker—he's up to 230—but the look of the eagle is still there.

A retired colonel, Doc is currently commandant at New Mexico Military Academy, the school where Roger Staubach logged time before moving to Annapolis.

New Mexico Military has room for 900, but it's a sign of the times little more than 500 attend today.

"School boarders are falling off everywhere because of the economy," says Blanchard. "But there's also the fact there is a general disinterest in the military and the simple fact that parents don't want their sons raised in a disciplined atmosphere. I'm concerned over the role parents are playing."

Blanchard is hoping, in time, the cycle will come full circle, a change in the lifestyles that will elevate the image of West Point and Annapolis to those storybook times of the Forties.

Talking of storybook times, the old heroes have scattered. Glenn Davis, Doc's "Mr. Outside," fulfilled his four-year service obligation, gave pro ball a whirl, and has been working in sports promotions for the Los Angeles Times. Arnold Tucker, the quarterback, recently completed 25 years in the service and is presently principal of a Miami high school.

Every now and then, on the Late Show, Doc's most painful memory returns to haunt him. Following the '46 season, Blanchard and Davis were dispatched to Hollywood where they had starring roles in a forgettable movie—"Spirit of West Point."

"The more Glenn and I practiced how to deliver our lines," says Doc, "the worse we got."

Recently, Doc's 19-year-old son saw "Spirit of West Point" for the first time.

"Dad," he said the next morning over breakfast, "you sure were a lousy actor."

Proving, as Shakespeare once said, "The evil that men do lives after them."

Winning Is Not Having to Say "Wait till Next Year"
December 3, 1973

Whenever I think back to Tulane 14, LSU 0 in 1973, I fondly remember Augie Cross, who not only bled purple-and-gold but also reacted to olive-green-and-blue as though it were an infectious disease.

Augie, a Metairie insurance salesman who founded the Year 'Round Tiger Booster Club in 1960, was such a staunch LSU fan that for years he refused to drive on Tulane Avenue in New Orleans, even if it sometimes meant crossing the intersection.

He told *Times-Picayune* sportswriter Marty Mulé once that he became a Tiger fan in homage to Huey Long, the Louisiana governor and self-proclaimed LSU football coach who got Augie's dad a job during the Great Depression.

"My daddy loved Huey Long for that, and Huey loved LSU, so my daddy did, too," Augie said.

As Augie's cachet grew among both LSU and Tulane fans, Greenie supporters would call his home and yell insults and obscenities. Still, Augie refused to get an unlisted number until one of the callers got fresh with his wife Marge.

For Augie, December 2, 1973, was the perfect time to take the phone off the hook.

. . .

The game ball tucked under his arm, Bennie Ellender, Tulane class of '48, had made his way through the reception line, pumping hands and giving bear hugs, past some squeezed oranges, a purple-and-gold stocking cap, two wrestling football players, many misty-eyed football players, several bottles of Cold Duck, yards of adhesive tape and assorted bandages.

Now he stood on the fringe of the bedlam trying to convey his feelings on the Green Wave's historic, drought-ending 14–0 conquest of LSU, one that changed the tense of Tulane ambition from can do to have done.

"What can I say," mused Bennie, "except isn't it wonderful not to have to say 'Wait till next year'?"

That about said it for all those frustrated Willow Street football followers who hated to be reminded Harry Truman was president when Tulane last beat LSU, 46–0, in 1948.

Suddenly, the famine was over and the goalposts—the wood of the '40s had given way to the steel of the '70s—came tumbling down. Significantly, it was over in the last game Tulane and LSU will play in that massive saucer of concrete and iron, the scene of so much joy and misery. And it was over in a game that will be a lasting tribute to a team that had to pick itself off the canvas after an embarrassing 42–9 whipping seven days earlier.

"I had faith and hope we could bounce back from the Maryland loss," said Bennie. "Football teaches you to contend with adversity. I think we demonstrated we had men who could get up off the ground after being knocked down."

Tulane also demonstrated something else. The varsity victory, coupled with an impressive, freshman upset of the unbeaten Baby Bengals on Friday, showed the deep inroads the Greenies have made in the talent market and must, for the moment, leave LSU supporters in a state of shock.

Saturday night it was a matter of emotion, preparation and ability coming to a boil.

It wasn't simply that Tulane pulled the rug from under a team favored by two touchdowns. It was how the Greenies did it: the way LSU has been winning games the last 15 years—with defense and depth.

Both Tulane scores came when the second unit was in the game, and the winning points came on a pass from a sophomore quarterback to a sophomore tight end.

It's my feeling LSU played with more emotion in losing this time than it did in winning last year.

This time, however, it was the Green Wave which forced the errors and kept the poise. While emotion is invaluable, it is useless without execution, and Tulane managed to set the tone for the evening in a first quarter that saw drives by both clubs end with missed field goals.

Near the end of the LSU march, with the Tigers playing a third-and-3 at the Wave 34, Paul Brock knifed through and nailed Mike Miley for a four-yard loss, the first of several big plays by the defense.

Later, you had Mike Trapani sacking Miley on third down at midfield and, even later, back-to-back plays in which first Dave Griener and then Rusty Chambers halted Brad Davis on third-and-2 and fourth-and-2 at the Tulane 30.

All of this trench warfare set the stage for Dave Lee's interception of an overthrown Miley pass which, in turn, set up Terry Looney's strike to Darwin Willie 19 seconds before halftime.

As it turned out, Terry Looney set himself up with a 14-yard scramble on third-and-10 when it looked as if the half would end scoreless.

So it was a case of Tulane putting one big play on top of another and going to the dressing room brimming with confidence.

Far from dead, LSU was going to test the defense again in a third-quarter stand which, I feel, was the turning point of the night.

The Tigers recovered a Steve Foley fumble at midfield and drove it to the 11, where Davis bulled to the 3 for a first down, only to have it nullified by illegal procedure.

Now it's third-and-7 and Mike Miley is rolling left. But yapping at Mike's heels is bloodhound Mark Olivari. Mark rides down his prey for a 13-yard loss, Juan Roca misses a 46-yard field goal try, and you could sense some of the steam going out of the Tigers.

Perhaps it was fitting that Olivari made the crucial sack. The pep-perpot middle guard has made offseason running along the Lakefront a glamorous pastime, and the religious way in which he and Steve Foley prepare themselves for a season—they'll begin running for 1974 on Jan. 20—has a contagious effect on the squad.

"Mark Olivari," says veteran trainer Bubba Porche, "is one of a kind." But Saturday it took a platoon of kamikaze efforts to kill the Tigers. Aside from ever-present Rusty Chambers, who was in on 16 tackles, you had two Blue Cross candidates in Dave Griener, who made two interceptions with an arm that's on the mend, and Charley Hall, who made a shoe-string sack of Miley on a leg that is less than 100 percent.

Losing with class, Charlie McClendon would probably peg the Green Wave performance at something over 100. He put it accurately when he said in his post-mortem: "They wanted it more than we did."

Beaming under his shiny dome, Bennie Ellender did not step out of character. His joy was restrained, suggesting if you had 500 Bennie Ellenders in a movie and someone shouted "fire" there'd be an orderly walk to the nearest exit.

Modestly, he accepted telephone congratulations from three of his colleagues—Bear Bryant, John McKay and Duffy Daugherty. Then, after a shower, he was greeted by his wife and his 73-year-old father who said: "I've never spent three more pleasant hours in this stadium."

Mr. Ellender was speaking for a large portion of the record crowd of 86,598. Two hours after the game, some of them were still milling around, waiting to shake the hand of the head coach.

"You know what LSU stands for?" asked one lady throwing her arms around Ellender. "It stands for L-S-zero."

Bennie chuckled. He was ready to unwind. He was still cool and boyishly bashful. And he was still carrying the game ball.

No. 1 Gamble: Power-I-Right, Tackle-Trap, Pass-Left
January 1, 1974

Bear Bryant could scarcely believe his eyes. No. 1 Alabama trailed No. 3 Notre Dame 24–23 with four minutes left in the 1973 Sugar Bowl, but the Crimson Tide had the Irish backed up on their own 3-yard line, facing a third-and-8.

It was then coach Ara Parseghian took one of the greatest gambles in college football history. Rather than run the ball again and set up a near-certain punt, Parseghian had quarterback Tom Clements fake the run and throw a rainbow pass down the left sidelines to reserve wide receiver Robin Weber, who had been used mostly for blocking and had caught only one pass for 11 yards all season.

When Weber made his shocking over-the-shoulder catch, falling to the ground on the Alabama sidelines, Bryant knew he had been outfoxed. "The way we had them backed up," Bryant said, "if I were a betting man, I would have bet anything we were going to win."

I will always remember what Bryant did after the game. He walked into the Notre Dame locker room and congratulated Ara. Then he asked to shake Clements' hand.

• • •

All evening long, those two celebrated faith healers, Ara and Bear, had been swapping miracles—extra points were being missed seemingly through a sorcerer's curse, fumbles were being swiped out of the air, a freshman was running 93 yards with a kickoff, a quarterback was catching a touchdown pass.

But now it all came down to a coach's decision, and coach Ara Parseghian had to make it.

Later, trying to reconstruct the most dramatic scene of the 1973 college football season, the intense Armenian leader of the Fighting Irish admitted two plays were running through his mind as No. 3 Notre Dame found itself two minutes away from wrestling the national championship from Alabama.

There were the Irish, hemmed in at the south end of Tulane Stadium, facing a third-and-8 at their 3-yard line—a classic possession down, which, as Ara put it, called for a high-risk venture.

"I was either going to have Tom Clements bootleg the ball around left end or we were going to the pass," said Parseghian.

Ara chose the pass, specifically "Power-I-Right, Tackle-Trap, Pass-Left," then he stood by to watch the football sail from the hand of Clements into the arms of wide receiver Robin Weber, who disappeared into the Alabama bench after a gain of 35 yards. The game ended six plays later.

Weber had caught only one other pass all year, in the season opener against Northwestern. His second catch helped make Notre Dame No. 1 and handed Parseghian his first perfect season as a head coach with a 24–23 victory good enough to have won a smile from Rockne, cheers from the Four Horsemen, and fight-song music from a Warner Brothers' orchestra directed by Pat O'Brien.

COLLEGE FOOTBALL • 97

Along with the game ball and the Sugar Bowl trophy, it might be fitting for Notre Dame to frame "Power-I-Right, Tackle-Trap, Pass-Left"—the play that helped undo the Crimson Tide and humanize Bear Bryant.

"No doubt it was the big play for us," said quarterback Clements, speaking to a knot of reporters as his MVP award rested on the shelf behind him.

"We used the same play for two points after our second touchdown," said Tom. "Think what would have happened if we hadn't made that. We would have been forced to go for the touchdown at the end."

The first time, Pete Demmerle, wide receiver to the left, broke to the outside and took a soft lob from Clements to turn 12–7 into 14–7. The second time Weber did the same thing as Alabama's cornerback froze, looking for the run.

"They were run-conscious both times," explained Clements. "And both times, the tight end—Dave Casper—was the primary receiver, not the wide man. The play is designed for the wide receiver to clear the area and for the tight end to cross over the middle behind him into the area he clears. It just so happened the wide receiver was able to run past the corner man who was coming up to stop the run."

A mature junior who passed up basketball offers from Maryland and North Carolina to play football for Notre Dame, Clements was the glue that kept the Irish offense together when things were getting sticky.

With nine minutes left, Bama suddenly vaulted into a 23–21 lead on one of those walk-on-water gimmick plays. On a third-and-7 at the Irish 25, Bryant substituted quarterback Richard Todd and halfback Mike Stock, whereupon Todd handed to Stock, who appeared to be headed around the right side on a sweep. But Mike stopped after taking a few steps, wheeled and tossed a pass to quarterback Todd, who was streaking down the left sidelines all by his lonesome, past an aghast Notre Dame bench.

"We knew what we were facing," said Clements. "There was plenty of time left. All we had to do was keep our poise."

Which the Irish did by driving from its 19 to the Bama 2, where Bob Thomas booted the winning points from the 9-yard line. On the way, however, there were some anxious moments. First, Clements seemed to be trapped for a sizable loss only to turn it into a first-down run. Then there was another of those third-down situations when Parseghian once again flashed his Las Vegas colors.

With a yard to go at the Alabama 45, Clements faked the run and threw to tight end Casper. "When it left my hand," said Tom, "I thought it was going to be picked off. I didn't get enough into it."

Downfield Casper, blanketed by two red jerseys, also was expecting the worst. "I saw the ball quacking," said Dave of Clements' wobbler. "I don't know what happened to the two Alabama players. All I know is I came back for the ball and made the catch with no trouble. Maybe they were watching me and not the ball."

It all added up to the biggest first down of the march—a 30-yard pickup that put the Irish on the Tide 15, setting up things for Bob Thomas.

"When their guy missed the extra point after their last score and it was 23–21," said Thomas, "I knew I might be kicking for it."

When his time came, the senior from Rochester, N.Y., hit what he called a chip-shot. "I didn't want to hit it too hard. That's how I missed the first extra point. When you punch it, you know the ball will curve on you, but I felt we were in so close it wouldn't matter."

It didn't. The chip-shot got home to make the Fighting Irish No. 1 by one point.

"Roll, Tide, Roll," shouted the white-shirted Notre Damers sarcastically as they filed into their dressing quarters. "Everywhere we went," said Dave Casper, "all we heard was 'Roll, Tide!'"

Today there's a change in the top song. It's "Ebb Tide." And "King Ara."

"Maybe," said one lady fan drained by the evening's dramatics, "I've been praying to the wrong coach."

Woody: Winnie Was a Winner
December 15, 1977

Woody Hayes is remembered for "The Punch," his out-of-control hit to the throat on Clemson nose guard Charlie Bauman in the 1978 Gator Bowl that cost him his job after 28 seasons at Ohio State.

I will remember the Buckeyes' coach for his rare love of history and books. How many football coaches could give a 15-minute dissertation—without notes or a Teleprompter—about famous military generals throughout history and how each one would have moved the chess pieces on the gridiron?

I spent a few days in Columbus prior to the 1977 Sugar Bowl interviewing Woody. It was like going back to school.

• • •

COLUMBUS, Ohio—As Woody Hayes pondered the question, the names came at intervals.

"Well, certainly," he said, "Winston Churchill would be one. Then there's that general you people down South have a particular dislike for, fellow by the name of William Tecumseh Sherman. Robert E. Lee, of course. And, listen, I've got one no one would think of. Karl Doenitz, the German admiral."

So there you have it—Churchill, Sherman, Lee and Doenitz—lumped together maybe for the first time.

Woody Hayes seemed intrigued by the question: What figures of history would have made great football coaches?

"Churchill would have been a natural," Woody was saying, warming to the subject with messianic zeal. "He not only had the ability to inspire, he had a knack of getting to the crux of things. That's an unbeatable combination."

He becomes misty-eyed every time he reads Churchill's pep talk to his countrymen during their darkest hour ... "We shall fight on the beaches, we shall fight in the fields and in the streets; we shall fight in the hills. We shall never surrender. ..."

With Sherman, it was more strategy than eloquence. "He formulated and developed and demonstrated a plan of attack which proved decisive in the Civil War. It was based on speed, deception and maneuverability, striking over a broad front with the use of a broad objective, which denied the enemy time to dig in. It took full psychological advantage of the confusion and defeatism it created in the enemy."

It created, Hayes will tell you, exactly what Stanford's T formation did in 1940, when it was revolutionary: one battlefield opponent after another.

Oddly enough, that same year, German generals who were students of Sherman's tactics were, says Woody, "blitzing Western Europe with Sherman's formations."

Hayes' selection of Lee was much like Churchill: the Confederate hero inspired devotion and respect among his troops, not with hell-raising oratory, but with a majestic presence.

Admiral Doenitz, the commander of the German U-boat fleet in the second war, is Woody's sleeper.

"I hate to think what would have happened if he had been running the whole show," Hayes said with emphasis, leaning forward in his chair. "He was your one-on-one leader. The reason the Germans were so successful with their wolfpack operations can be traced to Doenitz bringing in all of his U-boat captains after every trip and getting information straight from their lips. Person-to-person. He was able to stay on top of things and he planned accordingly. Because they knew they would be talking to the top man, the captains had the best brought out in them. That fellow knew his business. He would have made a helluva coach."

Over the years, Hayes has borrowed from world leaders and football coaches.

"There's always a history lesson," he insists. "When I talk to some coaches, I think of Herodotus, the Greek historian. He sort of got carried away with what he reported. Some coaches are like that. They might not be trying to mislead you, but they get carried away and paint a false picture."

The use of film, he says, brings to mind another Greek, Thucydides, who was "an exact historian, someone who believed in cause and effect." Movies don't lie.

Woody's close friendship with Vince Lombardi helped support a basic Hayes trait: unswerving certitude in your philosophy. From an even earlier friendship with Frank Leahy, Hayes picked up the basics in the center-quarterback exchange, which his Ohio State teams have been using from Year One—1951.

As someone who represents the Puritan ethic—do more tomorrow than you do today—Woody was shaped by a schoolteacher father ("He never had to flunk anyone because he brought out the best in everyone") and a mother who was "driving, honest, unyielding in her position."

His sister Mary was once George Jessel's leading lady on the stage. A brother, Ike, was an All-American at Iowa State and later an outstanding veterinarian.

Woody tells the story of Ike crying bitterly outside Cincinnati Stadium in 1949 after Woody's Miami (Ohio) team lost to the University of Cincinnati. "You were out-coached and your team got out-fought," Ike told his younger brother. "I'm going to be at this spot next year and, if you don't beat 'em, I'm going to beat the hell out of you."

The next year Miami won, 28–0.

When you survive the test of time, and win, as Bear Bryant and Woody Hayes have done for a quarter century, you find success based on one simple fact: they coach people, not football.

Hayes had a question for his listener. "Do you know what people young and old crave more than anything else?" Then he answered it. "Attention," said Hayes.

Woody gives it and, as he puts it, "You damn well better be sure I get it."

Hayes is appalled by the caliber of elementary and high school teaching in this country. Because standards have fallen, each recruiting crop has more of a struggle with the books. With simple words.

So how does Woody attack the problem? This year he inaugurated a class in "Wordpower" for his players. He taught vocabulary—from the time the players reported for fall practice, until regular classes began. "They liked it and I liked it," he said.

Also, Woody is showing up more in study hall. Where he continues to draw on lessons history has taught him.

"Just the other day," he said, "I was helping some players who had a class in theater. They came over, one by one, and I soon had a crowd around me. I did it by talking softly. They had to gather round to hear what I was saying. It got their attention, all right."

Hayes went on to say his tactics grew out of something Henry Ward Beecher, the clergyman, used in pleading the Northern cause in England during the Civil War.

"It was a tough job because England was suffering because the North's blockade cut off Southern cotton," Woody explained. "But Beecher worked his magic with audiences that could have been hostile. And you know how he did it? He began by speaking so low only the people in the front row of the auditorium could hear him. Then he got a little louder to bring in the second row. And then the third. And so on. When he finished, he had everyone in the place hanging on every word. That's what I tried to do the other day in study hall. Henry Beecher came through for me."

Even in Marriage, Coach Picked Winner
November 29, 1992

When Eddie Robinson passed Bear Bryant in 1985 to become the winningest college football coach of all time, his wife Doris brought some extra handkerchiefs.

"Lordy, that man's so emotional," she said. "He weeps at the drop of a hat."

When Eddie accepted the coaching job in 1941 at a school then known as Louisiana Negro Normal Institute, you had to stand to watch the football team play. There weren't any seats. He was a 22-year-old rookie coach with one part-time assistant, who doubled as the night watchman.

Eddie remembered the time Boston College came to New Orleans to play Tennessee in the 1940 Sugar Bowl, with a halfback named Lou Montgomery, a black halfback who could not play because of "existing circumstances."

Three days before that Sugar Bowl, Eddie played quarterback in an all-black amateur game for the Baton Rouge Patriots. Montgomery played halfback for the New Orleans Brutes.

Eddie recalled Montgomery as "some running back"—but one of the many blacks who never got a chance and, as Eddie put it, "just faded away."

That's why when Grambling played Southern in 1974 before 76,000 in Sugar Bowl Stadium, Eddie couldn't help but bawl like a baby.

"For the players," he said, "it was a game. For me, it was the walls falling down."

• • •

For Eddie Robinson, it was No. 380.

For Doris Robinson, the thrilling 30–27 Bayou Classic victory over Southern, before 70,000 in the Superdome, was . . .

"Let's see," said the wife of Grambling's football coach. "I've lost count. I haven't seen them all. But I've seen my share."

It figures.

Not only is Doris Robinson still married to the man she wed 51 years ago; she still goes around holding hands with the man with more victories than any college football coach.

Over the decades, one of the game's great ambassadors never misses an opportunity to ladle praise on his lifetime companion—"It's tough being married to a coach," Eddie will tell you—and it's easy to see why.

For two people born two months and 11 miles apart—Eddie in Jackson, La., Doris in Wilson, La.—they've helped keep one another far younger than their years which, in this case, is 73.

"I really don't deserve a lot of credit," says Mrs. Grambling. "Eddie doesn't drink, doesn't smoke and he loves his job. That's what keeps him going."

For how much longer?

Doris Robinson smiles.

"Who knows? It's gotten to where, while I worry about him, I don't worry him. Every time I try to give him a pill, he says, 'Do you have a medical degree?'"

Genetics suggests Robinson could be a candidate to approach the legendary Amos Alonzo Stagg, who coached into his 90s, a time when failing eyesight put him in danger of being trampled by his players.

A year ago, on the day of the Bayou Classic, Robinson lost his mother at age 89.

"Mama Lilly," says her daughter-in-law, "was a remarkable woman. She never lost her sense of humor. When the nurse was having a hard time trying to draw blood, she told Lilly: 'I hate to be doing this to you.' Lilly looked at her and said: 'That's right. I'd rather be doing it to you.'

"It was Mama Lilly who gave Eddie his gift of gab. And it was Mama Lilly who taught me how to cook. Eddie grew up eating her six-layer coconut cake with lemon icing. Loved to cook and bake. There she was lying in bed, near death, and all she could think about was getting out of the hospital to cook gumbo for homecoming."

Years ago, when Robinson received a Cadillac as a gift, he offered to drive his mother to work. She refused, saying: "I'm going like I always go—in the bus."

"Mama Lilly," says Doris, "taught Eddie never to put on airs. Even though his hair is thinning out, he never wears a hat. I don't think you'd ever catch him in a toupee."

The Robinsons met at McKinley High in Baton Rouge.

"It was at a church bazaar," Doris recalled. "He tried to impress me. Bought me five icebergs—little colored cubes—at a penny each. And you know what? I was impressed. Right from the start, he looked like the man I had dreamed about."

In the summer of '41, they crossed the Mississippi River, found a preacher in Port Allen, and exchanged vows. "We didn't want any big wedding," says Doris. "Eddie was headed for Grambling to coach all sports and to put on school plays."

A half-century later, the workload has lightened, but the hours are still long.

"The phone's always ringing," says Doris. "If it's not a coach, it's someone who used to play for Eddie. They're always calling or writing to thank Eddie for all he's done. Whenever Eddie gets to talking to them, or reading their letters, he starts bawling like a baby. Never saw a man cry so much."

Nowadays, Eddie has five grandchildren and two great-grandsons to open the tear ducts. Eddie Jr., who has an Eddie III, has been a Grambling assistant for 10 years.

"My Eddie was one of 12," says Doris. "He was the first one in his family to finish high school. That's why he has always preached education. That's why his players always keep in touch. That's why they love him."

What makes him special is that the number of victories he has rolled up in 50 years doesn't approach the number of lives he has touched.

With, of course, a helping hand from an All-American wife.

Brandt Got the Ball Rolling
December 1, 1999

I chuckle whenever I hear LSU fans, suffering from terminal agita triggered by the departure of Nick Saban to the NFL after the 2004 season, reach for creative ways to vilify the man who will go down as the greatest college football coach in history.

Consider what Saban did at LSU—turning around a program that had not won a conference championship in 13 years before he did it in 2001, his second season. The Tigers' 2003 national championship was LSU's first since 1958.

Did Saban deliver? Of course.

What I always will remember about Saban coming to LSU was the way he conducted his job interview with Joe Dean and the LSU brain trust: Saban asked the questions, not the other way around.

Saban was and is a man with vision—tunnel vision.

• • •

BATON ROUGE—Considering it all happened in less than a week, you might say the machinery moved at warp speed.

First there was a call from Gil Brandt, former personnel boss of the Dallas Cowboys.

"You better look into that opening at LSU," Brandt told Nick Saban, whose coaching past included two tours of duty in the NFL before winding up as the head coach at Michigan State.

Saban dialed his agent, Jimmy Sexton, in Memphis.

On the day before Thanksgiving, Sexton was making a local call to his longtime friend and business associate Sean Tuohy, a native New Orleanian.

Would Tuohy call Joe Dean and ask Dean to get in touch with Sexton?

Tuohy made the call. Five minutes later, Dean was getting a call from Sexton, who told a surprised LSU athletic director that Saban was interested in discussing the LSU job.

On Saturday, Tuohy was at the Memphis airport, picking up a delegation from Baton Rouge—Dean, Chancellor Mark Emmert, Board of Supervisors members Charles Weems and Stan Jacobs—and driving them to Sexton's home where Saban was waiting.

For 3½ hours, they talked. And 48-year-old Saban told them why he wanted to coach at LSU, why he'd prefer taking on the LSU challenge than continuing on at Michigan State for a sixth season.

In so many words, Saban delivered this message:

* "I have a better chance of winning a national championship in Baton Rouge than in East Lansing."

* "Louisiana is a highly fertile recruiting area where LSU is No. 1, unlike my state where Michigan always will be No. 1, and you're also competing with Ohio State."

Saban flew to Memphis armed with glowing reports on what he already knew: There are few coaching jobs better than LSU.

His offensive coordinator, Morris Watts, spoke from his experience as an assistant, first under Jerry Stovall, then under Gerry DiNardo.

But Saban didn't stop there. He spoke to Bill Arnsparger, who told him the same thing. Arnsparger, who coached in Tigertown for three years, addressed the mother-lode of Louisiana high school talent, the fan base, the fanaticism (when you win, of course).

By this time, Sexton had addressed the financial end with LSU officials.

A school that signed a future national championship coach in Paul Dietzel for $13,000 in 1955 was raising the bar to the ceiling.

It is handing Saban a five-year contract worth $1.25 million a year: $250,000 in base salary, $550,000 for radio, TV and Internet appearances, with additional guarantees from shoe contract and apparel deals, and the remainder from the Tiger Athletic Foundation.

And what was Saban promising?

The usual. Blood, sweat, dedication. Building the kind of program in which the players feel they own and represent the football team, on and off the field.

Saban made his first public appearance, as a Tiger, in a turtleneck that reflected an easy manner in the give-and-take, someone who's far more at home discussing football than finances.

Four years ago, he came close to taking the job as head coach of the New York Giants that eventually went to Jim Fassel. Two years ago, he came closer to becoming coach of the Indianapolis Colts, before it was handed to Jim Mora.

Saban had earned his spurs as a defensive whiz, first with the Houston Oilers, later with the Cleveland Browns, a team whose defense he helped turn from worst-to-first in the NFL.

Ask him, why not the NFL, and Saban became emotional for the only time in Tuesday's coming-out party.

Five hours earlier, he had told his Michigan State players he had decided to become coach at LSU.

Now he was saying why he preferred the college game: "Because the effect you have on young men's lives means something."

So now Tigertown waits. It waits for the magic to return in what will be a Tiger Stadium with 91,664 seats, a Tiger Stadium that Saban once remembered, as a youngster, as the home of the Chinese Bandits.

Saban was born Oct. 31, 1951. Which means, the night Tiger fans were celebrating Billy Cannon's 89-yard punt return against Ole Miss, Saban was blowing out eight candles on his birthday cake.

Tigers' Win Leaves Kentucky Fans Blue
November 10, 2002

I had to feel for Jim Hawthorne. The respected play-by-play voice of LSU football had the call in 2002 when wide receiver Devery Henderson put an exclamation point on one of the most improbable touchdown plays in college football history—the 75-yard "Bluegrass Miracle" from quarterback Marcus Randall that beat Kentucky 33–30 in Lexington.

Hawthorne understandably got excited when he saw Henderson's bumper-car reception. He blurted out the name "Jack Hunt" (who wore jersey No. 8) instead of Henderson (who wore No. 9) as the Tiger who had scored.

The LSU broadcast team later retaped the scoring play to give Henderson full credit.

That reminded me of something similar that happened during another incredible football moment. Just as Tom Dempsey was lining up to kick his game-winning, NFL-record, 63-yard field goal in 1970, a swarm of bees knocked the WWL radio transmitter off the air.

Sometime later, Saints broadcaster Al Wester did the voice-over that is now a classic part of the WWL radio archives.

Who says mulligans are good only in golf?

• • •

LEXINGTON, Ky.—Kentucky students, going a bit wacky, had spilled onto the sidelines waiting to welcome their heroes in blue.

Some had made their way to the south end zone and were going about the job of tearing down the goal posts.

On the Kentucky sidelines, head coach Guy Morriss was soaking wet from the winning ritual of a Gatorade shower.

Two seconds remained, but on television, Jefferson Pilot was flashing the final score to its TV audience: Kentucky 30, LSU 27.

That's how final this football game looked.

As Tigers quarterback Marcus Randall took the final snap, you could not blame the home team for touching off a fireworks display inside Commonwealth Stadium.

And then?

What happened next was the most unbelievable football finish I've ever witnessed, more incredible, really, than the legendary "Immaculate

Reception" that sent the Pittsburgh Steelers to a miracle victory over the Oakland Raiders in the 1972 NFL playoffs.

In the huddle, Marcus Randall called, "Dash, right, 93, Berlin."

It was a desperation "last play" call.

With LSU on its 25-yard line, with the Kentucky defense camping its secondary all the way to the 20-yard-line at the north end of the field, it all began with Randall fading in the face of a three-man rush, with Randall stepping up, planting his feet and letting it fly.

The ball was in the air for 68 yards. When it finally came down it was touched, first by safety Quentus Cumby at the Kentucky 25. Then it went between the hands of linebacker Morris Lane, then was tipped by cornerback Earven Flowers, winding up in the hands of Devery Henderson who juggled it at the 18. But he didn't gain possession until he was at the 15, finally running through the hands of cornerback Derrick Tatum on his way into the end zone.

Whereupon Jefferson Pilot made a final score correction: LSU 33, Kentucky 30.

"All you can say is this one was ordained for us," said Michael Clayton. "When something's ordained, no one can stop it."

It was ordained, all right. Neither Clayton nor the sure-handed Henderson was where he was supposed to be, after being jostled as they sped downfield into a forest of four blue shirts.

"We practice that play every week," said Henderson. "But it never works. Michael was supposed to be the tip man, but the tip guys turned out to be Kentucky players. How can you figure something like that? All I remember was bobbling the ball, then pulling it in, then running like hell."

It was such a sudden turnaround, Kentucky fans at the other end of the field were still celebrating, climbing the goal posts.

Losing coach Guy Morriss fell to the ground, his head in his hands.

Winning coach Nick Saban remembered watching the ball being tipped, "watching Devery make the catch and just keep on going."

"My first impulse," said Saban, "was to look back to see if there were any flags."

None.

His team had won a game it had given away in the fourth quarter, squandering a 10-point lead then watching the Wildcats kick a field goal in the final 15 seconds for an apparent victory.

So what were Saban's feelings?

"I felt we won the game, but I also felt we did not defeat Kentucky," he said. "I'm baffled that when we got on top 21–7, we could not put Kentucky away. I'm proud of the way we kept battling, but I wasn't happy about all the penalties (the Tigers had 13, the Wildcats five) that kept Kentucky drives going."

For much of the afternoon, Henderson kept LSU going. His speed turned a 1-yard shovel pass into a 70-yard touchdown for the Tigers' first score. His leaping end-zone catch produced a 30-yard touchdown that put LSU ahead seconds before halftime.

"No, I've never had a game like this," said the Opelousas junior, who caught five passes for 201 yards. "What happened at the end was still a blur to me. I know Marcus threw that ball as far as he could. And I know I was lucky to be where I was. One thing I'll never forget was hearing those fireworks go off as I was running downfield. I guess it all goes to prove this is a 60-minute game."

While some Kentucky fans left the stadium talking about the last second shot by Duke's Christian Laettner that knocked the Wildcats out of the NCAA basketball tournament, LSU remembered the two-out ninth inning home run by Warren Morris to win the College World Series.

It was an extraordinary outhouse-to-penthouse piece of history.

One scene said it all for the losing team: the sight of a Kentucky fan sitting under the goal posts he had planned to tear down.

He couldn't believe what happened.

Who could?

LSU linebacker coach Kirk Doll spoke for the staff: "The first thing I'm going to do when I get back to Baton Rouge is buy a lottery ticket."

Total Team Effort Puts Tigers on Top
January 5, 2004

In August 2003—five months before Nick Saban would hoist the crystal football emblematic of LSU's first national championship since 1958—I asked him what he thought about the team he was preparing for battle.

You would have had to search long and hard to find a more Jekyll-and-Hyde LSU team than the 8–5 squad from 2002. Four of LSU's five losses were by double digits: Virginia Tech (18), Auburn (24), Alabama (31), and Texas (15).

"I see something we haven't had to deal with in the past," said Saban of his 2003 team, "and that is maybe eight to 12 members of our freshman class moving up in the depth chart."

Coming into the season, the offensive line was the best Saban had in four years at LSU, and there was quality speed at all receiver positions and at running back. The big question mark was at quarterback, where Matt Mauck and Marcus Randall were going in with less than one full season as a starter.

To me, the biggest question was: Could a defensive front four that returned Chad Lavalais, Marquise Hill, and Marcus Spears apply the kind of pressure that shapes quality defenses?

Five months later, we had the answer.

• • •

Move over Trojans, there's a Tiger in the room.

A bunch of Tigers.

There's Lionel Turner, a blitzing linebacker, who flattened the Oklahoma kid who won the Heisman, Jason White, to sew up a 21–14 victory that gave LSU another trophy, the crystal football as the BCS champion of the planet.

There's Marcus Spears, who carried 297 pounds into the end zone with an interception that gave the Tigers their winning cushion.

There's Marquise Hill, another cat-quick defensive end, who made life miserable for the guys in red all evening long, knocking down passes and drilling ball carriers.

And there are those tireless speedsters in the secondary, Randall Gay and Eric Alexander and Corey Webster and Travis Daniels, who are either going for the quarterback's jugular or are running downfield tossing blankets on receivers.

Finally, there was Justin Vincent, whose 117 rushing yards made him the game's MVP, just as his 201 yards against Georgia made him the MVP of the SEC championship game.

The case can be made that LSU kept the Sooners in the game, first with a penalty that erased a field goal that would have put the Tigers up by 17 in the third quarter, later with an interception of an errant throw by Matt Mauck that set up the score that pulled the Sooners to within a touchdown.

It was fitting that Nick Saban's Tigers won a national championship with one defensive stop after another, a tribute to the architect who has made defense a mission, who has developed a disciplined consistency that has carried his ball club to the heights all teams dream about.

Consider this: Saban's defense held a team that averaged 461 yards over the season to 154 yards—52 yards of it rushing. LSU limited a team that averaged 45 points to a couple of touchdowns, one on a two-yard drive after a blocked punt, another on a 30-yard push following an interception.

They made a virtual basket case of Jason White, who was picked off twice, who struggled to complete 13 passes in 37 tries. They closed the rushing lanes, they made their blitzes pay off, and they never stopped coming.

Most significantly, they kept responding to adversity, which they've managed to do all year.

On the game's first play, there went Vincent popping up the middle, juking linebacker Gayron Allen five yards past the line of scrimmage, then setting sail for the end zone. What looked, for a moment, like an 80-yard touchdown gallop turned into a more modest one of 64 yards when a streaking Derrick Strait ran down the freshman on the Sooner 16.

Four plays later, the Tigers were playing a first-and-goal at the 1 when Matt Mauck could not handle the snap and fumbled it away at the 2.

Whereupon, two plays later, Corey Webster picked off a bomb launched by White at midfield and returned it to the Sooner 32. It took LSU four plays to punch it in, which Skyler Green did turning right end and scooting along the sideline from the 24.

The Tigers had made their first response. The second came after Oklahoma blocked a second-quarter punt and got life two yards away from the end zone. But it took the Sooners one-two-three-four plays (after a penalty) to punch it in.

An Oklahoma offense that had scored on its first possession 11 times during the season, and twice on its second, wound up moving two yards for its only first-half points, and they didn't do it until the Sooners' fifth offensive series.

The Sooners had been outgained, 204–50, and yet they had managed to tie at 7–7.

But back came the Tigers, this time with an 80-yard drive that had Mauck throwing strikes to Devery Henderson, Michael Clayton and David Jones, after which Vincent applied the exclamation point with another up-the-gut explosion, this one from 18 yards.

That was the story.

Response.

Defense.

Championship.

We'll never know how these Tigers could have done against the Southern Cal, No. 1 in the media poll, in a season that will produce split champions.

Nick Saban could not care less. To him, all that matters is the crystal football that will be sitting in LSU's trophy case.

"The crowd was unbelievable," Saban said. "I can't think of a better city for LSU to win a national championship."

Crystal Football Says Miles a Winner
January 9, 2008

So what do you do upon learning you're going to play for a national championship?

If you were LSU in 2007, you'd send a thank-you note to the Pitt Panthers. And don't act surprised. Or make apologies.

After Pitt pulled off one of the biggest surprises of a 2007 season-gone-wild with a 13–9 victory over No. 2 West Virginia in the final week, it was no surprise, at least to me, to see the Tigers' SEC championship victory over Tennessee fuel a leap from No. 7 to No. 2 in the final BCS standings, high enough to send them against No. 1 Ohio State in the BCS championship game.

But more amazing than LSU getting into the BCS title game was this from a Las Vegas morning-line guru: Whom would he have seeded No. 1?

"Florida," the Vegas insider said.

"But Florida lost three games," I said.

"I'm just telling you. Right now we'd make Florida favored over anyone on a neutral field."

That said everything about the SEC in 2007. Which is why LSU had no apologies to make, especially when its nonconference schedule included a wipeout of Virginia Tech, the ACC champions.

• • •

As you looked around the dais at the Marriott Convention Center, it seemed Les Miles had won everything but the Kentucky Derby.

There was no blanket of roses, but on the morning after, there was a blanket of trophies.

One for finishing first in the final Associated Press poll.

Another for doing the same in the final vote of the Football Writers Association.

Another from the National Football Foundation.

And there was that crystal football, the award, still aglitter, recognizing the national Bowl Championship Series champion.

Obviously, the coach of the LSU Tigers had had precious little shuteye since that 38–24 victory over Ohio State at the Superdome on Monday night.

After a postgame press conference at the Dome, where Miles lauded the losing Buckeyes and heaped praise on what he called "an overachieving LSU football team," Miles and wife Kathy took a brief timeout before heading for, of all places, Bourbon Street.

How did it happen?

"I just looked at her and said, 'Let's go have some fun.'"

If you're the coach of a newly minted No. 1, getting to a jam-packed thoroughfare in the French Quarter is a matter of a police escort in and a police escort out.

So there were Miles and his wife, standing on a balcony, in the wee hours of Tuesday morning, holding a crystal football aloft, introducing the spoils of the BCS to Bourbon Street.

Down below, it wasn't long before hundreds of purple-and-gold-clad crazies were into a Mardi Gras–type frenzy.

"It was wild, it was great, it was unbelievable," Miles said. "It's the kind of moment I'll never forget. Kathy loved it."

When someone asked the 54-year-old Miles how he might feel 25 years from now if he's invited to the Superdome and introduced as "the coach of the 2007 national football champions," his response was: "I hope I'm still alive in 25 years."

At the moment, he's very much alive, even though he admitted that what his team accomplished Monday night, in front of the largest crowd to witness a sports event at the Superdome, has not yet "sunk in."

In a way, joining the ranks of championship coaches has a way of changing the way you're regarded in your profession, yet Miles is enough of a realist to understand fans are always judging you on "what have you done for us lately?"

Miles knows he's in a league with a bunch of high-salaried tigers. Even though this season his Tigers defeated five teams coached by coaches who have won a national championship—Tennessee's Phillip Fulmer, Alabama's Nick Saban, South Carolina's Steve Spurrier, Florida's Urban Meyer and Ohio State's Jim Tressel—he knows that's a blip on the résumé.

He understands an LSU coach has a better chance than the coach at Michigan to win a national championship because of the mother lode of Louisiana talent. But he also understands it's tougher for an SEC team to get a shot at No. 1 than a team in the less-demanding Big Ten.

The man, whom many had tabbed as Michigan's next coach, came to a fork in the road recently and realized something "a Michigan man" never realized might be true: "The LSU job is not a steppingstone. It's a destination."

So, as Les Miles sails into 2008, he'll be playing mainly with his recruits, not Nick Saban's.

What are the big questions?

Cornerbacks, to begin with.

Then quarterback Ryan Perrilloux. Can he slip into the Matt Flynn leadership role?

The offensive line, running backs and defensive line are in good shape. But will the linebackers shape up?

Next season the schedule changes. LSU visits Auburn and Florida. And, just as challenging, the Tigers pick up Georgia, the likely preseason pick to win the SEC and contend for No. 1.

No, the Tigers will not go into 2008 as the No. 2 pick in the land as they did in 2007.

But, said Miles: "We expect to be strong next season."

As long as the talent keeps rolling in, from whistle stops such as

Breaux Bridge, Baldwin, St. Martinville, Edgard, Franklinton, Rayville and Elton, the sun will keep on shining.

How brightly?

That's the question.

One 2007 question was answered, at least for LSU fans: The Tigers played well enough Monday night to knock Southern Cal out of a possible No. 1 finish in the AP poll.

Forgetting that USC lost to poor little Stanford, it made sense, if only because LSU played and defeated five of the top 15 teams in the final AP ranking, while the Trojans played no one in the top 15.

Les Miles didn't have to share a championship, or a crystal football, with anyone.

Tide Deserves to Be Unanimous No. 1
January 10, 2012

I was on deadline up in the rafters of the Superdome press box, so I didn't have a chance personally to witness Les Miles' postmortem of LSU's 0–21 whitewashing at the hands of that team in red for the BCS national championship on January 9, 2012.

"Postmortem" is Latin for "after death," and in this case, the words absolutely fit.

Out of the corner of my ears, through the press box P.A., I could hear the Cajun Cannon, Bobby Hebert, warming to his Everyfan's task, asking the now 13–1 LSU coach, in so many, many words, "What the hell just happened?"

However inelegantly Bobby asked the question—is Bobby still talking?—that was exactly what every Tiger fan wanted to know.

Was quarterback Jordan Jefferson incapable of throwing the ball more than five yards downfield?

Did backup Jarrett Lee have emergency rotator cuff surgery in the locker room before the game?

That the Tigers' offensive implosion came at the hands of Nick Saban simply made the shattered dream of another national championship that much more difficult to swallow.

The good news is Bobby and Les have buried the hatchet. And, they have agreed to translate for each other.

And you thought *Swamp People* needed subtitles.

• • •

Co-champions?

Don't be silly.

The season has come to an end.

Yes, Alabama and LSU finished the season 1–1, but I say the final vote is in, and it should be unanimous.

It's Alabama No. 1, LSU No. 2.

While it would be wrong to brush aside the memorable 13–0 journey Les Miles' Tigers took into the championship game, this BCS champion carved itself a place in history with perhaps the most lopsided 21–0 victory one will ever witness.

For a minute, it looked as if Nick Saban's Crimson Tide was on the way to the most lopsided 15–0 win, but there went Trent Richardson turning left end and speeding into the end zone for the first touchdown in a 1-vs-2 Tiger-Tide series that produced 10 field goals, the last five by Jeremy Shelley.

How dominating was Bama on a night Saban became the first coach to hoist the crystal football a third time?

Well, when one comes away with a daunting series of edges—21–5 in first downs, 384–92 in total yards—and the other guys are not allowed to cross midfield until the final quarter, the case has been made.

There was quarterback A.J. McCarron making a case for MVP with 234 passing yards against a defense that was thinking more of stopping the run, especially Richardson. It gave McCarron enough time to pick his spots, using 23 completions in setting up four of the five three-pointers.

Miles, of course, was happy to make a case for his team.

"We had a great year with this football team, which made as quality a run as there was in the country," he said. "We played eight nationally ranked teams. . . . I think this team accomplished a lot. I think that's for the voters to go figure."

From the get-go, as the Tide defensive front virtually shut out the run, Jordan Jefferson became one of those one-against-11 victims who was sacked four times, harassed all game, with time enough to do only 53 yards of damage passing.

In the opening 30 minutes, there was the feeling one had seen this one before.

The difference was, in that first Game of the Century, the Tigers seemed to be putting up somewhat of a fight.

This time, while they appeared to be doing their best, it was only to a point, considering the offense had struggled to a single first down and been out-gained a whopping 225–43 by halftime.

The Tigers had to feel fortunate to be down by a mere 9–0.

It could have been worse had Brad Smelley, all alone on the first play of the second quarter, hung onto a pass from A.J. McCarron that had 38 yards and a touchdown written all over it.

Seven plays later, Michael Brockers was blocking a 35-yard field-goal attempt to keep LSU within a field goal.

Bama's defense suffocated LSU to an embarrassing 17 yards rushing, leaving a bewildered Jefferson to see if he could do anything passing. In seven throws, Jefferson got 26 yards on six completions.

McCarron, meanwhile, was going to the air 25 times, moving the chains with high-percentage short and middle-range strikes, using the run only occasionally for diversion.

"Coach told me to show some emotion," McCarron said. "I wanted the ball in my hands and do the job. I don't think I did anything special. I just felt it was in my hands and Coach gave me the opportunity. Coach told me to just go play your game. That's what I tried to do."

LSU's Tyrann Mathieu complimented McCarron's performance.

"When he did put the ball in the air, it was a good ball," he said. "It was tight coverage, and he was very accurate."

The Tigers were being shut out for the first time since a 31–0 loss to Bama in 2002. It marked the first time a team had been shut out in a BCS championship game.

Oddly enough, LSU was being shut out for the first time in a bowl game since losing by the identical 21–0 score to Ole Miss in the 1960 Sugar Bowl.

That happened to be a rematch, too.

But this time the stakes were much higher.

Be sure Tiger fans are circling the date, Nov. 3, Saban takes his team into Tiger Stadium next season.

When it comes to LSU and Alabama, there's always tomorrow.

Today, the Crimson Tide rules.

CHAPTER 5

PRO FOOTBALL

Action in the Patio Room
November 2, 1966

Archbishop Philip M. Hannan, a sports fan, came to pre-NFL New Orleans in 1965, and it didn't take long for the city's new Catholic leader to quickly assess his new flock.

"As a religion," said the archbishop, "I learned football ranked just behind Catholicism."

When the former WWII paratroop chaplain with the 82nd Airborne saw the size of the headline on page 1 of the *Times-Picayune* on November 1, 1966—"N.O. GOES PRO"—he wondered if World War III had been declared.

It was All Saints Day. The city had been awarded an NFL franchise, and Dave Dixon, who worked with Gov. John McKeithen to bring the team here, would shortly be asking the archbishop his view on calling the team the "Saints."

"Would that be sacrilegious?" Dixon asked.

"I told Dave I'd have no objection," the archbishop said. "But I also reminded him, from the viewpoint of the Church, most of the saints were martyrs."

Forty-four years later—on February 7, 2010—then 96-year-old Archbishop Hannan celebrated a game-day Mass for the Saints in Fort Lauderdale, Florida, before Super Bowl XLIV.

The word in Las Vegas was: Never bet against the prayers of a 96-year-old archbishop.

The Saints beat the Colts, 31–17.

• • •

Seventy-eight-year-old Maurice Chevalier, born 31 years before the National Football League was founded, got the better of the Pontchartrain Hotel's accommodations yesterday.

While France's ageless institution met members of the press in the elegant Henry Stern suite on the 11th floor, Pete Rozelle and his party had to settle for the Patio Room to make the announcement sports fans had been expecting for months.

Actually, the Patio Room, a few feet off St. Charles Avenue, is a lovely place to settle for. With walls of black shutters, irregular old brick and panels of velvet, with a gas-lit chandelier hanging from the ceiling, it formed an appropriate backdrop for a historic city's entry into professional football.

At exactly one minute past 11, Rozelle and party, wearing blue suits without shoulder pads, weaved past newsmen and television cameras, making their way to a rostrum on which sat a maze of microphones and tape recorders.

Jim Kensil of the NFL asked for quiet and introduced Congressman Hale Boggs.

Boggs introduced Dr. Herbert Longenecker, who said Tulane was happy "in making the events of this day possible."

Sen. Russell Long was next with: "I think I have some idea of what Mr. Rozelle is going to say."

City Councilman Moon Landrieu, representing Mayor Schiro, expressed the city's appreciation to the congressional delegation, Gov. McKeithen and Dave Dixon.

Tom Donelon said he was glad "Jefferson Parish played a part" in this great day.

Next, Gov. McKeithen declared, "This shows what we can accomplish by working together."

By now, it was nine minutes past 11 and we still didn't know—officially—what we had accomplished until Boggs introduced Rozelle.

Pete had come a long way since the first day I saw him—in the LSU dressing room after the Sugar Bowl on Jan. 1, 1960, attempting to land Billy Cannon, who, minutes before, had signed under the goalposts with the Houston Oilers.

Ironically, before Rozelle got into his remarks, he introduced Tex Schramm of the Dallas Cowboys and Bud Adams of the Oilers, the fellow who pilfered Cannon from Pete's Los Angeles Rams.

"I guess Halloween brings all sorts of shocking surprises, and we have one for you today," said the commissioner as one newsman wisecracked, "Good God, it's Cincinnati."

But then Rozelle said the secret words at 11 past 11 on All Saints' Day: "Professional football has voted a franchise to the state of Louisiana, the city of New Orleans."

This made it official although, unlike the Declaration of Independence, we had nothing to show for it.

Perhaps the most visible sign was the mist I detected in the eyes of Dave and Mary Dixon. Dave is the kind of fellow who would be smiling if he was up to his ears in quicksand and, seemingly, it took that kind of optimism to drag this city into major league sports.

Of course, Dave will not be completely happy until the passage of the domed stadium amendment next Tuesday, the passage of which he feels the NFL franchise assures.

"This," smiled Dave under the gas-lit chandelier, "is only the beginning for our great city."

It's only the beginning for our city—and for the owner Pete Rozelle selects within the next three weeks. If you can use the Atlanta Falcons as some sort of yardstick, the best estimate is a franchise costing $8.5 million spread over five years plus an extra $1.1 million, a figure that should be trimmed in view of the common draft, which will cut down unrealistic bonuses.

The $8.5 million is for what is technically known as "territorial rights"; yet, in a more tangible way, it means the 42 players a new club gets from existing teams. For example, New Orleans will pick three from each NFL roster (those that are unfrozen) excluding Atlanta's, making it the highest-priced meat market in the U.S.

Yesterday anyone near the Pontchartrain Hotel was suspected of being an owner. But I have a scoop for you: Maurice Chevalier is not interested. The Frenchman also had no suggestion for a name.

"My favor-eet sport ez box-eeng," said Maurice.

By Water, Blood, and Desire
September 18, 1967

I. Thou Shalt Not Cheer in the Press Box.

The First Commandment of sports journalism was chiseled in stone (by a faithful scribe) and brought down from Mount Grantland long before the invention of the Gutenberg press.

But on September 17, 1967, when the New Orleans Saints played their first NFL game against the Los Angeles Rams at Tulane Stadium, the First Commandment was violated by the biggest sinner of all, sitting front and center in the creaky press box.

Pete Rozelle stood up and cheered.

The NFL commissioner rose to his feet and slammed his fist on the table as soon as he saw rookie returner John Gilliam take the opening kickoff at his 6-yard line, make one cut, and then race up the middle untouched for a 94-yard touchdown, christening the franchise with a play paralleling the biblical account of Moses parting the Red Sea.

Pete had been New Orleans' best friend in securing a professional football franchise. He wisely convinced the league's owners that it would be prudent to satisfy Louisiana Sen. Russell Long, who was suggesting Congress might be interested in reviewing the NFL's protective antitrust exemption.

All of a sudden, New Orleans and Long got their team, leading eventually to Rozelle's original sin.

All was forgiven.

• • •

According to the Catholic Church, there are three kinds of baptisms—by water, by blood and by desire.

Yesterday afternoon, as the Saints were christened by the Los Angeles Rams on behalf of the National Football League, the home team qualified in all three categories.

Under a September sun that brought many of the 80,879 fans to instant broil, the Saints sweat, bled and battled their way into regular-season play against a physically awesome, talent-wealthy ball club that has the manpower to go all the way.

They were outgunned, outgained and outscored but, at the finish, they were carrying the fight to a superior opponent which, at times, resembled a blinking giant fighting off an aggravating pest.

"I don't believe this is an expansion team," cracked Merlin Olsen, one-fourth of the Rams' Fearsome Foursome. "It seems like they've been together a long time, hiding out somewhere playing in another league."

Quarterback Roman Gabriel corrected another misconception.

"I know a lot of people are going to say we took New Orleans lightly," he said. "Believe me, we did not. We knew we were in tough from the game in Anaheim. And that shot they got by returning the opening kickoff simply made matters worse."

John Gilliam's 94-yard sprint—it took him 15 seconds—and a 44-yard field goal by Charley Durkee looked as though they would send the Saints into halftime with a 10–6 lead, especially when the Rams faced a third-and-25 at their 30 with less than 30 seconds remaining.

Then, in perhaps the game's biggest play, Gabriel lofted a 48-yard beauty to Bernie Casey to put the Rams in business on the Saints' 22. Two plays later, Gabriel, looking for either Jack Snow or Les Josephson, found both covered and cracked the final 2 yards for a touchdown. One second showed on the clock.

"Before the play," said Roman, "we had six seconds left officially—two more than showed on the scoreboard. We had the ball at the two, so we figured to go for six or nothing."

The score gave the visitors a tremendous boost—as Kent Kramer's run with a Gary Cuozzo pass had lifted the Saints last week against Atlanta. But the Saints came right back to turn a fumble recovery on the third-quarter kickoff into another Durkee field goal and make it a new ball game.

"If there was one thing I liked," said Tom Fears, sad but smiling, "it was that we never lost our poise, not even when the Rams got those two second-half touchdowns. We made mistakes—and you can't make 'em against a great club like Los Angeles—but our men were sticking 'em at the end, and I felt like we kept our poise all the way."

Actually, the third-quarter fumble recovery was the only "gift" the Saints received all afternoon. Aside from being able to squeeze the ball into the end zone on the final scrimmage play of the half, the Rams had to travel only 17 yards for their go-ahead score in the third, and the Saints lost a possible TD (and the football) when the ball was knocked loose from Bill Kilmer as Bill was six yards short of a fourth-quarter touchdown. LA recovered in the end zone for a touchback.

Kilmer's fumble followed a 31-yard gallop after he was forced out of the pocket. "It look like ol' Bill was just trying too hard," said Norm Van Brocklin. "He was giving it all he had all afternoon."

Can an obviously juiced ball club come back after a game like yesterday's and play well against the Redskins?

"Hell, yes," said Bill. "In this game you've got to forget your defeats in a hurry. If we have the guts I think we have, we will play just as hard against Washington."

These sentiments were echoed by linebacker Steve Stonebreaker.

"I don't go for this business of bad breaks," said Steve. "In this game, you make your own breaks. All you can do is look ahead. If you start feeling sorry for yourself, you won't do anyone any good. You either go from one game to the next or you'll be a wreck."

Perhaps the most amazing statistic was the 125 yards picked up by the Saints on the ground, 38 tough yards going to Jimmy Taylor, who was bloodied in the second half but not slowed down.

"That cat's as good as he ever was," said Deacon Jones, who caught some of Taylor's action. "What you people got to realize is that it takes at least three years to build an offensive line—and to learn all about the people you're running behind. If you put Jimmy on the Rams, it would still take him awhile to learn how our guys block."

John Gilliam, whose 94-yard trip touched off yesterday's noisiest demonstration, knows how one Saint blocks.

"All I do is follow Les Kelley," said John. "On my touchdown, he threw a tremendous block at the 20 and I turned left. Nobody laid a hand on me."

From that moment, Gabriel knew it would be a long afternoon. "They stunted a lot and had me checking off," said Roman. "I thought their linebackers did one helluva job. Judging by the two games we've played 'em, I'd say, with that defense, they've got a good chance to beat anyone they play."

So did most of the 80,879. The balloon didn't make it at halftime. But the Saints are off—and hitting.

Ben Hur as "Cat" Catlan
November 8, 1968

As the president of the National Rifle Association in the late 1990s, actor Charlton Heston knew all about rifles. He also knew much earlier in life that he didn't have one—a rifle arm, that is.

When Heston showed up in New Orleans in 1968 to film *Pro* (the name of the incredibly forgettable movie later was changed, perhaps to protect the innocent, to *Number One*), he exuded the physical charisma of an aging NFL quarterback trying to hang on to his job by using his field smarts to counteract his diminished athletic skills.

Heston looked the part of quarterback Ron "Cat" Catlan. There was only one problem.

The Cat couldn't throw a football.

The producers didn't know where to turn, so they asked Billy Kilmer, a knuckleballer, to be Heston's passing guru. Quick, get me rewrite!

Jessica Walter, Heston's co-star and on-screen wife, came to New Orleans a few years after *Number One* was released and was preparing for a TV interview.

"Whatever you do, please don't ask me about that damn movie," she said.

• • •

When you figure he parted the Red Sea with the help of Cecile B. DeMille, painted the Sistine Chapel, defended Khartoum for the British Empire, captured Jerusalem's chariot derby behind four white horses and won the Battle of New Orleans, playing quarterback for the Saints should fall into the ho-hum category for Charlton Heston.

As a connoisseur of pro football, however, Chuck Heston especially digs his current role as a fading sports hero—quarterback Ron "Cat" Catlan—because he feels the "Cat" encountered a problem Moses, Michelangelo, Chinese Gordon, Ben Hur and Andrew Jackson would not appreciate.

"Bart Starr best expressed the unique pressures—physical and mental—confronting a pro quarterback," Heston was saying the other day.

"He said, 'By the time you mature in your job, get to know what to do and why you do it, you begin to peak out physically. From then on, it's a slow descent.' This doesn't happen in any other profession."

As most Saints fans know, Heston is in town for several weeks of shooting on "Pro," a United Artists flicker scheduled to be released next year, one telling the saga of a 40-year-old quarterback on the skids, whose hard-nosed attitude puts a strain on his marriage, and whose unwillingness to accept his decline creates a conflict with his coach, his teammates and a young Negro quarterback expected to succeed Catlan with the Saints.

In this case, the marriage of football and conflict, with a sprinkling of sex—but no stop-action—is the stuff Hollywood dreams are made of.

Between takes at the Saints' Lee Circle headquarters, 44-year-old Heston, tanned and athletic looking in a coffee-colored turtleneck, credited "Yat" Tittle for planting the germ of "Cat" Catlan in his dome.

"I was on a plane six years ago thumbing through a magazine when I came across this picture of Y.A. kneeling, helmetless, with blood trickling down his face," said Heston.

"Here was mute, but eloquent, testimony to a great athlete on the way out. I saw it as an idea for a film."

In a career that has taken him from ancient Rome, across sand dunes, to Inca country and under the big top, Chuck Heston has managed to out-Plimpton the George Plimpton of "Paper Lion" fame, someone who has made it fashionable to walk off the street onto the field of athletic combat.

For Heston, learning to be a quarterback has proven far more grueling, and painful, than his Academy Award role as the winning jockey in Ben Hur.

"It took me eight months to learn the secret of driving a chariot—bluffing the four horses into believing you could hold onto them," said Heston. "I drove a chariot like porcupines make love—very carefully."

As for quarterbacking, Heston began his apprenticeship under former Southern Cal QB Craig Fertig, spent time at the Saints' San Diego training camp last year and this year, and has worked closely with Billy Kilmer only to discover: "I am getting to a point where I'm beginning to have delusions of adequacy."

When he lofted a wobbly pass during shooting before Sunday's Cowboys game, a live audience of 84,000 wondered if he had taken any lessons.

The truth is he had been the victim of a Saints blitz the night before—one that left him with a fractured rib—making him a medicated "Cat" Catlan, playing with the assistance of Novocain.

"I've made a lot of action movies but this is the first time I've ever broken a bone," said Heston. "Once, during a Western, I chipped a bone in my elbow. "But this was strictly my fault. The first guy in got me at the thighs and, as I twisted, the second guy put a helmet in my ribs."

At 6-2 and 201, Heston has a quarterback's physical makeup, and he manages to keep in shape by running three miles a day—when he's not playing tennis, which he hasn't lately.

If you ask him to select his favorite quarterback, he'll pick Bart Starr—but tell you it's "an emotional choice" from a hot Packer fan.

"To me," says Heston, "the ideal quarterback would have the passing arm of Sam Baugh and Otto Graham, he'd be able to handle the ball like Tittle, he'd be able to run—when necessary—like Fran Tarkenton, and he'd have the leadership qualities of Graham and Norm Van Brocklin."

Hopefully, movie fans will remember "Cat" Catlan as a composite of this galaxy—in twilight. A longtime pro in his profession, Heston can be counted on for realism—a trick he learned from DeMille.

A stickler for detail, C.B. thought nothing of shooting, again and again, the exodus scene from "The Ten Commandments," one involving 9,000 extras and 5,000 animals. Then, when it came to casting the infant Moses, he depended on Charlton's expectant wife. Mrs. Heston gave birth to a boy, and Frank Clark Heston got the part.

Joe Kept Telling Us
January 13, 1969

I did not cover the first two Super Bowls, but I was there for Super Bowl III, which turned out to be a watershed game for the NFL and the upstart AFL.

When I look at the Super Bowl media circus today, it boggles my mind. In Miami in 1969, we interviewed quarterback Joe Namath of the New York Jets while he lounged around the swimming pool of the team hotel.

There were maybe a dozen reporters in a cozy circle around Broadway Joe. We didn't even have to goad him into making outrageous statements. We simply opened our notebooks and jotted down his prediction of a Jets victory over the Baltimore Colts: "I guarantee it."

And, then, on Sunday at the Orange Bowl, Broadway Joe delivered with a solid game—completing 17 of 28 for 206 yards—but his significant impact was

the way he audibled into the right play time and time again.
No. 12 was No. 1.

• • •

MIAMI—Fu Manchu, the National Football League learned yesterday, is alive and calling audibles at the line of scrimmage.

In a game that set clean living back 20 years, the boy bachelor who used to sport a $10,000 mustache, that $400,000 quarterback who brought the AFL in from the cold, struck a blow for bar rooms everywhere, to say nothing of the National Broadcasting Company, by practicing what he had been preaching.

Trouble was no one believed Joe Willie Namath. Didn't he tell Lou Michaels of the Colts—in an after-dark episode in a Fort Lauderdale restaurant last week—that the AFL had a flock of quarterbacks better than Earl Morrall, including himself; that he was going to pick Baltimore to pieces; that, yes, he hoped Johnny Unitas did get into the action because, as Joe put it, that would mean "the game is too far gone."

Because Joe said all of this about Baltimore's thundering herd, the press was alarmed that the boy in the white shoes would soon be needing a club plan with Blue Cross.

Today Joe Willie's credentials as a prognosticator are every bit as good as his passing arm—which yesterday was magnificent.

While Namath, a 49 percent passer in regular-season play, was turning into a 61 percent pitcher in the biggest game of the year, Michaels was busy missing three field goals—one from 27 yards—as Baltimore became the biggest upset victim since Tom Dewey got blown out of the tub by Harry Truman.

As I see it, the turning point in New York's deserving—and brilliantly conceived—victory was Lou Michaels' failure to break Joe's arm during their nocturnal tête-à-tête.

In a Jets dressing room aglow with television lights, tears flowed and sweat poured—from folks like Lamar Hunt, who founded the "other league" and helped nurse it through many a winter; from kewpie-doll Weeb Ewbank, who beat the organization he earlier directed to two NFL championships; from Sonny Werblin, who signed Joe Namath to help wipe out a sad-sack image.

From Namath, there was candor and, as usual, flippant humor.

"Okay, now, all you NFL writers—out," yelled Joe as he became submerged in a fourth estate tidal wave.

Like a football version of Cassius Clay, Joe was telling it like it is—why the Jets beat the Colts 16–7. But he was being more modest than boxing's mighty mouth, so you had to go to his teammates for the answer.

"I'm telling you," said offensive guard Bob Talimant, "he is the greatest guy who ever played this game. So cool it scares you. He picked up every blitz the Colts threw at him and pushed that ball down their throats. And he did it with audibles. Lots of times, he didn't call a play in the huddle. He'd just say: Be ready to go on 'one.' Then he'd look over the Colts defense and hit 'em where it hurt. He called audibles close to 50 percent of the time."

It seemed Joe's battle plan was to hit Baltimore at its right side—where Ordell Braase, 36, and Don Shinnick, 33, held forth. Was Joe attacking old age? Talimant said no.

"A great defense like the Colts is always going to be weak in one spot. The question is to find it at the right moment. This is what Joe kept doing. We ran left, not because of Braase and Shinnick, but because they were over-shifting to the other side. Joe also was able to hit the seams of their zone—where it was weakest."

The Jets' offensive line, which was supposed to crumble before Baltimore's awesome rush, qualified for offseason jobs with Brink's.

"I wasn't nervous before the game," said rookie guard Randy Rasmussen. "I was madder than hell. We felt that 18 points was ridiculous. But all week the papers kept it up. The line got together before the game and we all dedicated ourselves to protecting Joe. They weren't going to get to him."

The Colts did—twice—but this was insignificant alongside the wall they formed around their curly-haired playboy.

Don Maynard, the Jets' leading receiver, didn't catch a ball all afternoon—he had only three thrown in his direction—but he said this reflected "Joe's intelligent thinking."

"Joe just took what they gave him," explained Maynard. "He kept hitting those secondary receivers. We all felt before the game like the rodeo guys who said: 'There ain't a horse that can't be rode.' Look around this room and you're going to see 40 pairs of boots of guys who felt just like that cowhand."

Overshadowed by the manner in which Namath opened wounds in a defense rated the finest ever to come out of the NFL was a Jets defense that came close to blanking Baltimore for the first time in 50 games—back to the Chicago game of the '65 season.

"Morrall helped us," said trigger-lipped Johnny Sample, who would be even money against Cassius Clay in a talkathon.

"The cat was real easy for us to read. From the pictures, we learned how he looked off receivers. We got three of his passes and could have got a couple more.

Sample made a diving interception of a down-the-middle throw aimed at Willie Richardson on the 2-yard line, one which enabled the Jets to go into the dressing room with a 7–0 lead.

At the start of the second period, a weird theft helped turn the game around—and sent the Jets into a lead that they never surrendered.

On a third-and-4 situation at the New York 6, Morrall rifled one to Tom Mitchell in the end zone. The ball hit Mitchell in the shoulder pads, bounced 10 feet in the air and Randy Beverly, like an infielder gathering in a pop fly, made the catch. The Jets got the ball on the 20—and were off on a 12-play drive.

On the first running play of the third quarter, Tom Matte fumbled, the Jets recovered—and soon it was 10–0.

"That fumble was the turning point," offered Jet defensive end Gerry Philbin. "It looked to me the Colts seemed to get tired in a hurry after that. They were huffing and puffing."

In a way, the Jets' image-building conquest was the greatest thing that could have happened to pro football, a sport on the threshold of merger and possible future expansion.

Significantly, the game ball was presented to the AFL. Predictably, the MVP award went to Joe Willie, who, after the champagne has lost its fizz and the confetti has been cleared up, figures to earn a lot more than his $15,000 winning share.

East Side and West Side, he has Gotham at his knees. Will NBC make him a vice president? Will they name a scotch after him? Will success spoil—and the life of a gay boulevardier ruin—Joe Willie?

Time will tell. At the moment, Joe is much in demand. Late yesterday, as the Jet dressing room emptied of well wishers, someone asked Namath's whereabouts.

"Joe," said a New York official, "cannot be disturbed. He's busy posing for a stamp."

Dempsey's Impossible Dream
November 9, 1970

For 44 years—until the Saints' victory over the Colts in Super Bowl XLIV— Tom Dempsey's 63-yard field goal to beat the Lions in 1970 arguably was the shining moment in franchise history.

And I missed it.

After the Lions' Erroll Mann kicked a field goal with 11 seconds left to give Detroit a 17–16 lead, Buddy Diliberto and I made a beeline for Tulane Stadium's creaky press box elevator. From past history, we knew how slow the elevator was, so we wanted to give ourselves a little extra time to fight through the crowd to get to the locker rooms, which were located outside the stadium.

When we reached ground level, Buddy told me, "I'm going straight to the field and then I'll cut across."

I told Buddy, "I'm going to cut under the stands."

A few seconds later, I felt an earthquake. The steel bleachers were exploding. As I turned the corner, still under the stands, a man with a radio in his ear was shouting, "We won, we won, he kicked a field goal!"

Buddy never let me live it down.

One postscript:

Buddy had a running tug-of-war with Coach J. D. Roberts. Buddy swore that when assistant coach Don Heinrich told J.D. that the Saints had to kick the ball to win, J.D. at first sent in the punt team. (That can't be true.)

But this part is. "All I can tell you is," Buddy said, "Dempsey's kick set the franchise back 20 years. J.D. lived on that kick for three seasons."

• • •

For those who believe in Sunday afternoon miracles, as dished up by St. Jude, or Don Quixote's "impossible dream," it must have been something like sitting in the Polo Grounds in 1951 the day Bobby Thomson, with one swing, won the pennant for the New York baseball Giants.

History tells us that, after going bananas for maybe a minute, those stunned, delirious New Yorkers sank back into their seats to comprehend what they had witnessed.

So it was yesterday with the remaining faithful of a 66,910 crowd that saw Tom Dempsey's incredible, stupendous, fantastic 63-yard moon-shot field goal defeat Detroit, 19–17. And would you believe John Mecom Jr. saw it from the press box?

Most fans just sat there. Some of those on the field, like Doug Wyatt, did crazy things.

"I don't know why, but I jumped the fence behind our bench, ran into the stands and began shaking hands," said Doug. "Someone stole my helmet."

There were crying fans, and crying Saints, most of them trying to get a piece of Dempsey's very large anatomy, first pummeling him on the back and then lifting him to their shoulders.

"It was pretty hectic in there," related the engulfed Joe Scarpati, whose left index finger became a part of pro football history—a kind of launching pad for the longest field goal ever kicked in football.

"Joe picks out my spot, and this time he set me up a little deeper than usual—about eight yards back instead of seven," said Tom. "All I asked the line to do was hold them out about a second longer than usual."

Explained Mike Tilleman, who was down in the trenches: "Maybe it was because we were so keyed up, I don't know, but the Lion rush wasn't as strong as it was on our other field goal tries. I really think some of them felt we might fake it and maybe some of the others felt, if we kicked, there was just no way."

Scarpati knew Tom "had gotten hold of it" but he wasn't sure it had the range.

Standing on the sidelines, Billy Kilmer, who would have been a hero in defeat had Dempsey not done the impossible, observed: "It looked like it sailed off line and then came back and just got over that bar. God, what a powerful boot. What a wonderful sight."

With a wind at his back, Dempsey was not awed by having to give the ball a boost from the Saints' 37.

"When you're back that far," said Tom, "you naturally have to kick harder at it. What you've got to make sure is you hit it square to keep it on line. It's like a golf shot. When you try to kill the ball off the tee—and you don't catch it just right—you're off to the right or the left."

Dempsey, who has kicked 'em 65 yards in practice, booted a 57-yarder in the semi-pro leagues and last year kicked a 55-yarder against the Rams, a yard short of Bert Rechichar's NFL record—now ex-record.

The shoes from that 56-yard kick today rest in the Hall of Fame at Canton, and trainer Warren Ariail was preparing to mail a memento from yesterday's bit of history—the tape that encased Dempsey's kicking foot.

You've got to tape Tom tight, but not too tight," said Warren, displaying his trophy. "First you put on what we call 'pro wrap,' then some 'grease padding.' Then you encase that with elastic tape and top it off with adhesive tape."

The boot of the century not only launched Dempsey into the record book but launched new coach John David Roberts off to a 1–0 record.

"What can you say?" asked the husky young man who Tuesday was named Tom Fears' successor. "Everyone played their hearts out—Billy, the offensive line, the defense, just everyone. We had some penalties, but they didn't get to Billy once.

"When Al Dodd caught that pass and ran out of bounds with two seconds left, I was standing alongside Don Heinrich. Don said: "There's only one thing to do—let Tom kick it.' I wonder how many people gave it a chance."

In Detroit today, they are warmly second-guessing Lions coach Joe Schmidt for not letting the clock run down more before killing it. Following a march from the Detroit 14, the Lions set up what looked like the winning three-pointer for Erroll Mann.

There were 17 seconds left when Mel Farr, on third down, ran the ball to the middle of the field at the Saint 9. The Lions stopped the clock with 14 seconds remaining. After Mann kicked his 18-yarder, there were 11 seconds left.

When Al Dodd ran the kickoff out of bounds, eight seconds remained. When he caught a 17-yard down-and-out at the Saint 45, there were two seconds.

Enter Tom.

"I don't know why the Lions killed it so quickly," Kilmer said, "but, really, how could anyone figure on a 63-yard field goal?"

So, where are the Saints going?

"To six more victories," said Kilmer. "We can win all the rest if we keep carrying the fight and not making mistakes."

And where was Tom Dempsey headed?

"To get bombed," said Sunday's 265-pound hero.

And how safe is his record?

"Plenty safe," chuckled Dave Rowe after Tom was tossed the game ball. "A team would have to be nuts to try a 64-yard field goal, right?"

Right, David. Unless Tom Dempsey's on that team.

Mr. Allen's Rest Home
November 29, 1971

Billy Kilmer's career, in effect, was salvaged twice—first by going to the Saints in the expansion draft of '67, then by being traded to the Redskins, his ticket to Super Bowl VII.

With the Saints, he beat out Gary Cuozzo, who had cost the club a No. 1 pick. In Washington, he won the starting job when Sonny Jurgensen injured his shoulder, lost it to Sonny during the Super Bowl season of '72, then got it back when Jurgensen exited with a severed Achilles tendon.

Oddly enough, it was Jurgensen who put Kilmer through graduate school as far as passing mechanics were concerned. "It all came so easy to Sonny and so hard to me," said Kilmer. "My best asset was reading defenses, going to the right receiver. That's what kept me in the game."

Kilmer always laughed when reflecting on the January 1971 trade—just a few weeks before the Saints selected Archie Manning—that enhanced his career.

"The Saints thought they were burying me when they sent me to Washington, and I guess if Sonny hadn't gotten hurt, they would have succeeded," Kilmer said.

Kilmer led the "Over the Hill Gang" to the Super Bowl in 1972.

• • •

(Why are the Washington Redskins the surprise team of 1971? The following exclusive tells you why.)

WASHINGTON—As you near Fort Dullesville, by Dulles Airport, the sign says:

REDSKIN REST HOME

GEORGE ALLEN, DIRECTOR

VISITING HOURS 7–8 P.M.

I took a left and there it was, the shady retreat of Washington's professional football team, a group of men living out their lives with as much comfort as George Allen can provide, old men with thinning hair, men like Sonny Jurgensen, 37; Jack Pardee, 35; Boyd Dowler, 34; Richie Petitbon, 33; Tommy Mason, Myron Pottios, Ron McDole, 32.

"They're a wonderful bunch of old folks," the caretaker told me. "Ordinarily, when you get a collection of old geezers together, you get a few cranks. But Mr. Allen has managed to keep everyone happy."

How?

"By keeping their minds off the march of time. By not giving them time to think about hardening of the arteries. Mr. Allen, bless his heart, does it in a number of ways—with group singing, card socials, domino tournaments. On Friday nights, he has inaugurated a Jeanette McDonald–Nelson Eddy film festival. Also, for the men with crystal sets, he got a local radio station to revive 'Stella Dallas,' 'Portia Faces Life' and 'Flash Gordon.' Mr. Allen doesn't miss a trick."

I was particularly interested in the condition of Billy Kilmer, the 32-year-old quarterback. He had gone to the rest home from New Orleans where he had a number of infirmities—broken ankle, shoulder separation, torn muscles.

"Mr. Kilmer is getting along just fine," I was told. "He's over there playing checkers with Mr. Allen. It's Mr. Allen's way of keeping his quarterbacks alert. Mr. Allen usually watches while Mr. Kilmer plays Mr. Jurgensen, but Mr. Jurgensen has been in intensive care the last month."

What about practice for games on Sunday? How do the men learn their plays? I looked around and saw Mason, Pardee, Pottios, Petitbon and Dowler sitting on the veranda, some reading newspapers, some listening to Rudy Vallee records on the Victrola.

"This is their way of staying in shape," said the caretaker. "All of them have played the game for so long, little practice is required. Sometimes Mr. Allen will call them together and draw a play on the blackboard. He'll ask them if they've seen the play before. Everyone raises his hand. You have to realize these people have been playing the game for almost 20 years when you count high school and college. When they do throw the ball around on the front lawn, Mr. Allen has periodic breaks for Geritol and plasma."

What about speed? I wondered if Mr. Dowler and Mr. Pardee, for example, had been timed for 40 yards.

"There's no way of telling how fast they can run the 40. When Mr. Allen first got here, he did have wheelchair races. I believe Mr. Dowler did the 40 in 11.6, Mr. Pardee in 12.2, which is really flying for a 35-year-old linebacker, even in a good wheelchair."

Was there a sense of competition among the men?

"You bet. They hate to lose, every last one of them. The other night, Mr. Mason and Mr. Petitbon were playing cards, a game called 'Fish.'"

"Gimme all your fours," said Mr. Mason.

"'Fish,'" said Mr. Petitbon.

"Later, when Mr. Mason discovered Mr. Petitbon had a four of spades, but refused to give it up, they got into a big shouting match. Mr. Mason came close to breaking his walking cane over Mr. Petitbon's head. It was all Mr. Allen could do to keep them apart."

According to the caretaker, scenes like this are the exception.

"There's a real esprit de corps here. On most other teams, you have carousers. All of that is behind these men. We have a 9 o'clock curfew and no one has broken it. There has been only one minor fine levied. Mr. Pardee got a fruit cake from a lady fan and it had a bit too much whiskey in it. He had a couple of slices and fell over in his rocker. Mr. Allen fined him $5, and he hasn't been in trouble since. In fact, he went out and intercepted three passes against the Cardinals. Had his picture in all the papers."

But will morale suffer after the loss to Kansas City?

"I don't think so. What it means is Mr. Allen will be hanging up a few more signs. He's big on signs to pep you up."

A few samples were in evidence.

"God Loves the Redskins"

"Remember—Congress is Behind You"

"Custer Lost Because of Overconfidence"

I did find it strange that none of the under-30 Redskins, people like Roy Jefferson, Diron Talbert, Larry Brown and Charley Hathaway, were around.

"You mean the kiddies," said the caretaker. "They're busy right now working in another building. Sunday is a big day, you know."

"I realize that," I said. "The Redskins are playing the Saints.

"I'm not talking about football. The kiddies are busy making costumes for trick-or-treat. I just hope they don't overlook the Saints for Halloween. Mr. Allen never has had much faith in young whipper-snappers, and he'd never have forgiven them."

Watching the Budget in Dodgertown
August 9, 1976

Hank Stram oozed sartorial splendor. One day, post-Saints, when he was working as an NFL color analyst for CBS, I went to his house on the North Shore.

Hank ushered me into his master bedroom closet, which seemed to go on as far as the eye could see, like the catacombs or unincorporated Houston. When Hank needed more space for his shoes, suits, shirts, and sweaters, he simply annexed it—the right of eminent domain.

Hank had a heart just as big. Sometimes, he let his heart get in the way of good decisions. After drug-enslaved Chuck Muncie repeatedly missed the Saints' charter flights—his excuse was his "grandmother" had died unexpectedly—Hank finally got wise after the fourth or fifth missed flight.

"How many grandmothers do you have?"

• • •

VERO BEACH, Fla.—"Glad to see you," said Hank Stram, extending a welcoming hand.

He was standing at the entrance of the Saints camp in Dodgertown, a week after John Mecom Jr. had publicly complained of excessive spending.

Stram invited me down for an in-person inspection. "I want for you to look around and make your own evaluation," he said. "Everything we've done here has been done with the aim of creating a winning atmosphere."

He motioned to me to follow him to his golf cart. "This is a golf cart?" I asked.

"Well," said Hank, "some may find it pretentious. I call it comfortable."

It was air-conditioned, with red leather upholstery, a bar, piped-in stereo. On the side, neon lights blinked: "Saints 13, Oilers 10." Hank told the chauffeur to proceed to command central.

"I was a little dazed by John's comments," he said. "But everything is just fine now. We both understand one another. He saw Saturday night what I mean by a winning atmosphere."

"Who are these people?" I inquired as we pulled up to a building on a tree-shaded lane.

"They're just finishing up with the landscaping," said Hank. "I'm having some boxwood planted in the shape of a fleur de lis."

"It's going to be beautiful," I said.

"I'm glad you like it," said Hank. "These little touches are what make for a winning atmosphere. Let's go inside."

"Wow, this is really something," I said as I sank in a lush, wall-to-wall carpet, into which was woven all of the NFL logos.

"It's just a bit of home away from home," said Hank.

It looked like a nice home. A Baccarat chandelier hung from the ceiling over a Louis XVI desk, a period piece cluttered with football books. Cut into the walnut paneling on the wall was a 40-inch television screen. With a flick of the switch, it enabled Stram to watch practice film, movies of last week's win over Houston, movies of Buffalo, this week's opponent, and highlights of Kansas City's win over Minnesota in Super Bowl IV.

At the moment, Otis Taylor flashed across the screen. He had caught a pass in the flat, a Viking missed a tackle and Taylor was on his way to a Chiefs touchdown. "Go, Otis!" shouted Hank, rising out of his chair.

Hank walked over to the corner of the room where a soft blue light caressed the Super Bowl trophy, resting on a Chippendale cabinet.

After a few moments, seemingly in meditation, Hank turned to me and said: "Let's have a bit of lunch."

"Fine," I said.

Hank had removed his Gucci shoes and slipped into more comfortable slippers, made, I learned later, from East African lizard. On each slipper was embossed: "Beat Buffalo."

Just as I began to feel uncomfortable in my Thom McAn loafers, the butler appeared, white coat, Saints emblem, black-and-gold pants.

"We'll have a light meal now," said Hank. We began with leek and watercress soup. Then a green salad, a small portion of Trout Veronique, and Sabayon for dessert. The wine was Bâtard-Montrachet, 1970.

"It was delicious," I told Hank. "You can sure tell the difference from Boone's Farm."

He excused himself to plan the afternoon workout. An hour later, he was barking instructions to his players in a well-organized drill.

Midway through the practice, he removed his Pierre Cardin windbreaker.

After it was over, Hank's Bill Blass shorts were soaked. The coach looked pleased. "I think we got a lot accomplished. We're right on schedule."

In the distance, the team managers were collecting the 81 practice footballs of soft Italian leather, and hand-stitched blocking dummies, each bearing the picture of a Buffalo player. "It's a way of familiarizing yourself with the enemy," said Hank.

We made a dinner date following the evening squad meeting.

"Well, what do you think?" Stram asked his guest.

"I think everything is first class, Coach. If appearances mean anything, the Saints are on the right track. I hope Mr. Mecom shares this feeling."

"I think John does. I understand how badly he wants to win. I think he now understands you begin by creating the right climate."

Hank was relaxing in an Oleg Cassini dinner jacket. His two Super Bowl rings sparkled. On the giant screen, Joe Kapp was being sacked by Curly Culp and Chief banners were waving in Tulane Stadium.

"That day will come again," said Stram.

The butler appeared. He was wearing white tie, tails, an NFL patch on his jacket.

"Dinner is served," he said.

It was a festive setting. A violinist strolled through the room playing Strauss waltzes, interspersed with snatches of "When the Saints Go

Marching In." We sipped Chateau Lafitte Rothschild from a Waterford crystal goblet, bearing a score from the past: "Chiefs 23, Vikings 7." We dined on Beef Wellington with sauce Perigourdine. The decorative Wedgwood china had a picture of coach Stram with his arm around Len Dawson. For dessert, we had flaming Baked Alaska carried by the assistant coaches.

"We have a great spirit here," said Hank as we sipped an Amaretto later.

"It's obvious," I said. "I don't see how Mr. Mecom can object."

There was a knock at the door. The butler announced: "John Mecom Jr."

Mecom was beaming. He gave Stram a big hug. "That win over the Oilers was worth every penny," said John. "It was one of my biggest moments in sports."

Mecom had been diving for treasure off the Florida coast. He told Stram there is a good chance he'll find more than one million dollars in gold pieces on a Spanish galleon that went to the bottom in 1628.

Suddenly the violinist began to play.

"Where did he come from?" asked Mecom.

"From Austria," said Stram.

"Does he kick field goals?" asked Mecom.

"No," said Stram. "All he does is play the violin. We're paying him well, but he adds to the winning atmosphere."

Mecom looked over at me as he headed for the door. He looked at the chandelier, the TV set, the carpet. "If I don't find those gold pieces, I'm in trouble."

It Could Have Been Worse . . .
December 12, 1977

For Archie Manning, this was pretty much the Death Valley of his 11 years as an NFL quarterback in New Orleans: Tampa Bay 33, New Orleans 14.

The expansion Bucs entered the 1977 game having lost 26 consecutive games over nearly two seasons. As coaches looking for motivation love to do, Buccaneers coach John McKay jumped on an offhand pre-game remark by Manning, something to the effect that losing to Tampa Bay would be disgraceful, and turned it into bulletin-board material.

As the clock wound down on the victory, Bucs defenders serenaded Manning with a chorus of "It's disgraceful! It's disgraceful!"

And, it was. Hank Stram was fired a week later.

McKay was a quote-a-minute. Once when asked after a Tampa Bay loss what he thought of his team's execution, he replied, "I'm all for it."

That goes ditto for Stram.

• • •

No, there have been worse disasters.

• In 1887, a flood in China left 900,000 dead.

• In 1556, an earthquake, also in China, killed 830,000.

• In 1737, an earthquake, this one in India, was responsible for 300,000 fatalities.

So keep this in mind when you contemplate the score—Tampa Bay 33, New Orleans 14. Keep in mind Johnstown, the Hindenburg, the Titanic, Little Big Horn.

Was not Tampa Bay the best 0–26 team in professional football?

Hadn't it already broken loose for three points in six home games this season?

Although the coach had complained his team could not score against a strong wind, who was to say it could not score, again and again and again, in the windless Superdome and controlled 70-degree weather?

Doesn't anyone believe in the law of averages?

And New Orleans hospitality?

The Buccaneers had suffered enough. They were beginning to give Jean Lafitte, Captain Hook and Long John Silver, not to mention Short John McKay, a bad name.

Ask yourself: Is there anything more saintly than losing to the worst team in the league, a 12-point underdog, by 19 points?

In their Monday Morning Quarterback Club, you may be sure Peter and Paul, Matthew, Mark, Luke and John are blessing their namesakes for playing the role of Good Samaritan.

"It's better to give than receive."

In this case, six interceptions, three of them accounting for all of the Bucs' points in the second half.

"Blessed are the meek."

In this case, a Saints' offense which kept giving Tampa the ball in the plus side of the field by not making a first down during the first 24 minutes.

"Allow others to do unto you what you have been trying to do unto others."

In this case, win.

"Blessed are the no-shows."

In this case, 4,140 missing from the crowd of 40,124.

Are you there, Hank Stram?

"No question this is the lowest I've ever been as a coach."

Stram said it with feeling and, in saying it, he spoke for the 11-year-old franchise.

Until yesterday, there were two other contenders in the race for what you might term abysmal milestones: a 62–7 loss to Atlanta in the opening game of '73, a 42–17 loss to Chicago to cap a 2–12 finish in '75.

Now the Bucs go to the head of the list.

"You can't believe how ready this team was to play before the game," Stram was saying. "They were raising so much hell in the dressing room, I thought some players were fighting.

"But we go out there and strangle by the thumb. As soon as they got those points, we could feel it. The longer we went without points, the more pumped up they became."

Even at halftime, down 0–13, Stram said the mood was good. But that changed in a hurry on the Saints' second play of the third period when Mike Washington picked off a Bobby Scott pass in the flat and scooted uncontested 45 yards.

"It was a quick out," explained John Gilliam. "The guy gambled and it paid off. If Bobby had checked, and then thrown, we would have had six instead of them."

But Scott had looked right and then turned and threw left—in one motion. He had no string on the ball, and the Bucs had all the points they needed.

In essence, the Saints lost this one weeks ago, when they began compiling a tome of breakdowns—offense, defense, special teams. They have found so many ways to lose, they expect to lose, which made it no surprise they began to press when the Bucs got out in front, 6–0.

You don't allow teams to run back punts all the way (Packers and

Chargers), trick you on a fake field goal (Cards), hit the upright on place-kicks (Packers and 49ers), return critical kickoffs into scoring position (Jets) without it taking its toll.

Hank Stram has not done what you would expect a coach to do: bring his team strongly down the stretch. It has been just the opposite.

While the Saints do not have the personnel of a contender, they have not executed with the kind of precision you expect from a franchise making even modest progress.

Where did Stram lose the handle this year? Has he been too soft? Too timid about making changes?

Those are questions Stram must ponder. Also, owner John Mecom Jr. will have to ask himself that in a post-season appraisal. Mecom left yesterday's game in the fourth quarter and headed for Florida—not Tampa.

"He will review the entire situation after the Atlanta game," explained one club official, looking ahead to the end of the season.

For now, the brightest news is the Saints' magic number is one.

Requiem for Saints' No. 8
October 17, 1983

Bum Phillips had a simple explanation for the trade: "I didn't trade Archie because he couldn't play quarterback. I traded him because he couldn't play left tackle."

The 1983 trade of Manning to the Houston Oilers for left tackle Leon Gray unceremoniously ended the unfulfilled Saints career of a quarterback who spent most of his Sunday afternoons running for cover or gazing wistfully at the blue sky of Tulane Stadium or at the Superdome gondola while buried under another pile of defensive linemen no one could block.

Archie never complained. He never pointed fingers.

It was heroic stuff.

Archie and his wife Olivia raised three sons. You may have heard of them.

• • •

Well, we'll never know, will we?

We'll never know just what kind of quarterback Archie Manning would have been with—how many times have you heard it?—"a good team."

It makes you think of the classic movie scene, the one in "On the Waterfront," when Marlon Brando, a stumblebum of a fighter, is riding in a car with his brother, bemoaning his plight in Palookaville, a career gone by the boards.

"I coulda been a contenda," Brando said.

The what-might-have-been tugged at the heartstrings, just as Manning's Friday farewell did out on David Drive, a red-eyed, redhead quarterback saying goodbye to the only pro team he'd ever known.

All along, Archie Manning has been all class, and the personality trait of a thoroughbred was never more obvious than it was in this requiem for his career as a Saint.

"Bum asked me if I'd like to talk to the team," Archie said in a halting voice, "but I just couldn't do it. I'm having trouble just talking."

The saddest part of the story was the final scene of his Saintly life was tarnished by the kind of indelicacy you try to avoid in such situations. Manning first heard unconfirmed reports of his trade to the Oilers from inquiring media Thursday night—word had been leaked by friends of owner John Mecom Jr.—and it wasn't until 12 hours later he got the news from his coach.

It was a tainted ending, as was last week's episode, when Manning got the word he would not be starting against the Cardinals, not from Bum Phillips but from King Hill, his quarterback coach.

So life goes on. As you move beyond the end of an era, and Archie's class exit, the preeminent question remains: Was it a good trade for the Saints?

I'll say this: I think the trade was good for Manning, good for his mental state, his confidence having eroded in the wake of the dizzying events at quarterback.

Whether it's good for Bum Phillips depends on two things: how effective Leon Gray is as a starting left tackle, how fortunate Bum is in keeping 36-year-old Ken Stabler healthy.

Bum admits he's rolling the dice, taking a "calculated risk" with Guido Merkens, the backup quarterback for the time being.

I'm positive on one point: The biggest mistake the Saints can make can be made by only one man, by John Mecom, if the clouds get darker and he has another fit of pique and fires Bum Phillips. Considering the fragile quarterback setup, the Saints could be looking at a disastrous season, but if it comes, it is not time to change oars once again. You ride it out. You don't start another era.

"You don't get ahead by standing still," Bum explained.

Which is one thing you could never accuse Bum of doing. The truth of the matter is the Saints' cause, Archie Manning's, would have been better served had he been traded years earlier. Not only would Manning's value have been higher (a No. 1-plus), his chances of winding up with a contender may have been enhanced.

When Billy Kilmer was dealt to the Redskins, the feeling was he was being buried in Washington under all those monuments. So what happens? He winds up as the knuckleball triggerman for the Over the Hill Gang in Super Bowl VII.

Manning's future does not look quite so enticing. The Oilers have the look of an unmade bed, wandering aimlessly in the NFL jungle, with a coach, Ed Biles, whose days may be numbered.

Of one thing you may be sure. Despite diminished physical skills, Archie will give it his best shot. Long on pride, the 33-year-old Ole Miss legend wrote the textbook on offseason work, pushing the body, punishing the body after a string of broken bones, after two bouts with shoulder surgery.

In a dozen autumns, the best he could show was an 8–8 year. But the images linger . . . Archie, in his rookie debut, rolling into the end zone, past Deacon Jones, on the final play of the game to upset the Rams as 80,000 fans rocked Tulane Stadium . . . Archie, still a rookie, running past Lee Roy Jordan, running past Bob Lilly, as the Saints upset the soon-to-be-Super Bowl champion Cowboys.

It was vintage Manning and, surely, Saints fans thought, NFL trophies were just over the horizon.

But, no, there was one era—J. D. Roberts—and another—John North—and another—Hank Stram—and another—Dick Nolan—and another—Bum Phillips.

More than anything, Archie Manning was victimized by this game of musical chairs, moving Roger Staubach to observe: "If I had gone through a fraction of the changes Archie went through, I would have been a basket case."

For Archie, the isolated memories, the roar of the crowd on Willow Street, will have to suffice. "I never liked to talk about what a tough time I had here," he was saying Friday. "I have no complaints. The city has been good to me. I'll always have a special feeling for New Orleans. No one can take that away."

And how would he like to be remembered?

He recalled a talk he once had with his dad about athletic achievements, how nebulous they can be as time moves on. He said he came away from the conversation with one message.

"I'd like to be remembered as a good guy," said Archie.

He will.

"I've Seen This Game Before"
February 1, 1988

Eddie Robinson was a father and grandfather. On this 1988 evening in San Diego—after his best Grambling quarterback ever, Doug Williams, had destroyed the Denver Broncos in Super Bowl XXII with a 35-point, second-quarter explosion—Eddie was in full parental glow.

Standing to the side of the podium where the Super Bowl MVP was holding court, Eddie soaked in every word.

Eddie was the father who had worked three or four jobs to pay for his kid's college education, finally getting to watch his son walk across the stage in cap and gown to receive his diploma.

Years of draining, weeding, cutting, and lining the Grambling football field—and thousands of fatherly conversations with hundreds of kids who made it because they listened and worked hard—had all been worth it.

A father's dream fulfilled.

• • •

SAN DIEGO—After a salute to Bob Hope, a national anthem by Herb Alpert and a scoring strike by John Elway, Super Bowl XXII became the property of the Washington Redskins and Douglas Lee Williams.

Suddenly.

Brutally.

146 • THE BEST OF PETER FINNEY, LEGENDARY NEW ORLEANS SPORTSWRITER

Emphatically.

It was a public massacre, 42 points to 10, the kind that left a trail of orange blood inside Jack Murphy Stadium, the kind that shot holes in the Elway legend, the kind that carved an alcove for the Washington quarterback in Roman numeral lore.

As the Redskin defense began tomahawking Elway and his protective cocoon, Doug Williams went on the kind of historic tear most folks expected from a No. 7, not a No. 17.

According to the scenario, it would be Elway's Day. Afterward, the Golden Boy of Mile High country would pose for a stamp, have his picture painted on the Goodyear Blimp, have a peak in the Rockies christened Mount Elway.

It all began with that kind of look—a 56-yard touchdown pass on Denver's first play, followed by a field-goal drive featuring Elway strikes from the shotgun.

And then?

And then Doug Williams stood tall, much taller than the 6-foot-4 it says next to the name of the Hall of Fame quarterback from Grambling.

On Saturday, Williams underwent root canal surgery.

In the first quarter on Sunday, he slipped while retreating into the pocket and limped to the sidelines with a twisted knee that would be placed in a brace in the second half.

By that time, the Broncos had fallen from a stream of arrows out of the Doug Williams quiver.

"Goodness me," gushed Grambling's Eddie Robinson as he stood off to the side of the game's MVP in the winning locker room, "I've seen this game before. I've seen that man get warm and hum that ball on a line. I guess the thing I liked best was the way he followed the game plan. He never got ruffled. He always went to the right man."

After limping off, and surrendering the football to Jay Schroeder for two plays, Williams returned with a fastball to Ricky Sanders that was a 30-yard pass and 50-yard run.

That was it.

The Skins were off the canvas and off on a rampage.

Moments later, Williams was hitting Gary Clark for a score, Timmy Smith was going 58 yards for six, Sanders was catching another, this time for 50 yards. When Clint Didier grabbed a Williams throw in the end zone shortly before halftime, Doug Williams had passed for a Super Bowl record-tying four touchdowns. Terry Bradshaw of Shreveport, La., did it in SB XI. Doug Williams of Zachary, La., did it in one quarter; actually on one leg.

Richie Petitbon, whose defense suffocated Elway with front-four heat and a variety of blitzes, said he had never seen a quarterback have a better day of practice than Williams had Wednesday.

"He hit everyone on the numbers," said Petitbon. "I had the feeling he was going to have a real big game. He's a real trouper."

As Williams was throwing for 218 of his 340 yards, John Elway was becoming unglued. As the score went from 10–0 Denver to 21–10 Washington, Elway was completing only two passes in 11 attempts, and both were shovel passes behind the line of scrimmage.

"Our plan was to make him throw from the pocket," said Petitbon. "Damn if he didn't throw from the pocket and hit us with a quick score right away. I think our guy (Barry Wilburn) got a little lazy on that one. After that, we settled down and really got into it."

The plan was to apply heat with five men, the four down linemen and a linebacker, corner or safety. Aside from five sacks for 50 negative yards, the Skins had Elway looking over his shoulder, hurrying throws, waiting to get kissed from menacing bodies belonging to Alvin Walton, Dexter Manley, Monte Coleman and Charles Mann.

This one was as one-sided as a train wreck. A Redskin parade.

In the afterglow, the winning pitcher was standing as tall as he did on the football field.

If he was a better quarterback in Washington than he was at Tampa Bay, it was because of the guys in front of him, it was because of a guy like Timmy Smith who would run for 204 yards after Doug handed him the ball, it was because of Washington's version of The Three Amigos—Sanders, Clark and Didier—who caught four touchdowns worth of passes.

All week long, Doug Williams exuded a special kind of class. In his moment of triumph, he was the same man, poised and humble.

"This is great, a dream," said Williams. "But I can't wait to get home and see all my friends."

Zachary is waiting.

Voodoo Man Takes a Shot at Montana
September 10, 1990

Well, I tried.

Before the Saints hosted the 49ers in a 1990 Monday night game, I called on a French Quarter voodoo shop to get a possible explanation for the misery the Saints defense and Saints fans were experiencing having to face Joe Montana twice a year.

As it turned out, the voodoo curse imparted before I left lasted for about $58\frac{1}{2}$ minutes. Whenever the Saints played Montana, 90 seconds—especially the final 90 seconds—were the equivalent of a lifetime.

Three times in the final six minutes, Montana had been handed the football, and three times the Saints' defense had forced the world champions to three-downs-and-out. But a fourth time was too much rolling of the dice. Montana set up Mike Cofer for a game-winning, 38-yard field goal in the final seconds.

49ers 13, Saints 12, voodoo priest 0.

• • •

VOO-dat say gonna beat dem Saints!

Because extreme situations call for extreme measures, there I was last week, in the French Quarter, in the presence of Chango Oshun, a voodoo priest.

What about it, Chango?

I suggested he was the last hope.

Specifically, I was wondering if this descendant of Marie Laveau might be able to do something about Joe Montana.

A hex perhaps. A benign curse. Anything.

Obviously, the Saints need help.

The memory of Montana carving up the Denver Broncos eight months ago in the Superdome, as he lifted the San Francisco 49ers to dynasty status, was still fresh.

Even fresher was the thought of the home team's suspect defensive line, a Pat Swilling in need of an engine tuneup, a finely tuned Jerry Rice running zigzags around Toi Cook.

It was the kind of dreadful Monday Night Football scenario that would be playing in living rooms coast-to-coast, courtesy of ABC.

Unless...

So what about it, Chango?

"Come with me," he said, leading the way into a dimly lit area behind a Voodoo Museum on Dumaine Street. A painting of Marie Laveau, wearing the kind of earrings Angela Hill would kill for, dominated one wall. There were tiny dolls, wax candles and gris-gris bags.

Chango took his seat behind a curtain. "Did you bring a picture of the man?"

I had.

Suddenly, Chango is examining an 8-by-10 glossy of Montana. He's holding it up to the candlelight. With dark brown darting eyes, he stares holes through No. 16. After awhile, Chango breaks the silence. He looks up and says: "This man has a nasty attitude. A very nasty attitude. But he can be handled."

Immediately, I felt relieved. Immediately, the Saints plus 4½ took on a different look.

"When is the game?" asked Chango.

"September 10," I said.

Chango wrote the date on the back of the photograph. He began meditating. He mumbled incantations. He took four cara shells in his hand, shook them and threw them on the floor.

They came to rest next to a bowl with a silver object surrounded by four toy automobiles and the butts of two cigars.

"Those are offerings to Eluggua, the African warrior," Chango said.

I placed my offering—money—next to one of the cigar butts.

All right. But what did the cara shells say?

"They say the Saints will win the game. They say Montana will be slowed down."

Chango was still holding Montana's picture, still meditating.

I reminded Chango about a story telling of voodoo priests bringing harm to someone by taking a photograph of the person, burying it face down, while burning a black candle.

"I do not bring physical harm to anyone," Chango said. "I am involved with Santarie, a Latin American religion. I am in tune with Santa Barbara, god of lightning and thunder and passion. All I'm telling you is Mr. Montana will be slowed down. He will be handled. The Saints will win."

Good enough for me.

Chango claims he was born with mystical powers. "I was mixing herbs when I was 10," said the native of Paulina, La., who has been practicing voodoo here for 16 years. "I am a Glapion. Marie Laveau was an ancestor."

The city's legendary Voodoo Queen was nearing 90 when she died in 1881. At rituals along Bayou St. John, she danced with a snake called Zombi. She sometimes beheaded live roosters. From her house on St. Ann Street, she placed curses and removed them, told fortunes and dispensed hexes known as gris-gris.

In one form or another, voodoo has been practiced here since the late 1700s. Chango, who was initiated into voodoo in Haiti, takes his job seriously. "I'm not afraid of no sucker or no momma," he says, sounding a little like Muhammad Ali. "And I feel like no one in the world owes me a damn thing."

Chango likes strong coffee and strong tobacco. He likes fine clothes, some of which he makes himself.

He also likes Wild Turkey.

"When I go," he said, "I want to be buried with a bottle of Wild Turkey."

So you figure Chango can't be all bad. You figure Joe Montana, the $4 million quarterback, might be in for some trouble.

As kickoff nears, the one problem could be keeping the owner of the 49ers, Eddie DeBartolo Jr., out of the Voodoo Museum.

For $35, you can buy a Ju-Ju necklace, with accompanying rabbit skull. It's designed for protection against any curse.

Which means? Which means, if you see Montana wearing a rabbit skull necklace, you might want to lay the 4½.

As for me, I'm taking a shot on Chango. Why not? NFL defenses haven't done anything against No. 16.

VOO-dat say gonna beat dem Saints!

It's Sad to See Simpson on Such a Downhill Run
June 19, 1994

The world saw it as it happened. It was less a chase than it was voyeuristic theater of the absurd.

How else could anyone explain the helicopter shots of this white Ford Bronco tooling down an L.A. freeway?

At the wheel was Al Cowlings, a close friend of O.J. Simpson. In the backseat, holding a gun, was The Juice himself, apparently despondent to the point of suicide—or worse.

O.J. was a marketing icon. Did he really murder his estranged wife and her unsuspecting male friend in a classic case of sexual jealousy?

The Bronco finally came to a halt inside the walls of O.J.'s compound. O.J. has lived in a gated community ever since. Three squares a day, striped sunshine.

• • •

NEW YORK—Those long gallops in the sunshine for the Southern Cal Trojans. Yes.

And those nimble scampers in the snow for the Buffalo Bills. Of course.

You knew they would be forever a part of the O.J. Simpson highlight film.

So would the Simpson smile. The Heisman Simpson. The Hall of Fame Simpson. ABC's Monday Night Simpson. And NBC's Sunday Afternoon Simpson. The Hertz Simpson dashing through airports. The Hollywood bit-part Simpson in "Towering Inferno" and "Naked Gun."

But never, ever did we dream the historical cassette of O.J. Simpson would one day include a 75-mile trip in a white Ford Bronco along California freeways, a police escort in soft pursuit of a wanted-for-murder fugitive holding a gun to his head.

Nothing in the world of sports has ever had to move aside, as Game 5 of the NBA championships did Friday night in Madison Square Garden, for what probably was O.J.'s Last Run.

Earlier in the afternoon, a friend of Simpson had read what appeared to be a suicidal letter from a disturbed person passing out final thank-yous.

"Ahmad," went one line, "I've never stopped being proud of you."

At courtside Friday, there was Ahmad Rashad, in his NBC blazer, watching a monitor that kept going from the action inside the Garden to the white Ford Bronco carrying one of Rashad's closest friends.

By the time the Knicks had closed with a 16–3 run to win, 91–84, and take a 3–2 lead in the series, a drained Rashad was still glued to the monitor as he watched the fuzzy nighttime picture of a surrounded O.J. finally stepping out of the Bronco and turning himself in.

With former USC and Buffalo teammate Al Cowlings at the wheel, Simpson's bizarre journey joined Game 5 in the first quarter, weaving its way through cheering crowds along the freeway shouting, "Juice! Juice! Juice!"

Two hours later, O.J. was in custody and Derek Harper of the Knicks was talking of the "fantasy life athletes live."

"It's not really a real life," Harper said. "We stay at the best hotels; people wait on us hand and foot. When your playing days are gone, you have to realize you're not invincible. That you're a human being. When you feel you're bigger than that, you run into problems."

Problems money—or celebrity—won't cure.

O.J., apparently, had it all. He was married to a high school princess—Nicole Brown—who gave him two healthy children. They lived in a $3 million mansion. As some bicoastal couples, they shared an oceanfront home in California, a condo in Manhattan.

Annual vacations to Hawaii were all-expenses paid, courtesy of Hertz. They'd ski at Vail and Aspen. Each drove a Ferrari.

This was the Simpsons' life, before O.J. and Nicole split two years ago.

So how do you, or can you, explain a man charged with two brutal murders, his ex-wife and her friend?

If such an affable-on-the-outside guy like O.J. is indeed guilty, what could trigger such rage?

The question went to a clinical psychologist who has made a special study of the evolution of behavior.

"Generally," he told me, "sexual jealousy is a major factor in spousal abuse. It is the main cause 52 percent of the time. It is at least a part of the cause 92 percent of the time.

"More men see women as sexual possessions than the other way around. Many abusers see their wives or girlfriends as sexual objects who cannot be given up. Sometimes a pathological attachment is developed.

"In O.J.'s case, assuming he is guilty, a number of factors could have come crashing together. It's possible he could not deal with their failure to reconcile and he could not control his possessiveness. Suddenly, she's there with another man . . ."

Triggering perhaps an uncontrollable rage.

"There are many people in jail because of one violent crime, people who are not capable of committing another. A crush of circumstances. You might compare it to someone who rushes into a burning building to save his child. Ordinarily, that person might think he'd be incapable of doing such a thing."

What did he derive from O.J.'s letter that struck many as a goodbye message?

"To me," the psychologist said, "the most telling thing was O.J. saying, 'If we had a problem, it's because I loved her so much.' This goes right to the heart of sexual jealousy."

In the eyes of this psychologist, there isn't any doubt O.J.'s life would have been better served had he gone into therapy after Nicole called the police in 1989, after Simpson left Nicole bruised and battered, with a hand imprint on her neck. It wasn't the first time.

But O.J. got off with specified hours of community service.

Why do many battered wives keep returning to their husbands?

"Usually for two reasons," the psychologist said. "Because they love them and because they think they'll change."

Now it turns out O.J. might have a lifetime to ponder what he once told Parents Magazine about life in the fast lane.

"I've seen too many guys get lost in the glamorous world I move in," O.J. said. "My family helps me keep in touch with who I really am."

Is Kicking Situation Such a Serious Problem?
August 25, 1995

Over the years, the Saints have had some incredible characters with questionable football IQs, especially those who limped through the doors of their old practice facility on David Drive. When you're a lovable loser for so many decades, bad things seem to happen.

Archie Manning tells the story about the kick returner, a preseason pickup from the Raiders in the 1970s, who arrived the day of the game with a parrot. The parrot held such esteem in the player's heart that he carried it everywhere he went, even giving it pride of position by allowing it to perch on his shoulder. Before the game, the player placed the parrot in a cubbyhole above his locker.

The returner then went out and fumbled away two kicks. The Saints lost, and the returner's short Saints career obviously was over. Sadly, he returned to his locker to discover the life of his parrot also had ended.

For some reason, the great stories usually revolve around the kicking game.

• • •

With the ghost of Morten Andersen growing more ominous with every swing of the leg, with Chip Lohmiller's inability to make an extra point, with Cary Blanchard suspect beyond 45 yards, with Norm Johnson having pledged his instep to the Pittsburgh Steelers, I have a question:

Is there enough time for the Saints to hold a Kicking Karavan?

Think of the fun. Think of the stories.

If your memory goes back that far, it was the Dallas Cowboys—the "old" Cowboys—who came up with the caravan idea in 1967, which happened to be the year the Saints were hatched.

In Dallas at the time, the Cowboys were looking for someone to replace Danny Villanueva, whereupon, in typical Texas fashion, off went personnel boss Gil Brandt in a private plane, on a Hollywood-type talent hunt that would hit 28 cities, cover 10,000 miles and touch the lives of approximately 1,300 candidates. A real slice of life, it turned out.

In Memphis, a guy in a khaki uniform came rushing onto the field and asked if he could kick out of turn. "I've got a bus waiting for me," he explained as he handed a Cowboys official the coin money-changer off his belt. He kicked three squibs in street shoes, then raced back up the hill to his bus, to the warm applause of his passengers.

Showing up at various pit stops were dishwashers, bellhops, postal clerks, mechanics. And die-hards. In Columbia, S.C., when a young hopeful flopped as both place-kicker and punter, he inquired: "Y'all signing any holders?"

Naturally, Villanueva didn't think much of the caravan idea. "Gil Brandt probably thought that somewhere in this beautiful country of ours, there has to be a better kicker than me. So they blow $70,000 trying to find him, and they wouldn't give me a $500 raise."

What gives the current plight of the Saints an ironic twist is the manner in which the franchise's two biggest place-kicking heroes made their exit.

Before Morten (six-time Pro Bowler) Andersen was lost in a salary cap gamble, Tom (63-yard) Dempsey was gone through the infinite wisdom of J. D. Roberts. At least the Saints wanted to re-sign Andersen. Roberts, incredibly, ran off the man whose record kick won him his first game as an NFL head coach when he was called in from the Richmond Roadrunners of the Continental League to replace Tom Fears during the 1970 season.

Packing a misguided Marine psyche when it came to understanding kickers, Roberts cut Dempsey the following year for failing to make a pre-scribed weight, ignoring the fact that half of Tom's right foot was missing, ignoring the fact Tom kicked best between 265 and 270 pounds.

Even more unbelievable was Dempsey's losing his job in the exhibition season, to someone named Skip Butler, who had kicked off three times out of bounds and who had made one field goal from 12 yards (when the goal posts were on the goal line).

Interestingly, Dempsey was signed by the Eagles and brought up from the taxi squad for the 10th game of the '71 season. In his first four games, he was 10-for-14, including a 57-yarder against the Redskins and a 52-yarder against the Lions. He finished '71 12-for-17, a .706 percentage that was best in the NFC.

It was always Dempsey's feeling that no one man can win a game, but a kicker could lose it. "If you had a game where the quarterback threw three interceptions, a wide receiver had three drops and a kicker missed three field goals," he used to say, "the kicker would get most of the heat. It's the nature of the profession."

It's also the nature of the profession that kickers will forever be driving coaches up the wall.

Errol Mann, who kicked for the Broncos, Packers, Lions and Raiders, used to say, "It takes a different breed of personality to be a kicker: mentally deficient."

Onetime kicking coach Harvey Johnson finally came to the conclusion: "If you really studied kickers, you'd find that as children, they were left alone too much."

Who can forget Jeff "Wolfman" White, who lasted one exhibition season with the Saints?

There was the night, under a full moon in Tulane Stadium, that short and hairy-chested Wolfman kicked three field goals in a 16–10 victory against the Oilers.

After the game, in the showers, White gave out repeated wolf sounds—something like "aaoooooh." When reporters gathered round with questions, he climbed on a bench and began jumping up and down.

A few days later, Wolfman was cut by Coach John North. Asked why, North got right to the point: "He scared the hell out of me."

Favre Fever Running Wild in Hometown: Green Bay Star Puts Kiln in the Spotlight

January 18, 1997

Brett Favre's father Irvin was a high school football coach for 29 years, 24 of them at Hancock North Central in Mississippi, where he coached his three quarterback sons.

As he watched the NFL star of his middle son rocket into orbit, Irvin was forced to explain why he didn't let strong-armed, and strong-willed, Brett fill the air with passes. Why was Brett locked into a wishbone and a wing-T offense, handing the ball off to his running backs?

"Because," said Irvin, sounding more like a coach than a gushing dad, "we had a kid who was a 1,000-yard rusher, and we kept winning with what we were doing."

Brett's stats were not the kind to entice the big-time football colleges, which is why he wound up at the only Division I-A school to go after him, Southern Mississippi, where Curley Hallman rode four seasons of Favre's virtuosity to the head coaching job at LSU.

From 1995 to 1997, Brett was the MVP of the NFL. Not bad for a wishbone quarterback.

• • •

KILN, Miss.—At Rooster's Cafe, as management tries to decide what dish will be designated the "Brett Favre Special," the short odds are on Favre's favorite, the stuffed rib-eye.

Even though Favre has never set foot inside, the Broke Spoke, a biker's bar, has claimed him as one of their own, an autographed picture of the Green Bay quarterback holding a place of honor.

At the Park Ten Sports Lounge, a bowling alley in nearby Diamondhead, a "Favre Wall" enshrines the native of a community named for tar kilns (or furnaces) built in the late 1800s on the banks of the Jordan River.

The folks at "Lyons Insurance—Log & Dump Trucks & Mobile Homes" eagerly await the erection of a huge highway poster: "Welcome to Kiln, Hometown of Brett Favre."

A Brett Favre Doll, made of cheese and priced at $5, will go on sale next week in Bay St. Louis.

At 9:10 a.m. Friday, a Packers pep rally will delay the start of classes at Hancock High School, probably the first pep rally to be covered by "A Current Affair" and "Hard Copy," which is providing students with green and yellow pompons.

As purple, green and yellow decorations for an early Mardi Gras begin to appear, the purple lights are muted in many outdoor displays, leaving no doubt where this green-and-yellow whistle-stop stands for Super Bowl XXXI.

Favre Fever has run amok.

It ran a high temperature last season, when the man in jersey No. 4 helped steer the Packers into the NFC Championship Game against the Dallas Cowboys. But with Green Bay playing for a world championship for the first time in 29 years, as Irvin Favre puts it, "Man, this is a whole new ball game."

The father, and once the high school coach, of the Green Bay quarterback is trying to temper his emotions, sitting at home in a Packers sweatshirt, near a dining-room table whose centerpiece is a yellow foam-rubber cheesehead.

"I have never seen fans like those Green Bay people," mused the elder Favre, someone not easily impressed. "You have to think of most rabid college fans, and then double the intensity. They welcome snow, ice and sleet like a warm friend. They never met a wind chill they didn't like. I don't think Bonita and I could have made it through last week's game if we didn't get to sit in a box. The people sitting outside not only sat for four hours; when it was over, they didn't want to leave. It's incredible."

When it came to tailgating in a minus-15 wind chill, the quarterback's mother admits to being a wimp. "I like bratwurst all right," she said, "but, as soon as I could, I was inside a car with the heater on. It's going to be interesting to see how Packers fans who've never watched a game in a dome react."

At the moment, Mrs. Favre is reacting to a run on cheeseheads. "I've been on the phone to Green Bay trying to order as many as I can get my hands on. I'm guessing we'll have at least 100 Kiln cheeseheads, whether they get a ticket to the game or have to stay here and watch it on TV."

As for Irvin Favre, a man who coached for 29 years and is two years into retirement, his challenge comes Sunday, when he tries to survive "the dream of a lifetime."

A full-blooded Choctaw Indian who married the daughter of the man who ran Benny French's, a onetime restaurant-bar in Henderson Point, the elder Favre watched Brett grow up above the bar, riding his tricycle, bumping into pool tables as the beer drinkers patted him on the head.

Coach Favre saw his son blossom, first as a fifth-grade quarterback "with a fire in the eyes that never went away," then as a QB at Hancock High and the University of Southern Mississippi. "I'm really not surprised how far Brett has come," he said. "When he was a high school senior, we were unbeaten, but we had to go to Long Beach, where we had never done anything. We're down by 13 with six minutes left, and Brett takes us in for two TDs. We win by a point.

"Even though we were a running team, he took us 65 yards in two minutes throwing the ball," he said. "At Southern Miss, he's a 17-year-old freshman riding the bench. He comes in against Tulane in the second half and brings the team back from a two-touchdown deficit. That started it all."

The three sons and one daughter of Irvin and Bonita Favre were excellent students. Brett went 10 years without being absent or tardy. After Atlanta traded him to the Packers, Falcons coach Jerry Glanville portrayed Favre as unruly, someone he said "was probably kicked out of kindergarten." Whereupon he received a stinging letter from Favre's 89-year-old kindergarten teacher.

During the last two years, the former Falcons bench-warmer has been winging it despite some vicious physical treatment and a bout with an addiction to painkillers. Ask Mrs. Favre how her son has stayed healthy, and she'll tell you it's all because of Frank "The Cat" Trapani, proprietor of a Gulf Coast restaurant, "Trapani's Knock-Knock."

"Mr. Frank was Brett's biggest fan," Mrs. Favre said. "He prayed the rosary every day that Brett would do well and remain healthy."

In failing health at age 80, Trapani spent Christmas day in a hospital room ablaze in Packers colors, opening his presents, every one tied to the

Green Bay quarterback: statues, sweaters, jerseys, helmets, photographs. He died shortly after midnight.

"His dream was to see Brett play in the Super Bowl," Mrs. Favre said. "On Sunday, he'll have the best seat in the house. He'll be up there praying the rosary for my son."

Hall's Slighting of Shaughnessy a Travesty
January 25, 1997

Football genius.

Two words that tend to be tossed around indiscriminately. Whenever Richie Petitbon hears them, he is amused by the idle gushing.

In his NFL tour of duty, more than three decades as player and coach, the man who once ran the Redskins' defense reserves that kind of label for someone who died in 1970.

"When it comes to football," says Petitbon, "Clark Shaughnessy is the only one I'd call a true genius. And that's because, from what I saw of him and what I heard of him, no one had more of an impact on the game."

But Clark Shaughnessy never made it to the Pro Football Hall of Fame.

• • •

Today they'll vote the Class of '97 into the Pro Football Hall of Fame. And one more time, Clark Shaughnessy will not be among that number.

If you consider a small alcove in Canton, Ohio, something special, then Clark Shaughnessy is the forgotten man of professional football, someone who hasn't exactly fallen through the cracks, but, better yet, has fallen through a manhole.

Brett Favre and Drew Bledsoe owe a debt to the eccentric genius, along with such ancestors as Terry Bradshaw, Joe Montana and Bart Starr, all the way back to Sid Luckman.

The same applies to people such as Ben Coates of the Patriots and Keith Jackson of the Packers, all the way back to a guy named Bob Shaw.

When Shaughnessy brought the modern T-formation to the NFL, then to college football, he revolutionized a game which, more than 60 years later, still bears his signature, and will do so into the next century.

So why isn't Clark Shaughnessy in the Hall of Fame?

George Halas, that's why.

It's quite simple. The father of professional football was not someone to share even a small slice of the limelight. Halas was smart enough to sign Red Grange, which thrust the game into the public consciousness. And he was smart enough to recognize Shaughnessy's fertile brain, which placed a halo around Halas' head. But Halas also was smart enough to keep Shaughnessy, and his pioneering thinking, off in the wings while Halas was taking bows at center stage.

In Super Bowl XXXI, the Packers and Patriots will not be using the Halas T, an outgrowth of the T-formation Halas' Chicago Bears introduced in the 1930s. They'll be using Shaughnessy's T, the formation Shaughnessy was developing as coach of the University of Chicago and as a paid "consultant" of the Bears. They will be using Shaughnessy's three-receiver alignment (split end, flanker, tight end), which Shaughnessy introduced as coach of the Los Angeles Rams in the late '40s. And they'll be using, in some fashion, defensive terminology Shaughnessy began refining as the Bears' defensive consultant in their championship year of 1963.

"As great as his offensive contributions were," said Hall of Fame coach Sid Gillman, "you could put Shaughnessy in the Hall of Fame for his pioneer work in coming up with defensive buzzwords. He's the one trailblazer who deserves to be called a genius."

Through the years, Shaughnessy had no one to carry the public relations ball. He couldn't care less. He was too busy tinkering in his lab.

When you look back on the watershed moment in the history of professional football—Bears 73, Redskins 0 in the championship game of 1940—Shaughnessy remains little more than a footnote. In the two-hour TV documentary devoted to the NFL's first 75 years. Shaughnessy received less than one minute for his role in a game that changed the face of football.

Consider: In their final regular-season game of 1940, the Bears lost to the Redskins, 7–3. In distress, Halas dialed for help. He called Palo Alto, Calif., where Shaughnessy, who had left the University of Chicago to take over a Stanford team that had won one game in '39, had knocked college football on its ear.

Stanford, and the T-formation, was on the way to a Rose Bowl date with Nebraska. Because the NFL championship would be played on Dec. 8, Shaughnessy had time to answer Halas' SOS. He hurried to Chicago, took one look at the Redskins' defense on film, and came up with a game plan that would make use of a man-in-motion to exploit Washington's tendencies. The result: 11 touchdowns, 505 yards, 73 points.

Shaughnessy returned to California to complete a perfect season with a Rose Bowl victory. From that moment on, football was never the same. Two years later, Vince Lombardi became the first high school coach in New Jersey to junk the single wing for the T. More importantly, Notre Dame's Frank Leahy, despite heated opposition, decided to junk formations introduced by the sainted Knute Rockne and go to the quick-hitting T.

At Army, Earl Blaik followed the parade, just in time for the era of Doc Blanchard and Glenn Davis. In time, the converts would be joined by Paul Brown at Ohio State. The modern T became a prairie fire. Shaughnessy had taken the game, kicking and screaming, into an era that eventually would put the single-and double-wing formations into mothballs.

Shaughnessy wasn't finished. As head coach of the Rams in '49, he wanted to come up with "something new" for his second game against Halas' Bears. The wrinkle turned into Tom Fears at split end, Elroy Hirsch at flanker, and Bob Shaw at what would later be called tight end. It was a three-receiver set Shaughnessy first used as Tulane coach in the '20s.

By 1963, Shaughnessy had become Halas' defensive consultant, utilizing knowledge that the Bears, and defensive coordinator George Allen, parlayed into an NFL championship.

Richie Petitbon, the Bears' All-Pro safety, remembered how amusing it was to watch Allen pick Shaughnessy's brain. "Shaughnessy was a paranoid genius," Petitbon said. "Bill George, who called our defensive signals, was the only one Shaughnessy allowed to take notes in our meetings. He was afraid someone would steal his stuff. We were doing things in the early '60s no one else was doing."

Shaughnessy and Halas had a love-hate relationship. "They were both strong-willed," Petitbon said. "One day they had a big-time argument, and Shaughnessy just up and quit."

In later years, after Halas' deserved place in Canton was secure, his blessing would have been enough to win a place for his longtime consultant who changed the game forever.

It was a blessing that never came.

With Ditka, There Are No Illusions
January 29, 1997

When Saints coach Jim Mora finally had enough after getting off to a 2–6 start in 1996—calling his team "diddly-poo" and resigning the next day—Buddy Diliberto started banging the drums on WWL Radio for Tom Benson to hire Mike Ditka, an icon without a team since being fired by the Bears after the 1992 season.

One day, Buddy asked me to drive with him to Baton Rouge. He had gotten an appointment to speak to Gov. Edwin Edwards.

I didn't know exactly what was going to happen, but I'll never forget the scene. As we walked into the governor's mansion, in a side room was the governor's shirtless son, playing cards with a group of his buddies.

Then we were ushered into the governor's chambers. Edwin looked over at his wife Candy and introduced Buddy to her. "This is Buddy Diliberto, the radio man from New Orleans who talks funny."

In early January 1997, Buddy got his wish—Ditka was hired.

In this case, caveat emptor. Buddy never lived down the train wreck. He couldn't. His fingerprints were all over the locomotive.

• • •

When he was coaching the Chicago Bears, Mike Ditka, in an idle moment, got right to the point on who Mike Ditka is.

"I'm a dinosaur," he said, "and I'm glad I am."

It made me think of Jurassic Park.

Since Mike Ditka was the third high-profile hire in the history of the Saints, you asked yourself a question about him: Will this dinosaur survive in a place where dinosaurs Hank Stram and Bum Phillips perished?

Remember?

With two Super Bowl appearances, and one championship, behind him, Stram was 54 in 1976 when the Saints, after a 2–12 season, called on him to do the things he had done with the Kansas City Chiefs. Hank went 4–10 and 3–11 and coached no more.

Bum Phillips arrived following the 1–15 season of '80, a cracker-barrel, tobacco-chewing, beer-drinking story-teller whose misfortune in Houston was having his finest teams at a time the Pittsburgh Steelers had theirs. In five seasons in New Orleans, the best Bum could do was 8–8, after which he retired to his Texas farm.

Now here comes Mike Ditka onto the Saints scene at the same age Bum was, age 57, a scotch-drinking, cigar-smoking, gin-rummy-playing, dice-shooting football coach oozing compulsive charisma from every pore.

He checks in after four years of the good life, in the TV booth talking football, on the golf course playing Michael Jordan for more than a $5 Nassau, before the cameras hawking merchandise.

He checked in saying a number of things.

"My aim is not to win later, but to win NOW."

"If you live in the past, you die in the past."

"This is not an ego deal. I'm not on that kick anymore."

But let's face facts. It is ego that has brought Mike Ditka back to the sidelines, an ego that tells him, at age 57, with a heart attack behind him, with two artificial hips, with football-scarred knees, he can do a job no one else has done here in 31 years: Take one small step toward the Super Bowl with a minimum of one playoff victory.

Ditka was offered a five-year contract. He wanted three, suggesting three years was enough time.

When he made a teary farewell after his Bears went 5–11 in '92, Ditka talked like a coach who would return only if some owner spoke the magic words: Total Control. In Tuesday's coming out party, he talked like someone who'd have no problem with Bill Kuharich, president and general manager, calling the personnel shots, indicating, when it came to draft choices or free agents, "sanity will prevail."

This much we know: Ditka will run the football operation, he'll run it his way, and he'll run it, I'm guessing, as one of the highest-salaried coaches in the league. If Tom Benson is not paying Mike Ditka $2 million-a-year, he's paying him close to it.

Ditka probably was the most popular 5–11 NFL coach to get the ax, if only because Michael McCaskey, grandson of George Halas, the man who hired Ditka, was considered a Yale-educated buffoon when it came to running a franchise.

Even though he was a Chicago legend during six seasons as a tight end, he was a controversial choice as head coach. In his fourth year, his Bears won the Super Bowl and his defensive coordinator-slash-personal enemy took off to become a head coach.

"I'm elated," said Ditka of Buddy Ryan's departure.

Which was vintage Ditka.

So what brought about Ditka's ultimate demise in Chicago?

Bear-watchers claim it all goes back to the strike season of '87 when the head coach embraced the replacement players, a decision that cost him the allegiance of the veterans who were the core of the '85 championship team. Ordinarily, you'd think a blue-collar guy like Ditka would be in favor of the players getting all they could. However, as one of the NFL's great over-achievers as a player, Ditka felt too many veterans were pampered and over-paid. And said so.

Ditka admitted Tuesday he "lost" the '92 team, lost it early in a 5–11 season when he ripped into quarterback Jim Harbaugh for calling an audible that resulted in a Vikings touchdown, turning a 20–0 Chicago lead into a 21–20 Minnesota victory.

He was always a raging presence. He drove quarterback Mike Tomszak into therapy. After a defeat in '83, he broke his right hand punching a filing cabinet, and then implored his team to "win one for lefty." Some felt he was loyal to a fault, keeping some assistant coaches around who wound up "doing him in." Others felt he spread himself too thin, going full-blown commercial, opening restaurants, making an appearance on "L.A. Law" and hawking Iron Mike cologne.

When you go 5–11, of course, they can always find a reason.

Now we'll see what the dinosaur can do with the personnel Jim Mora left behind, personnel Mora and Ditka discussed over the phone on Tuesday. "We talked mostly about the negatives," said Ditka.

In time, as he surveys the film, I'm sure Iron Mike will find lots more.

As for his health, no problem, he says. As for gambling, he said sure, he likes to gamble, but never on a sports event. "Just remember," he explained, "Vince Lombardi loved to play the horses."

So there. Take Iron Mike as he is. Or don't take him at all.

And fasten your seatbelts. It's going to be a bumpy ride.

Hey, Coach, a Quarter for Your Thoughts
July 17, 1998

It all went so bad, so fast.

Mike Ditka agreed to coach the Saints to scratch a five-year itch that wouldn't go away during his exile from the NFL sidelines. His $2 million-a-year contract paid for a few cigars and a few laughs.

Iron Mike opened a steakhouse. He put his jugular veins and his vocabulary through intense workouts. And he lost much more than he won, often looking befuddled by the way in which he could not "find a way or make a way."

It was apparent from the beginning: Ditka had left his heart in Chicago. He was merely double-parked in New Orleans.

• • •

I agree with Mike Ditka, a visitor to New Orleans. "Why don't they clean the streets?" he asks in the current issue of Sports Illustrated, which is a question I've sometimes asked myself as I walk the French Quarter, where I grew up and now reside.

Rather than get bent out of shape, I've found it's always good listening to the views of a visitor, in this case a visitor from Chicago who also happens to coach the New Orleans Saints.

Another visitor, the coach's wife, Diana, tells of having to "cover my nose" on a walk along Bourbon Street, something locals do many times, also something Saints fans were doing last year as they watched the team coached by Diana's husband turn the ball over 55 times.

It made me wonder what Diana might tell Mike about New York while riding a limo around some homeless people near Times Square in the wee hours. Probably: "God, what an awful city."

No question Mike the outsider has rattled some offices in City Hall. Nothing wrong with that. Many locals will agree with him. He was talking Ditka-speak.

Keep one thing in mind. Mike and Diana, at the moment double-parked in New Orleans, will always be Chicago folks who can't wait to get back "home." Which is understandable.

In most of us, civic pride runs deep, so let me say right here, when you factor in weather and murder rates, when you total up the respective warts—I've seen cleaner cities than New Orleans—I'd still never trade this River City for the city off Lake Michigan. But that's just me. Mike would disagree.

In May, my wife, Deedy, and I spent a week in Ditka's town—a great place, Chicago, even though, on a stroll down Rush Street, I saw two guys throwing up on the sidewalk outside the kind of sleazy oasis Mike might find uncomfortable today, but the kind he probably visited, many times, when he was playing for the Bears.

After reading every word of the SI article, if anything came through, it's that Ditka always will be honest in his feelings, he'll always be steeped in blue-collar tradition and values, he'll always shoot from the hip, and, in this case, he began to show his age—58.

In olden days, Ditka the player, a Hall of Fame boozer, on a visit to Pat O'Brien's would have looked past any refuse or tottering bodies, in a race to the bar.

But time marches on. Now you find the former altar boy has rediscovered religion—nothing wrong with that—and, in the words of assistant coach Danny Abramowicz, "he wants to evangelize." Quite laudable.

Ditka says he'll never use the F-word again (wanna bet?) and, after the flap created by the SI story, he vowed this would be the last (magazine) interview he'd ever do (wanna bet?).

This comes from a celebrity-coach whose job now is to prove he is more football coach than celebrity.

Funny thing, celebrity.

One Super Bowl victory for the New York Jets made Broadway Joe Namath as much, or more, of an eternal celebrity than Terry Bradshaw or Joe Montana, just as one Super Bowl victory for the Bears, along with a tour of duty on NBC, made Ditka more of a celebrity than Chuck Noll, a coach who won four Super Bowls for Pittsburgh.

In Ditka's case, it's because he's brash, he's up-front and he's goofy-smart; that is, he represents street smarts blended with frequent eruptions of goofiness.

"The people in this city are negative, and that bothers me," he tells Sports Illustrated. "Before you can win, you have to believe you're worthy."

That's goofy. Is he saying the reason the Cubs haven't won in years is because their fans are negative? Is he saying the Bulls have won and won and won because their fans are worthy?

In Super Bowl XX, here in the Superdome, Ditka's Bears beat the daylights out of the Patriots, not because of Chicago's fans, but because of possibly the finest defense in NFL history.

Given what they have received on the football field since 1967, Saints fans have been as "worthy" as any on the planet. Are they negative? Of course. Why shouldn't they be?

They were a lot less negative when Jim Mora took the franchise into four playoffs. And a little more negative when they lost four times.

Now we have Ditka, in the pulpit, talking of a winning season, the playoffs, making "believers" of us all.

To that I say, amen.

Let Billy Joe Hobert start throwing for touchdowns. Let Lamar Smith run for 1,500 yards. Let the defense finish near the top of the league. Let the offense cut last year's turnover number in half. Let the playoffs begin.

Then what would you have?

You'd have more than Tom Benson doing the boogie. You'd have fans looking to touch Iron Mike's garment (purchased in Chicago, of course). And you'd have fans reaching for the nearest broom, asking the coach: "Mike, where do I sweep? Do I begin in Jackson Square? Who's got Royal Street?"

Erxleben Shanking 'Em in the Business World, Too
May 19, 2000

I try not to laugh when I think of the football career of Saints kicker/punter Russell Erxleben. Goodness knows he got into plenty of post-NFL trouble for promoting shady financial schemes that cost investors millions and landed him in prison.

But as a purely football subject, Erxleben has a bronze bust in the Saints' Draft Day Hall of Shame.

I remember former Saints assistant general manager Harry Hulmes telling me how he argued vigorously against the Saints gambling a first-round pick—the 11th overall selection in the 1979 draft—on the Texas Longhorn with the prodigious leg.

Harry's main argument—which went unheeded—was that if you missed on Erxleben, you essentially were screwing up two vital positions.

After Erxleben's flame-out rookie season, he went back home to Austin, Texas, sat down for an interview, and blamed his place-kicking miseries on his snapper and his holder.

When the story caused a flap here, Erxleben was mystified. He thought he was speaking only to an Austin audience. He had no idea his words might travel beyond the Austin city limits, let alone across state lines.

No doubt ol' Russell never heard about that famous Hall of Famer, a guy named Marconi.

• • •

In North Carolina, wide receiver Rae Carruth of the Panthers is in jail, awaiting trial on a charge of being implicated in the murder of his girlfriend.

In Georgia, linebacker Ray Lewis of the Baltimore Ravens is sitting through selection of a jury that will determine whether he is guilty in the stabbing deaths of two men.

In Wisconsin, Green Bay tight end Mark Chmura could be facing jail on a charge he sexually assaulted a 17-year-old girl during a party following her high school prom.

In each case, let's say, the jury is out.

Not so in Texas.

Not so in the case of white-collar, hook-em-Horns crime.

In Texas, Russell Erxleben, the first-round pick of the Saints in the 1979 draft, has pleaded guilty to conspiracy and fraud in a foreign-currency scam that bilked as many as 800 investors out of more than $40 million.

On June 22, Erxleben is scheduled to learn how long he will spend in federal prison, this after a plea agreement last year when he was informed he could be facing up to seven years and a fine of $17 million.

What is it that Barnum said—about a sucker being born every minute?

The incredible thing is, not that Erxleben's venture went belly-up, but that investors were attracted to someone whose business résumé was as impressive as his performance as the Saints place-kicker.

Before the wall came tumbling down on something called Austin Fortex International, Erxleben had filed for personal bankruptcy, had been indicted on felony bad-check charges, had lost more than $200,000 in a clothing store venture, and failed in a telecommunications rebilling company that bought blocks of time from long-distance companies at discount rates, then resold them.

Somehow, for many, the name Erxleben remained magic.

Consider the thumbnail sketch when he delved into the volatile world of foreign currency trading:

"Mr. Erxleben prepared himself in the most elite rank of collegiate and professional football. The same mental discipline he applies to international foreign currency trading made him a three-time All-American football player at the University of Texas. The careful analysis and intense preparation he incorporates into each trade each day, he put into his every punt, field goal and extra point, including the 67-yard field goal, which still stands as the collegiate record."

Go ahead and laugh.

The money rolled in. Erxleben got started with a $500,000 loan from an Austin-based Longhorn, a lady. The lure was get-rich-and-richer. The risk huge profits or catastrophic losses. Erxleben spent football Saturdays watching the Longhorns in a $60,000 luxury suite bought by Austin Fortex. When Michael Jordan came to Austin, Erxleben was part of a foursome that paid $36,000 to play golf with the superstar. According to Erxleben, a low handicapper: "We bet $100 a hole."

Which was petty cash alongside what was happening to Austin Fortex. One day, the records would show, $5.6 million was lost. Another day, a $4.8 million loss in six hours. Another day, $1.8 million in a few minutes.

When the company went into receivership in 1998, it was charged with selling unregistered securities and with the failure to tell investors it was losing millions in its trades.

Two years later, as Erxleben awaits his fate, law firms involved in Austin Fortex have enabled investors to recover 65 percent of their money.

"I'm devastated," he said. "It just got completely out of hand."

Which just about sums up Erxleben's tour of duty with the Saints. The franchise made him the league's first million-dollar kicker, handing him a six-year contract that included a $300,000 signing bonus. Coach Dick Nolan joined the choir in singing the praises of the 6-foot-4 Longhorn who had a 44-yard punting average and was nailing field goals beyond 50 yards.

Unfortunately, Erxleben could not adjust to place-kicking without a kicking tee or with the NFL football, a far cry from the overinflated ones he boomed as a collegian.

From the get-go, the Texan became your classic basket case. In his NFL debut, an exhibition game against Miami, he missed field-goal attempts from 35 and 32 yards and later shanked a punt that traveled 19 yards and set up the Dolphins' winning touchdown. In his regular-season debut, against the Atlanta Falcons in the Superdome, the game was tied 34-all in overtime when Erxleben, in punt formation, watched the snap sail over his head. He went back to pick up the ball, and attempted to throw a pass as he was being tackled. A Falcon picked it off and ran it in for the winning points.

As a Saint, Erxleben would make 4 of 8 field-goal attempts. He'd spend the last three of five seasons with the team punting only. In a harbinger of things to come, when Erxleben signed, the Saints loaned him $150,000, upon which the kicker signed a promissory note agreeing to repay the amount, plus 6 percent interest, in 10 annual payments. When Erxleben failed to meet terms of the agreement, the Saints sued.

Finally, a sad historical note. Until the Oakland Raiders surprised everyone last month by taking Florida State's Sebastian Janikowski, Arkansas' Steve Little, drafted by the St. Louis Cardinals in 1978, and followed by Erxleben a year later, were the last kickers picked in the first round. Little died last year of liver disease at 43. When the Cardinals released him in his third season, after he made 3 of 8 field-goal attempts, Little went on a drinking spree, was paralyzed in a car wreck, and spent his last 19 years as a quadriplegic.

Erxleben was at the funeral. "I can't believe it," he said of his Southwest Conference rival. "It seems like just yesterday we were lighting it up."

How It All Began ... for Peyton
December 19, 2004

Talent evaluation is such a crapshoot. I recall Jim Mora telling me, years later, that when the Indianapolis Colts had to decide between selecting Peyton Manning or Ryan Leaf in the 1998 draft, the feeling inside the Colts' building was almost a coin flip.

Can you imagine that? If the choice between a future Hall of Famer and an immature blowhard is not crystal clear, then what does that tell you about the effectiveness of the millions of dollars spent on scouting every year?

You just never know. Never.

There is one person who will never forgive Peyton for returning for his senior season at Tennessee. (Peyton had earned his degree in three years but still had a year of eligibility left.) After the New York Jets suffered through a 1–15 season, Bill Parcells was hired as head coach, and the Jets had the first pick in the '97 draft.

When Peyton declared his intentions to return to Knoxville—the announcement was carried live on ESPN—Parcells' desperate screams echoed throughout Weeb Ewbank Hall.

• • •

It was a dark and stormy night.

The opening line to the Great American Novel?

Not exactly.

But it does tell you how it all began, Sept. 6, 1991, on a football field in Reserve, the day Peyton Manning threw his first touchdown pass in varsity competition.

"The weather was miserable, miserable, miserable," remembered Tony Reginelli, at the time the head coach at Isidore Newman School.

"On the bus ride there," recalled Frank Gendusa, Newman's offensive coordinator, "it got so bad we had to pull over. When the game started, it was so muddy you couldn't tell where the ball was."

In the first quarter, Newman had the ball on Riverside Academy's 19-yard line. That's when Peyton Manning, a 6-2, 160-pound sophomore, came to the line, gave his helmet a tap, and threw a pass to his brother, Cooper, a 6-4, 185-pound senior receiver who was running a post pattern.

Touchdown Newman.

It was to be the first of Manning's 92 touchdown passes in high school.

He threw 96 more in four seasons with the Tennessee Vols.

At the moment, after almost seven seasons with the Indianapolis Colts, he has thrown 223 touchdowns at the pro level, including 46 this season, leaving him two short of Dan Marino's single-season NFL record at Miami.

What it means is Peyton Manning's next touchdown pass in competitive football will be No. 412, dating back to those Manning-to-Manning days with the Newman Greenies.

"I was one of those typical receivers," Cooper said. "I wanted the football all the time. I remember the first pass he threw me in that game at Riverside. Hit me in the numbers and I dropped it. In games we had our own signals, ones we made up playing in our backyard. Peyton would touch his nose, hit his helmet, stuff like that. On that first touchdown he saw the defender playing me up tight, so he figured I could get open running a post."

Cooper caught a second touchdown pass that stormy night in Reserve, turning a quick toss from Peyton at the line of scrimmage, followed by a juke move, into a 34-yard score. "That time," Cooper said, "Peyton saw the guy playing way off me and he gave me the 'hitch' signal."

The Manning-to-Manning combo produced all of Newman's scoring in a soggy 14–6 victory.

In his only season catching his brother's passes, Cooper Manning pulled in 73 receptions, 13 for touchdowns, and averaged 17 yards per catch.

"Cooper was the class clown," Gendusa said. "Peyton was just the opposite. He was serious about everything. In the huddle, Cooper would tell jokes just to break the ice. And he was always telling his brother, 'I'm open, I'm open, throw me the ball.' I'm sure it was nice for Peyton having a brother you grew up with as your primary receiver."

Cooper was born when Archie Manning was playing for the Saints, and it wasn't long before he was showing up at the training facilities, a son his father remembered as someone who liked the sauna and the whirlpool, but more than anything, enjoyed having his ankles taped.

"Cooper would have made a fine college receiver," Gendusa said. "It's really sad he never got a chance to play at Ole Miss. An ailment that created a numbness, traced back to a narrowing of the spinal canal, something he was born with."

Gendusa remembered sending tapes of Cooper to schools that had shown an interest in him. "We sent one to Texas, and a coach there called back and said, 'That Cooper kid looks like a nice prospect. But, tell me, what do you know about that quarterback?' Peyton was already making a big impression."

With Manning at quarterback, Newman went 34–5, but never made it into the Class 2A championship game in the Superdome. In Peyton's sophomore season, he threw a last-minute interception in a semifinal loss to Haynesville, the eventual champ. In his junior year, Newman lost to Pickering in the quarterfinals when an exchange student from Spain kicked a 43-yard field goal in the final seconds. In his senior year, against Northeast High of Zachary in the quarterfinals, Peyton threw for 396 yards as Newman lost to a team coached by Doug Williams.

Today it's a bittersweet split-screen for the Manning clan, with young brother Eli suffering growing pains in New York while Peyton closes in on Dan Marino's magic number of 48.

It finds Cooper and his father bouncing around this weekend, trying to touch all the bases. As fate would have it, Peyton will chase Marino's record in a Sunday game in Indianapolis against the Baltimore Ravens, the team that chewed up Eli and the Giants last week.

Cooper spent Saturday in New York, watching Eli and the Giants take on the rampaging Steelers.

"Right now," Cooper said, "I figure Eli needs me a lot more than Peyton."

No question about that.

Benson, Have FAITH in N.O.
September 5, 2005

Anyone who smelled it will never forget it.

The Katrina smell.

Mold, death—the brown, lunar landscape.

"One dead in the attic."

No life.

Into this life-changing event came Tom Benson. The months after Katrina were not Benson's finest hour.

To be charitable, no one knew if a billion-dollar business would be able to flourish again in a city of the dead. Tom Benson considered his options, which meant looking at life through an accountant's monocle.

He flirted with San Antonio. That did not sit well with people who were burying their dead and piecing their lives back together.

Abandoned refrigerators, sealed in duct tape, cropped up like mushrooms on every neutral ground in the city, the refrigerators with the spray-painted signs: "Do Not Open—Benson Inside."

Ultimately, we are judged not by words but by actions, and Tom Benson, with a large assist from NFL commissioner Paul Tagliabue and fellow league owners, did the right thing.

• • •

Have "FAITH."

In the days before Hurricane Katrina, that was the message the Saints sent to the most loyal following in the NFL.

In our post-Katrina world, as I see it, FAITH is a message that should be embraced by Tom Benson, immediately. Not next week, not next month and definitely not next year.

So what should the owner of a franchise that has called New Orleans home for 38 years be telling us, at a time a devastated Big Easy floats in some sort of primeval ooze?

Tom Benson should tell us he will lead the charge to make our Superdome football-friendly again.

He should tell us it's his intention to keep the team there indefinitely.

He should tell us, as a resident of a city that gave him life, and prosperity, he has FAITH in the future of that city, FAITH that New Orleans will recover and become a living symbol of what FAITH can accomplish.

He should tell his season-ticket holders who already may have lost everything but FAITH, that the Saints will play as many, if not all, of their home games in LSU's Tiger Stadium, not in San Antonio's Alamodome.

When it comes to FAITH, Tom Benson finds himself in a unique position, keeping in mind NFL owners carry different levels of clout.

And, right now, as the owner of a team in a city drawing international focus, Tom Benson can become a Big Easy immortal by doing the right thing. Which is?

Well, for someone who did business in San Antonio, it would be easy for Tom Benson to use Katrina as a kind of escape hatch to set up shop— permanently—in the home of the Alamo.

That would be a horrendous decision in this change-of-life time. In the wake of 9/11, Commissioner Paul Tagliabue made sure the NFL did everything possible to heal the wounds of terror. Now Tom Benson, with the commissioner's backing, should be finding a way for the New Orleans

Saints, not the San Antonio Saints, to begin waving "We Have FAITH" banners. Obviously, in this case, it's a one-man bottom line.

It's Tom Benson's team, Tom Benson's money and Tom Benson's call.

In the pre-Katrina days, when he was beating the drums for a new stadium, Tom Benson did his best to trash the Superdome as obsolete, light years behind the state-of-the-art facilities springing up around the NFL.

Of course, he was trashing a facility good enough to hold six Super Bowls, one as recently as three years ago.

He was trashing a facility he inherited, debt free, one that allowed his franchise to keep its bottom line among the top half of a 32-team league.

As we speak, the Superdome, as a hurricane shelter, is experiencing its darkest days through no fault of its own.

In a way, it became the No. 1 whipping boy of the national media through no fault of its own.

I listened to one media idiot say, when evacuees were bused from the Superdome to Houston's Astrodome, "they were able to shower, something not available in the Superdome."

He forgot to mention a simple fact. New Orleans was without power. Without power and without water. If the Superdome had 50,000 showers, they would have been useless.

So, yes, the Superdome took a hit.

That's exactly what would make this Tom Benson's finest hour.

Standing up, making a "restored Superdome" his top priority in the fight back from a force-of-nature catastrophe, he would have carved out a fitting tombstone.

"Here Lies Tom Benson. He Kept The Faith."

Tagliabue Holds Fate of Saints in N.O.
September 9, 2005

There is a special place in hell—or maybe in Antarctica—for grave robbers.

Just a few days after Katrina, Red McCombs, who owned the Minnesota Vikings before selling the franchise and moving to San Antonio, saw a chance to rob a grave.

He thought he could get the Saints to relocate to San Antonio. This was 10 days after Katrina. Bodies still had not been recovered; 200,000 homes were under water; a historic city was on life support.

McCombs ultimately failed, but not before revealing who he was.

• • •

I didn't know a vulture had four legs.

"This is a great opportunity for the city, and we need to seize the moment, jump into it with all four legs," said Red McCombs.

That's Red (The Vulture) McCombs, former owner of the Minnesota Vikings, speaking from his hometown, which happens to be San Antonio.

"Every effort needs to be made to tie up the Saints for this season, including having people stand in front of the Alamodome singing, 'When the Saints Come Marching In.'"

What class.

In a stricken, evacuated, underwater New Orleans, they've only begun to count the dead, and here you have a former NFL owner dancing on the coffin, telling the San Antonio Express-News he believes a permanent move of Tom Benson's franchise would be supported by league owners.

Red The Vulture. What a sleazeball.

There's a time for everything. This is not the time to talk about moving a franchise—permanently—from a city that has served as the host of nine Super Bowls.

This is a time to open your arms to those who have lost homes, lost loved ones, lost everything, which is exactly what the city of San Antonio has done.

It has been open arms to Tom Benson's football team, in the way of practice facilities, also to an estimated 12,000 of the displaced, in the way of shelters, rooms for the elderly, tons and tons of food and runaway charity.

In San Antonio, you have someone like Famous Washington, a pharmacist who grew up in New Orleans, sheltering 16 members of his extended family, from 9 months old to 77 years old.

In San Antonio, you also have Red (The Vulture) McCombs.

Millionaire McCombs, a longtime friend of Benson, bought the Vikings a few years ago and unloaded them after failing to get a new stadium.

Now he's saying, if Benson wants to make a permanent move to Alamo

City, he'll get the green light from the owners because, as McCombs puts it, "Tom sits on the Management Council and has a lot of clout."

What do I think?

In the post-Katrina world, I have little doubt Benson would like to relocate to San Antonio.

Forever.

But what about Paul Tagliabue, commissioner of the NFL?

That's the billion-dollar question.

Because a vote of the owners would stop a move, because the commissioner owns the ultimate clout, Tagliabue sits in an emperor's chair.

A city that has been the crown jewel among Super Bowl hosts has suffered the greatest catastrophe in the history of this country, assuming you place what happened on 8/29 above 9/11.

All of which leaves the commissioner facing several questions:

How crucial, how fair to the future of the NFL, is keeping the Saints in Louisiana over the short term, in New Orleans over the long haul?

If it turns out Katrina KO'd the Superdome as the Saints' home, where can the team play on an interim basis while a new home is being built?

What part—financially—would the league play in a "new" Superdome?

Given the circumstances, what part might the federal government be willing to play in such a revival?

Looking down the road, waiting for a renovated Dome, or a new one, in New New Orleans, all sorts of options would face the gypsy Saints of, let's say, 2006 and 2007.

Perhaps playing all home games in Tiger Stadium?

Perhaps scattering them among Baton Rouge, Shreveport, Mobile, Jackson?

And San Antonio?

Keep in mind, while the (North) Carolina Panthers, whom the Saints play Sunday, were waiting to move into their new home in Charlotte, their interim home was across the state line, in Clemson, S.C.

Who knows what the future holds.

In a long-term manner of speaking, Katrina has made it a moment of truth.

For Tom Benson.

For Paul Tagliabue.

For the moment, my message to Red (The Vulture) McCombs is simple: Stop doing the boogie on a fleur de lis grave.

It's unbecoming.

Let's see how it all plays out.

New Orleans is down.

But not out.

How do I know?

Well, Paul Prudhomme is planning to show up Friday, leading a caravan of trucks to his offices in Elmwood.

"We've got generators, food and trailers, and we'll be in a parking lot cooking for anyone who needs it," he said. "We're going home, baby."

Benson Needs to Let City Show a Pulse

December 4, 2005

Two months after Katrina, Paul Tagliabue talked about the "human issues" coming out of an "unprecedented natural disaster." He talked about the future of the Saints being "a small part of a much bigger puzzle."

He talked about Katrina calling for such things as "coming up with a new model," using a committee of owners to bounce ideas off one another and "think out of the box."

Was the commissioner concerned, if the Saints left a city struggling for survival in the wake of Hurricane Katrina, that the NFL's image would suffer some sort of Category 5 hit?

"I'm not big into images," Tagliabue said. "I'm big into reality."

If there was a post-Katrina hero in New Orleans, it was none other than Paul Tagliabue, a buttoned-down lawyer with a missionary's heart.

He brought together Tom Benson and Gov. Kathleen Blanco, who didn't always see eye-to-eye, around the idea that a revitalized Superdome would jumpstart the New Orleans recovery rather than siphon money away from recovery.

Tagliabue was right. And, he was a hero.

• • •

Paul Tagliabue and Tom Benson, it says here, will spend part of today ~~in Baton Rouge,~~ in Tiger Stadium, watching a football game.

Tiger Stadium is a place the owner of the Saints, and his football team, have been carried into this season, let me put it nicely, kicking and screaming by the NFL commissioner.

I think that's an accurate statement.

It's also accurate to say, once Katrina laid a haymaker on the Big Easy, Benson told the organization it was finished in New Orleans forever, it would move to San Antonio, and play all of its 2005 home games there.

Anyone who disagreed could leave.

Tagliabue raised his hand.

"I disagree," he said.

Because the owner could not fire the commissioner, as he would sack his top front-office executive, the Saints are playing Tampa Bay today in the home of the LSU Tigers, 80 miles from Benson's hometown, which has given unbelievable support to a franchise that has produced seven winning seasons, and one playoff victory, in 38 years.

I believe that's accurate. You can look it up.

So what did Tagliabue tell Benson?

I don't think he told him, "Tom, if you abandon New Orleans now, after such a catastrophe, you'd be an embarrassment to yourself and the National Football League."

I don't think the commissioner said: "Tom, what's wrong with you? Are you crazy? You're a public-relations disaster. Get a grip on yourself."

I think Tagliabue probably said something like: "Tom, please don't turn your back on your fans. The Saints are a part of their lives. No owner has ever taken such a hit. And no one can say how long it will take the area to recover. But let's talk to the other owners and see what the league can do to help. They all have great sympathy for what you're going through. But right now common sense tells you that you've got to play some of your home games in Baton Rouge."

Against his business instincts, Benson bought common sense.

For the time being.

You might call this weekend visit by the commissioner, and the Saints owner, step two.

The big question: Can Tagliabue, in what seems like another common-sense pitch, sell Benson on returning to the Saints' Airline Drive headquarters, which would put the team no more than an hour-and-a-half ride to 2006 "home" games in Tiger Stadium?

What gives in 2006?

No doubt Benson, unlike Tagliabue, wants to make San Antonio the team's permanent home. There is talk of another "split season" next year, some games in San Antonio, some in Baton Rouge.

Logic suggests, when it comes to headquarters, Benson's virtual state-of-the-art facility on Airline Drive, with indoor and outdoor practice fields, makes more sense than what's available in San Antonio.

At the moment, with the Saints having to surrender their space in the Alamodome because of the NCAA volleyball tournament, the team's locker room will be moved to a high school baseball field. The weight room will be located under a tent on the baseball field's parking lot. The front office will relocate to a city water works building.

Even if Benson can find headquarters elsewhere in the city, it will be no match for Airline Drive.

In a post-Katrina world, Benson made the correct decision in moving his operation to San Antonio. It made sense. It was his best option. However, with a city under water, a city hungering for any kind of emotional life raft, Tagliabue made far more sense in scheduling than the knee-jerk reaction of a distressed owner.

In my world, a world that would bring the Superdome into play, here's what I would like to see: I would like to see Benson commit to playing his 2007 home schedule in the facility that was the home of six Super Bowls.

I would tell Benson: Do this, give the city, give the Superdome, a shot to demonstrate there is still a heartbeat here for the Saints.

If there isn't, if the results are disastrous despite league assistance, if the NFL deems New Orleans a lost cause financially, then tell Benson, who would be 80, he can bid his hometown farewell. Tell him he's free to go to San Antonio, anywhere at all, with the Big Easy's blessing.

For 20 years of untold NFL riches, the gift of a small market that embraced a Hall of Fame losing franchise, all I'm saying is Benson deserves to give New Orleans, the Superdome, and the long-suffering Who Dats one last shot.

Benson would call it the longest of third-and-longs.

Maybe he's right.

It's either accurate to say the post-Katrina Saints can survive in our town or it's sheer fantasy.

Tagliabue seems to be saying: Let's see.

Dome Sprouts from Dixon's Big Dreams: Bringing the
Facility Back to Life in Year "Another Miracle"
September 25, 2006

When the Superdome hosted its first Super Bowl on January 14, 1978, a 27–10 victory by the Dallas Cowboys over the Denver Broncos was watched by a worldwide television audience of more than 201 million, largest ever for a sporting event.

For the first time, more than 75,000 watched inside the stadium from luxury box suites that would become a prerequisite for future Super Bowls.

Dave Dixon, the father of the Superdome, was there.

What did Dave remember?

"I probably cried more than I ever have at a football game."

That was, until September 25, 2006.

• • •

"At my age," said 83-year-old Dave Dixon, "I weep easily."

Well, he'll be weeping tonight, tears of joy, watching the franchise he helped bring to the city play its first post-Katrina football game, and do it in the home that sprang from the fertile mind of an idea-gushing Mount Vesuvius.

"There would be no New Orleans Saints without you," said Commissioner Pete Rozelle, looking Dixon in the eyes on Nov. 1, 1966, All Saints Day, the day the Big Easy was awarded its ticket to the NFL.

Years before, his wheels had begun grinding away, a Dixon dream that would open its doors in 1975, a Superdome that would host six Super Bowls, four Final Fours, mega-entertainment events, conventions, trade shows, enough to generate in excess of $3 billion in business over its 31-year life.

You can say no single person had a greater impact on this city than the man who never stopped dreaming.

This is the guy who founded the United States Football League, a temporary burr under the NFL's saddle, and co-founded World Championship Tennis with Lamar Hunt, bringing colorful outfits and the tiebreaker to the sport.

This is the man who, a year ago, chased to Memphis, Tenn., by Hurricane Katrina, looked on in horror at the scenes, inside and outside, the giant mushroom on Poydras Street.

"You bet I cried," he said. "The Superdome had become the symbol of a city's nightmare, all those people begging for help. But you know what? As awful as those scenes were, I'm sure the Superdome saved some lives, just by affording shelter when the city was swimming."

Then Dixon began hearing stories it might be wise for New Orleans to "wash away the nightmare" and tear down the Superdome.

"I had no idea the extent of the damage," Dixon said. "But I could not believe anyone could contemplate such a thing. Thank God, common sense prevailed. Thank God, Commissioner Paul Tagliabue came to bat bigtime for our city, the Superdome and the Saints. The New Orleans Saints.

"Look what we have now. We have another miracle. In one year, the Superdome has come back from the dead. It's still there on our skyline, our Eiffel Tower, ready for some football. It's out there, in front, leading the city's comeback."

On returning here months after the storm, to a flooded home, the first thing Dixon did was drive. Lakeview. Lower 9th Ward. St. Bernard. Arabi.

"Just looking at the water lines was enough to blow you away," he said. "Tears. Then, in St. Bernard, I saw this man, all by himself, with a power saw, cutting some trees. That one scene reminded me what someone once told me, about there being something mystical about New Orleans. I believe it. It will take time, but, you watch, New Orleans will surprise the doubters."

The road to a Superdome in a corporate-poor city surprised a lot of folks.

In the 1950s, Buckminster Fuller, an internationally known architect, was commissioned to design a domed stadium for the Brooklyn Dodgers. Never got off the drawing board, mainly because the Dodgers were off to Los Angeles.

"It stirred the juices," Dixon remembered. "Then, when the Astrodome opened in '65, I went to Houston and saw what amounted to a covered baseball field. The Astrodome was baseball first, then football. In New Orleans, it had to be football first."

In John McKeithen, Dixon would meet the governor of his dreams, a rabid LSU football fan who reminded Dixon in an early conversation that "football has always been king in Louisiana." Dixon knew that. But he never gave a thought to what the governor said next: "In this state, Dave, telling voters football is king is akin to political wisdom."

Came the day Dixon made his domed stadium pitch to a governor, lying back in his chair, eyes closed, feet propped up on a table.

"I talked for 30 minutes, pointing out what a dome would do, not only for the city, but the state. I was trying to sell a man from north Louisiana where plenty of voters look down on our town. I'm talking away, and it looks like the governor's fast asleep. Finally, I stop. He opens his eyes, says, 'Is that it?' I nod. The governor gets up, raises his fist, slams his hand on the table, and shouts, 'By God, we're gonna build that sucker.'"

It was built for a final tab of $163 million, following some delays, inflation, political infighting.

"It was a project without scandal," Dixon said. "One of the best moves we made was having the deans of the architectural schools at LSU and Tulane get together and select the architect. The late Buster Curtis designed a building that would stand the test of time, a building for the ages."

With bonds to build the Dome facing a statewide vote, Dixon, along with a cardboard model of his dream, hit the road. In 46 days, he'd make 76 speeches, to groups large and small. The vote was 5-to-1 in favor of the bond issue.

The loudest, and most powerful, critic was state Sen. John Schwegmann, a millionaire who owed his riches to a chain of grocery stores. Mary Dixon convinced her husband that Schwegmann, as yet unannounced, was planning to run against McKeithen when McKeithen ran for re-election.

"I'll take care of the senator," McKeithen told Dixon. A few weeks later, addressing a convention of Southern Baptists in Shreveport, McKeithen said Schwegmann would make a fine candidate. He talked about Schwegmann being enormously wealthy, beholden to no one, someone who would become even richer because he had just pushed the passage of fair trade laws that would allow him to buy all the liquor he needed direct from the distilleries.

"There was a hush over the crowd," Dixon said. "It was a masterful speech. If John Schwegmann had any dreams of running against John McKeithen, which he did, he chose not to. But I will say this: His opposition wound up making the Superdome more expensive."

An expensive item Dixon championed was a replay screen that would hang from a gondola at midfield.

It sent Dixon to Europe, a trip he'd remember for a song. "A company in Switzerland sold us on the fact it had the technical expertise," Dixon said. "That night we go to a café, and there's a guy playing an Alpine horn. What's he playing? 'When the Saints Go Marchin' In.' The next night I'm in Rome, waiting for Pope Paul VI to make an appearance for a general audience. While I wait, a group of schoolchildren from France began singing, in French, the melody, 'When the Saints.' Couldn't believe it. That's when I learned the music goes back to a French tune around the 16th century. The other day I find out 'When the Saints' is the fight song for St. Michael's High School in Union City, N.J. That's Paul Tagliabue's alma mater. It's a small world."

Saints' Diehard Doing More Than Lip Service
January 12, 2007

In 2006, David Thiele was a waiter at Zea's Rotisserie & Grill—and a Saints fan.

This was the year after Katrina, and everyone on this side of a St. Louis Cemetery No. 1 tomb was piling on the team's bandwagon. Drew Brees propelled the Saints to a 5–1 start and took them all the way to the NFC Championship Game in Chicago.

Several years before—in the Aaron Brooks era—Thiele's Saints' mania had driven him to the tattoo parlor one night to have the inside of his lip branded with a fleur-de-lis tattoo.

Thiele was no lip-service Who Dat. He had faith long before he showed Drew Brees his Who Dat credentials.

• • •

He doesn't have a Drew Brees jersey.

Not yet, anyway.

But David Thiele does own two things.

The most famous bottom lip in town, thanks to the Saints' quarterback. And a special autograph: "David, Who Dat? No. 9. Drew Brees."

David Thiele is the waiter who served Drew and Brittany Brees last week at Zea Rotisserie & Grill, a restaurant in the Clearview Shopping Center.

An ordinary lunch became a topic of conversation when the quarterback tossed out a playoff-week story regarding his ever-evolving wonderment of Saints fans.

"The waiter came over and said, 'Man, I'm a diehard Saints fan,'" Brees said. "And I said, 'I've heard that a lot.' And he said, 'No, check this out.'

"He pulled his lip down, and he had a tattoo of a fleur de lis on the inside of his lip. Then I believed he was truly a diehard fan, because I don't know how many people would do that."

In this case, it was the age of the tattoo that suggested how diehard this 23-year-old zealot happened to be.

"I got my lip tattooed four years ago, when Aaron Brooks was the quarterback, when the Saints lost their last three games to miss the playoffs," Thiele said. "That ought to tell you something."

It does.

When Brees and his wife walked into the restaurant, it tells you how a nervous young waiter collected himself and put an emergency game plan into action.

Keep cool. Don't let the customers bother him. See that he eats proper.

"My table opened up just as they decided to seat him," Thiele said. "I was giggly the whole time. He had the dinner duck. He had corn grits, but it had a ton of butter, and he's allergic to dairy products. I had to bring back the corn grits. Can't have cream or stuff like that. I said, 'Drew, we need you in the best shape you can be. Let me take those back and get you something else.' So he ended up just getting regular corn."

Privacy was another matter.

"People kept coming over to the table," Thiele said. "I was saying to everybody, 'Go sit down and let him eat his duck.' People kept pestering him for autographs. I tried to be as professional as I could. Made you realize how tough it is being a celebrity."

At crunch time, with the game-clock winding down, Thiele decided to throw his Hail Mary pass.

"I didn't want any other people to see me showing my tattoo while they were eating," he said. "So I knelt down by the table and pulled back my lip. Drew said, 'Is that for real?' And I said, 'No, it's fake. I went and put it on in the bathroom because you're here.' We ended up talking and cutting up. I told him, 'You take the pain for us on the field, and I took a little pain for y'all on my lip.'"

186 • THE BEST OF PETER FINNEY, LEGENDARY NEW ORLEANS SPORTSWRITER

"I had a little alcohol in me the night I got it," he recalled. "It hurt. But once they started sticking my lip, my whole face went numb."

Although Thiele does not believe in voodoo, he's beginning to think the tattoo living inside his bottom lip is a good omen for the Saints' sixth voyage into the postseason.

"The lady that gave it to me told me it would go away in six months because my mouth heals so fast," he said. "It hasn't faded. It's gotten better. Sharper.

"I remember my worst moment as a Saints fan was the 2005 season after Katrina. That's when I was hoping my tattoo would heal and go away. But look what happened. Now everyone has a smile on their face, win or lose. That's why I've got good vibes. That's why I like to say we're going straight to the Super Bowl. It's incredible. I've never seen them do this good. It's like a weekly miracle. They kick butt."

After Katrina, Thiele got a job repairing roofs. A few months later, he was off to Tampa, where he soon came to realize the "beach life was not for him."

When Sean Payton's Saints began "kicking butt," he was back telling friends, "I'm not going anywhere ever again."

Thiele and his fleur de lis were back home.

To stay.

Win Was a Long Time Coming
January 25, 2010

The Saints' NFC Championship Game victory over the Minnesota Vikings was a fun time to remember that ancient Who Dat franchise.

With the first pick in the 1967 draft, the expansion Saints passed up defensive lineman, and future great, Bubba Smith by trading the pick to the Baltimore Colts for quarterback Gary Cuozzo, who would be beaten out for the starting job by Billy Kilmer, acquired in the expansion draft.

In 1972, the Saints became the first, and only, team in NFL history to hire an astronaut as general manager. Said owner John Mecom on the arrival of Dick Gordon, who had circled the moon: "The image of pro football is changing."

In a 1973 game against the Chicago Bears, quarterback Archie Manning tried to sneak it over from the 1—but the ball popped out, slipped through the hands of a dozen players, and was recovered by the Saints around midfield, setting up a third-and-52.

In 1975, when cornerback Bivian Lee dropped an interception in the first regular-season game played at the Superdome, he said: "It's a lot brighter in here during the day compared to our preseason games."

The Saints couldn't draft, but they got extra credit for some intriguing names that dotted the all-time roster: wide receiver Jubilee Dunbar, cornerback D'Artagnan Martin, kicker Happy Feller, and punt returner Jitter Fields. The 2009 Saints stood on the shoulders of such giants.

• • •

The Saints are going to Miami to play one more football game against Peyton Manning and the Indianapolis Colts on Feb. 7.

Believe it.

It is now history.

A franchise that lost more games than you can count because of place kicks that went wide right or wide left beat the Minnesota Vikings 31–28 in overtime, winning its biggest ever, with a down-the-middle 40-yarder that traveled from Poydras Street toward Girod Street.

At age 23, Garrett Hartley, whose right foot put the Who Dats in a Super Bowl, was not around for the jeers and tears surrounding the onetime Keystone Kops of the National Football League, the Gang That Couldn't Kick Straight.

Here's a franchise, born on All Saints Day in 1966, that took 21 years to celebrate its first winning season, 35 years to win its first playoff game, 42 years to have a chance to play for a world championship.

Suddenly on Sunday, there's a confetti shower inside the Superdome and you're thinking of those melancholy Sundays gone bye.

You're thinking of Al Hirt and his trumpet, trying to ease the sorrow at Tulane Stadium.

You're thinking of the pigeons, and the fireworks at those halftime shows, and you're thinking of a winning 63-yard field goal.

You're thinking of those miserable, long-ago losses to the Atlanta Falcons, thanks to those game-ending Big Ben plays.

Finally, all the comedy, all the catcalls, all the misery during the reign of the bag heads, have given way to Kismet.

Somewhere, up there, Buddy D is smiling.

Here we have Hero Hartley telling us he dreamed Saturday night of making the game-winning kick.

Here we have Sean Payton telling us his advice to his kicker was simple: "Just aim for the fleur-de-lis sign behind the uprights."

Fortunately, all Brett Favre could do was stand there and watch.

Favre had spent the day passing for a touchdown, and setting up three other scores for his Vikings in one more amazing display by a 40-year-old triggerman.

It took an outstanding effort by the Saints' defense to keep Favre from throwing for more than 310 yards, to intercept him twice, to force a season-high six fumbles and recover three. What helped make Favre effective were three touchdowns and 122 rushing yards by Adrian Peterson.

Meanwhile, Drew Brees, under mounting pressure as the game went on, found time to throw for three touchdowns, then engineer the crucial field-goal drive in overtime.

It was a drive given life by Pierre Thomas, who was playing with three broken ribs.

Thomas got it going with a 40-yard return of the overtime kickoff and, later, with his team facing fourth-and-1 at the Vikings' 43, went airborne for 2 yards that kept the chains moving.

Sunday's fireworks began with a rousing first half that saw the Vikings march 80 yards, a stretch during which Favre displayed his mettle by doing an excellent job in shutting out the Saints' 12th man.

With the crowd at fever pitch, No. 4 went about business by mixing several short completions with rushes of 8, 11 and 6 yards before Adrian Peterson galloped the final 19 yards as he ran through the arms of Darren Sharper.

The Saints' response was immediate, not to mention familiar, with Brees going to the air three times for modest yardage, before he hit Pierre Thomas in the right flat, then watched Thomas turn medium yardage into a 38-yard touchdown with a sharp cutback through three Vikings.

Whereupon, it was Favre's turn to see what he could do, and he responded by taking the Vikings 73 yards, ending the drive by threading a 5-yard bullet into the hands of Sidney Rice on third-and-goal.

Brees was not finished.

At the start of the second quarter, facing a third-and-10 at his 36, Brees hooked up with Reggie Bush for 28 yards. Three plays later, he was breaking out of the pocket to hit Devery Henderson for a 9-yard touchdown to tie it at 14-all.

In the closing minute, after Bush fumbled a punt to give Minnesota the ball at the Saints' 10, Favre got Reggie off the hook when he and Peterson failed to make connections on a handoff, the ball came loose and Scott Fujita made the recovery.

The teams would match touchdowns in the third and fourth quarters, with the Vikings twice rubbing out 7-point leads.

It was that kind of war down to the end.

At least one New Orleans-based Who Dat, who goes by the name of "Jimbeaux61," has already made his plans for Super Bowl Sunday, which happens to be nine days before Mardi Gras.

Says Jimbeaux61: "Breakfast will be beignets and café au lait at the French Market. A two-block walk for Bloody Marys at Margaritaville. Catch a Mardi Gras parade on Canal Street. A shrimp po-boy at Johnny's in the Quarter. A hurricane at Pat O'Brien's. Stroll over to the Superdome parking lot for tailgating. Early dinner at Galatoire's. More hurricanes at Pat O'Brien's. Watch the Saints beat the Colts at the Absinthe House. Back to Canal Street for another parade. Close out the night on Bourbon Street. Sleep till Tuesday. Get ready for the draft. Geaux Super Bowl champions."

Who Dat Men Pay Tribute to Buddy D, Celebrate Saints' Appearance in Super Bowl by Parading Their "Wears"
February 1, 2010

As Buddy D journeyed on from the print media at the *Times-Picayune* to careers in television and radio, a half century of Buddy D memories had a way of stacking up into a mile-high mountain.

Trying to choose one, I always found myself going back to the day in the 1950s, returning from a morning press conference in Baton Rouge, when I was at the wheel and Buddy was in the backseat, hidden behind the *Daily Racing Form,* busily handicapping the first two races at the Fair Grounds.

The man had a date with the Daily Double.

The fun began when a limo passed us and Buddy spotted a man, alone in the backseat, who turned out to be similarly occupied.

"Hey," Buddy said, "that's the governor."

Sure enough, it was Earl Long, also holding a *Racing Form*.

Buddy had me pull alongside. He rolled down the window, waved his *Form* at Uncle Earl, and, for the next several miles, it was an unbelievable sight, a couple of animated kindred spirits, sharing thoroughbred information along Airline Highway.

Friends loved to point out that Buddy died on January 7, 2005, and was buried on January 11. Not bad numbers: 7 and 11.

• • •

"Who Dat in Heaven—Buddy D."

That's what the sign said outside the Oceana Grill on Conti Street.

On the stage, a Pierre Thomas jersey was hugging a Sam Mills jersey.

A Drew Brees jersey was playing the trombone. A Marques Colston jersey was playing the trumpet. A Will Smith jersey was sipping suds. A Heath Evans jersey was carrying a mini–Who Dat on his shoulders. An Arnie Feilkow sign was doing the boogie.

They were part of a jam-packed crowd waiting for Buddy's Brawds to show up. On the parade route, from the Superdome to the French Quarter, they represented the finish line of the parade of men-in-dresses, in this case, all the way from thrift-store skirts to an elegant $14,000 wedding outfit.

Think about it.

All this because of a throwaway line from a Big Easy–bred legend.

"If the Saints ever make it to the Super Bowl," Buddy Diliberto once promised, "I'm going to wear a dress and dance through the streets."

Well, there they were Sunday, thousands of men in dresses, dancing from the Dome into the Quarter, with thousands and thousands looking on.

A week before a Super Bowl, ask yourself, was there anything like this, or close to it, in Cowboy Nation, in Patriot Nation, in 49er Nation, in Redskin Nation, in Dolphin Nation, in Viking Nation?

This was a tribute to the memory of an endearing Mr. Malaprop.

Throughout a career that began at The Times-Picayune and went on to television and radio, Buddy D could be a critic, but he was no mean-spirited critic, no critic eaten up with ego.

He was someone who refused to take himself seriously, who was quick to admit mistakes, never reluctant to join his legion of admirers in poking fun at himself, at his tongue-twisting, at those endless malaprops.

There was the day he introduced Joe Yenni, the mayor of Kenner, as "Joe Yenner, mayor of Kenni."

Meaning to say "secondaries," he once announced "quarterback Dan Fouts retired today after 15 seasons of terrorizing NFL secretaries."

And there were those throwaway lines:

"That's a mute point."

"That's just the chip of the iceberg."

"The Saints led in time of obsession."

"If the Saints can make the trade, it will be a good one, like mañana from heaven."

When it came to injuries, a player was out with "a torn lee nigament." On another day, a shoulder operation might be called one to remedy "a torn rotary cup."

A visit to Children's Hospital once prompted his observation about "those courageous boys and girls lying there, hooked up to their RVs."

Buddy D sailed through his sea of squirrels with passion, with frustration, with optimism, always with a smile.

The day Iran took scores of U.S. hostages, he telephoned me with an immediate observation: "That would have never happened if Iran had an NFL franchise."

At the time of the missile crisis involving Cuba, I told Buddy there was concern the U.S. and Russia might go to war. "I'm not worried about any war," he said. "They're talking about canceling the LSU–Ole Miss game. That's serious. If that happens, I'll never forgive that guy Khrushchev."

I was a guest on his TV show the night he greeted me with: "Wait till you see what I got for the folks out there."

What he had was the unveiling of the bags, during the 1–15 season of the 'Aints. When he put the bag on his head midway through the show and kept right on talking, I asked him if the station was using subtitles. He laughed, but went right on, never missing a beat.

In Buddy D's world, a faux Dr. Kevorkian was part of a cast of call-in characters that included, among others, "Bubba on the magic carpet," "Abdul the tentmaker," and "Sid from Jefferson."

Dr. Kevorkian was Frank Cusimano, a retired fireman, who became the radio voice of the doctor known as "doctor death" in relation to assisted suicide.

After a blowout loss during the Mike Ditka era, fans were calling in threatening to end it all by jumping from the terrace in the Superdome. Buddy kept telling them he understood their misery.

"I'm sitting there, listening to all the doom and gloom, and I decided to call in," said Cusimano. "When Buddy got on the line, I introduced myself as Dr. Kevorkian. I told him I was interested in helping miserable fans. I told him I had a crisis line. All they had to do was dial 1–800-BAD-TEAM. Buddy thanked me. He said, 'Doc, the way things are going, you're gonna have more business than you can handle.'"

Buddy used to joke that the best thing about dying was "getting a chance to watch all the games on TV."

Better than that, knowing who's going to win.

I'm trying to picture Buddy's first conversation with St. Peter, asking for a full confession. My guess is Buddy began talking point spreads, talking about all the losers he bet on, talking about how he's now in a position to cash every bet.

I'm imagining the look on Buddy's face when St. Peter reminded him, while he'd be the first to know who wins, and by what score, "it will be too late to make a bet. That's the rules."

St. Peter did say one thing: "In five years, the 2009 Saints will be playing in the Super Bowl."

Buddy D: "Pete, I don't know what kind of funny cigarettes you saints smoke, but tell me who will they play, and what will the spread be?"

St. Peter: "I can't tell you. After hearing your story, I joined Gamblers Anonymous."

One for the Ages: The Saints Stamp Their Place in Sports History with Huge Win on NFL's Biggest Stage

February 8, 2010

I was there on September 17, 1967, when John Gilliam returned the opening kickoff in the Saints' first regular-season game for a 94-yard touchdown.

Tulane Stadium erupted, and in the press box, NFL commissioner Pete Rozelle bolted out of his front-row seat to lead the ovation.

I mention that because on February 7, 2010, at Sun Life Stadium in Miami—44 seasons and a lifetime of misery later—one of the biggest plays in Saints' history was greeted with stone-faced silence and disbelief.

As soon as cornerback Tracy Porter jumped the slant route run by Indianapolis wide receiver Reggie Wayne, a New Orleans–area native, to intercept the pass thrown by Peyton Manning, another New Orleans native, it was clear that Porter would run untouched for a 74-yard touchdown return that would salt away the 31–17 victory.

No one in the press box gasped. No one even made a noise.

No one could believe his or her eyes.

For me, the only black-and-gold vision to match that came a few days earlier during Super Bowl XLIV media day at the stadium. As a cradle Who Dat, I scarcely could believe the work of folk art emerging from the green grass. There, in the north end zone, an NFL paint crew using spray guns drew the improbable vision in black capital letters, 20 feet tall: "SAINTS."

After finishing the black letters, the artists then worked on filling in the negative space with gold paint. The spray paint could have been 24-karat gold.

Anyone from New Orleans can tell you the Super Bowl never was exclusively about football. Reflecting on those days in 2005 when a great American city went wet and dark, I can bring only two words to mind: horrors and heroes.

Newly arrived coach Sean Payton and quarterback Drew Brees, a pair of out-of-towners, gave the Saints passion, purpose, and swagger. They lifted hearts. They touched souls.

They painted the end zone.

• • •

MIAMI GARDENS, FLA.—HOW ABOUT DAT?

Here's how it will be remembered: On a picture-post card day that wound its way into a crystal-clear evening, the New Orleans Saints gave their city, and its far-flung Who Dat Nation, the greatest moment in their long history.

Go back as far as you please and there has never been anything like it.

Look down at the green carpet inside Sun Life Stadium and it's raining black and gold confetti.

I'm trying to find Sean Payton in the crowd.

There he is.

It's LOVE DAT time.

The coach is kissing Drew Brees, his MVP quarterback.

Now I'm trying to find Tracy Porter.

He's over there, pointing to the number on his jersey.

Number 22.

It's HUG DAT time.

Porter is grabbing Darren Sharper.

And why not.

The planet has stopped spinning, at least for a WHO DAT moment.

The Saints are the world champions of professional football.

And that's only part of the story.

The Saints defeated the Indianapolis Colts 31–17.

And that's only another part of the story.

It's how Sean Payton's football team did it.

It's how they rose up to defeat Peyton Manning, a quarterback out to embellish a legend.

What they wound up watching is the other quarterback taking a giant step in establishing a legend of his own.

The Saints did it with the kind of aggressive passion that has been their hallmark.

It all began with the head coach calling an onside kick to open the second half.

It continued with the Saints recovering, with Brees marching the Saints 58 yards to their first touchdown and into a 13–10 lead.

After Manning took his team 76 yards to put the Colts up by four, one of Garrett Hartley's three 40-plus yard field goals brought the Saints within a point going into the final period.

Which is when WHO DAT TIME arrived.

Never was the hand of a poised Drew Brees more evident in the biggest drive of this championship game.

In traveling 59 yards in nine plays, Brees hit seven receivers, Pierre Thomas, Devery Henderson, Reggie Bush, Marques Colston, Robert Meachem, David Thomas. Finally, he hit Jeremy Shockey for the touchdown.

Then, incredibly, he found another pair of hands, Lance Moore's, for two points and a seven-point cushion with nine minutes to go.

All of which set the table for a game-breaking WHO DAT MOMENT that will remain forever golden.

With plenty of time to draw even, Manning had taken the Colts to a third-and-5 at the Saints' 31 when he hummed one of his fastballs in search of the trusted hands of Reggie Wayne.

The football found instead the sure hands of Porter, and there he went, a sea of daylight in front of him, going 74 yards into the end zone.

"It was great film study by me, great jump, great play," said Porter, not modestly, but accurately.

They were words echoed by the man who threw the pass.

"He made a great play, that's all I can say," Manning said.

It was fitting that the sixth interception returned for a touchdown by Gregg Williams' defense this season helped sew up a championship.

It was also fitting that Brees closed out a magical year with the kind of magic that has endeared him to WHO DAT hearts since he came aboard four years ago to find a new home in a city he loves.

"I'll say it again," Brees said. "God puts you in a position for a reason, and me coming to New Orleans was a perfect example. It was a calling to come to a city like that. We were not only rebuilding a team, we were rebuilding a city, a region, a mentality. We've been through so much, but we're going to come back stronger. It's unbelievable."

It is.

"Drew Brees was magnificent," Payton said. "It's part of the team we saw all year. Drew is an MVP for a reason. I keep thinking for all the people back in New Orleans that waited so patiently for this. We're going to have a good time on Bourbon Street tonight."

Spoken like a true WHO DAT.

One thing for sure, on Bourbon Street, Sean Payton will have plenty of company.

CHAPTER 6
GOLF

Big Eater Nicklaus Man with Mission
March 21, 1961

Jack Nicklaus is the greatest athlete—and one of the most gracious persons—I ever had the pleasure to interview. He was just 20 when I first met him at the Western Amateur at New Orleans Country Club, but it was clear he was poised to change the face of golf. He was still 16 months removed from the first of his 18 professional major championships—the 1962 U.S. Open at Oakmont, where he took down the king, Arnold Palmer, in Arnie's Pennsylvania backyard.

One tidbit about Jack: He has a photographic memory, not just for remembering every shot he ever faced on a golf course, but also for names. He can go years without seeing someone and recall the person's name. I guess that's just another example of his laser focus.

• • •

The puzzling thing about watching Jack Nicklaus walk down the fairway after hitting his golf ball out of sight is trying to figure out how someone so large ever grew up in football-mad Columbus, Ohio, and attended Ohio State without putting on a helmet and jersey.

The man who will battle Arnold Palmer for golfing supremacy in the 1960s is blue-eyed and blond—but carries no bathing beauty measurements.

He is 5-foot-11, weighs 210 pounds—mostly muscle—and has the thick arms and neck that remind you of an All-American tackle.

His physique is understandable. Eating rates right up there as a major hobby for the 20-year-old prodigy Bobby Jones labels the best amateur to come along in a long, long time.

Yesterday as Nicklaus (pronounced Nick-lus) played a practice round at Metairie, I asked Barbara, his wife of less than a year, if her husband had a favorite dish.

"Yes," she smiled, "food."

He has been known to quench his thirst with three bottles of chocolate milk between nines and thinks nothing of having a side order of French fries with a spaghetti dinner.

You might say that the temptation New Orleans offers a knife-and-fork man of his reputation would make him a poor bet for the Western Amateur championships beginning tomorrow at the New Orleans Country Club.

However, the form sheet indicates otherwise.

"Blob-o"—as he is called by his Ohio State fraternity mates—rates no less than a co-favorite with United States amateur champion Deane Beman in the 144-hole medal-match play grind that ends Sunday.

His impressive credentials mark the friendly, modest young man as the finest amateur golfer in the world.

In 1959, he won 29 of 30 matches against the best in the business.

Last year, although he was upset in the first round of the U.S. Amateur, he finished two strokes behind Palmer in the U.S. Open with a 282—the best score ever turned in by an amateur in that pressure spectacle.

Three months later at the Merion Country Club near Philadelphia, Jack led the U.S. to victory in the Eisenhower Cup matches, which attracted amateur teams from all over the globe.

He did it in spectacular fashion, shooting 66–67–68–68 (269) over the same course it took Ben Hogan 287 strokes to negotiate in winning the 1951 Open. When Nicklaus attacked it, Merion still had its 117 traps and measured the same as it did nine years before—6,694 yards.

The intriguing aspect about Nicklaus is the challenge he has accepted: He wants to win the big ones as an amateur—the Open and the Masters.

"Naturally you learn more from playing against the pros than in an amateur tournament," says Jack. "But after you have learned how to play, you can improve by working hard on your game.

"You pick up intangibles from the pros—how to finesse the ball around and how to save strokes. And you learn to think. I believe thinking is 80 percent of the game."

One of Nicklaus' major assets is an ability to approach golf as a game but, at the same time, retain a fierce competitive thirst. He seems to be a fellow who can forget his bad shots.

In last year's Open, he was leading on the 67th hole when he missed an 18-inch putt because of a ball mark on the green.

"I decided to charge the putt—to hit right over the mark—but the putt hit the bad spot and spun off line. That's the way it goes."

Off the tee, Nicklaus hits the ball with the savage-like ferocity of Palmer. For all of his power, he seems to have good control.

His short game and putting (he uses a specially designed Scottish putter and bends over the ball like the Hunchback of Notre Dame) are considered strong.

Jack's golfing career was launched by an odd twist of fate. His father, a Columbus pharmacist who is part owner of four drug stores, fractured an ankle playing volleyball and turned to golf to strengthen it.

Ten years old at the time, Jack went along for the walk, became interested and began taking lessons. Three years later, he broke 70 for the first time and, at 15, he qualified for the National Amateur—something he has done ever since.

Young Nicklaus never gave football a tumble because he was unable to find other boys willing to devote the practice time he felt the sport deserved. He chose golf because he could practice all day, every day.

Daddy Nicklaus has financed Jack's annual junkets (expenses come to roughly $5,000 annually) and gave him a down payment on his new $22,000 home in a Columbus suburb as a wedding present.

Currently, young Nicklaus is getting established in the insurance business and figures he'll have to make $25,000 a year to be free to play in the big tournaments—amateur and professional.

He plans to face the pros about six times a year—the first stop at Augusta next month.

So far as the immediate business at hand, Jack sees nothing unfair in the Western setup, which calls for four match-play rounds following 72 qualifying holes of medal play. Upsets are common since one bad round will put you on the sidelines.

"It's still the best format," says Jack. "You're not supposed to have a bad round, that is, if you want to play championship golf."

Trevino: Throwback to Thirties
April 15, 1970

I wrote this column before Lee Trevino drove from Lakewood Country Club to City Park, where he put on a dazzling golf exhibition. Everyone knew Lee had the most repeatable swing in golf since Ben Hogan. Somehow, his crazy setup and gyroscope swing plane produced laser after laser, with a slight left-to-right ball flight.

On the No. 1 tee at City Park East, surrounded by about 200 fans, Trevino joked that people didn't think he could hook the ball. He then set up five balls in a line: his first swing produced a big fade, then a little fade, then dead straight, then a slight draw, and then a big hook.

Lee saved his best for last. He pulled out an oversized glass Dr. Pepper bottle—probably the size of a 2-liter today—which was covered in tape at the bottom. That was the "club" he used to hustle bets at the par-3 course in Dallas where he ran the golf shop.

Lee threw the ball up in the air, cocked his arm, and delivered a wallop, hitting a shot, dead straight, that traveled 125 yards. And he did it again and again.

Don't ever bet this man.

• • •

When Lee Trevino shocked everyone but Lee Trevino by winning the 1968 U.S. Open, it was as if Bastille Day had come for every public course in America.

Today most of your pros come barreling off academic lines, nurtured in campus kindergartens and bank-rolled by well-heeled sponsors.

They represented a changing of the guard—from the days Hogans, Nelsons and Demarets played their way out of caddie poverty. Tommy Bolt liked to call the new breed "those flippery-wristed-youngsters"—youngsters with a diploma in one hand and a 7-iron in the other.

In Lee Trevino, who lasted seven and a half grades at Vickery Elementary in Dallas, we had a throwback to the '30s, a Mexican-American from the other side of Great Society's tracks who last year won $130,000 playing a gentleman's game.

Yesterday, as Lee picked at a dish of ice cream before heading for a Dr. Pepper–sponsored exhibition at City Park, he checked the latest PGA mutuels. He was leading the money parade with $84,272, a $17,000 edge over his closest pursuer and $30,000 more than Masters champion Billy Casper.

"Hey, you know, I don't think they're going to catch this Mexican," said Lee. "I think I'm going to have a good summer for a change. I'll only be on the tour three years in August, and I've never had a good summer yet."

This he blames on the mental strain the Masters course exerted on his low-ball shots, a strain he claims he doesn't want to undergo again.

Billy Casper, for one, feels Lee is foolish to blame the course, explaining: "The Masters layout hurt me when I faded the ball, but now I hook it and I'm okay. Lee is a whale of a player who could win anywhere."

If Lee has painted himself into a corner by sticking to this "I'll never return" edict, he isn't flinching.

"I love those Augusta galleries," he says. "They're knowledgeable, courteous and they love me. But I don't want to go for the flag, when it's on one of those ant-hills, hit a great shot, and wind up off the green. That's how it happened. Last year, I was playing with Kermit Zarley. On the sixth hole, I flew it at the stick. It hit 2 feet from the cup and I wound up with a 35-yard wedge shot. "'Hey, Kermit,' I said, 'I'm never coming back here again.'"

A decision to turn his olive-skinned back on golf's sacred pasture shook up the game's hierarchy as much as his Open victory. "God, I got all kinds of calls from the PGA brass," says Lee. "If I had decided to skip Cleveland or San Diego I wouldn't have heard from anyone. I can't understand why they got so excited."

Should he stick by his decision, it would automatically eliminate any chance of Lee ever winning the big four. "I'd like to win another U.S. Open and I'd like to win the PGA," said the poor man's Horatio Alger. "And, you can put this down, I'm gonna win the British Open. Maybe this year."

Lee has played in two but, as he puts it, "I haven't been properly cranked up."

"This year I'm going over to play St. Andrews with Sean Connery, you know Mr. Double-O-Seven. Then I'm going to take a week to get ready."

His plans include a unique departure in habits. "I'm planning to play both the large ball and the small English ball," says Lee. "I'll use the large one on the par fours. I can cut it better and make it bite. I'll use the small one on the par fives and the long par threes. It goes farther. When I need a three-iron, I'll hit a four. Mark it down. I'm gonna win that mother."

In the fall of '68, Trevino hit Great Britain with the impact of a meteor. He arrived in London wearing a green checkered sports jacket, cowboy boots and a sombrero, shouting to photographers: "You ever seen a pigeon-toed cowboy before?"

This was for the Alcan tournament. Next stop was the Piccadilly Open, whose officials became alarmed the flamboyant Texan might turn their tournament into a circus. Trevino was warned to wear a coat and tie.

His agent paid a visit to Peter Maas, Ltd., outfitters of dukes, princes and kings. He bought Lee patent-leather shoes, striped pants, swallowtail coats, opera capes, opera hats and a pearl-handled cane. Trevino arrived at the Savoy in a Rolls-Royce driven by a uniformed chauffeur.

Says Lee: "It was the greatest put-on ever."

Trevino estimates his Open victory will eventually bring him "in excess of a million dollars" but he isn't banking on it changing the personality of the grandson of a Mexican gravedigger.

"I'd rather be with those people who pay five bucks to join the gallery, than have some president of the board buy me a drink in the clubhouse," he says.

Lee's grandfather passed away earlier this year at 80. He had helped Lee's mother raise five children by digging graves from sunup to sundown. Lee didn't begin playing golf in earnest until he returned to Dallas after a hitch in the Marines.

"I had a job at a par-three course," says Lee. "I'd get up every morning at five to play the municipal course at Tenison Park. In dirty Bermuda shorts and bare feet. The mosquitoes were bad. After a round, I'd go down to the river and put mud cakes on my legs and arms. Then I'd get cleaned up and go to work. When business was bad, I'd play a few quick rounds on the par-three."

Which is where he gained fame by taking on all-comers with a Dr. Pepper bottle. No hole was longer than 100 yards and Lee, driving with the bottom and putting with the butt-end could go nine holes in 29 blows. He never lost and, if he could get eight matches a day, it more than paid his $3 rent.

Claudia Ann Trevino pushed the button that sent her husband into financial orbit. In 1967, she mailed her husband's $20 entry fee to the U.S. Open. He survived two qualifying rounds and, in his first tournament outside Texas, he finished fifth and collected $6,000. The next year, at Rochester, he became the first man in Open history to shoot four straight sub-par rounds. He's won five tournaments since to lose any flash-in-the-pan tag.

This week at Lakewood, he hopes to better last year's 33rd place finish, seven shots behind winner Larry Hinson. "The course is in great shape," says Lee. "The biggest hazard for me is Bourbon Street. I was down there the other night with my wife. Boy, those are some shows you got here, I was beginning to get a crush on one of the showgirls when I found out she was a man."

Still Spry at 82: Pioneer Turpie Recalls Greats
April 28, 1962

It's hard to believe that the quiet, unassuming senior selling Cokes at the seventh-hole snack bar at City Park once caddied for Harry Vardon, gave golf lessons to the richest man in the world, and helped design New Orleans Country Club.

But George Turpie, a wee Scot, was a huge part of New Orleans sports history.

• • •

He caddied for Harry Vardon when the mighty Scot won his first championship.

He flipped a coin that may have determined the destiny of Chick Evans.

He taught John D. Rockefeller Sr. how to play.

He refereed the 1919 Southern Amateur when Bobby Jones made one of the most talked-about shots in New Orleans history.

He sired the only girl from Deep Dixie to win the Southern women's championship.

And he won't budge an inch when comparing the greats of his day to the Palmers and Players of the space age.

All of this, from George Turpie, one of the oldest pioneers of the game in this country, whose twinkling eyes and mincing step mark him as another living example of that recipe for long life—golf and fresh air.

The snowy-haired Scot, born just a few blocks from St. Andrews, the cradle of modern golf, celebrated his 82nd birthday last week collecting tickets at the soft-drink stand near the seventh hole of the St. John course.

The saga of this golfing trailblazer actually began at another soft-drink stand, this one near the ninth hole at St. Andrews where his dad worked when not plying his trade as a shoemaker.

"I had four brothers and four sisters," he says. "All of us played. In fact, every able-bodied boy and girl swung a club."

George caddied during his grammar school days, and it wasn't long before he reached his first milestone at 15.

"I carried Harry Vardon's clubs when he won his first British Open in 1895," says Turpie. "What hands that man had—large and powerful. When he was eating, he actually was ashamed to put them on the table they were so big."

George crossed the Atlantic in 1898 to assist brother Harry, who was head pro at Edgewater Country Club in Chicago. Shortly thereafter, he hit the headlines, but it had nothing to do with golf.

"I had a little black mongrel named Jack that woke me from a deep sleep and wound up saving my life," says George. "The clubhouse was on fire, and I was lucky to get out the window before the whole place collapsed."

Turpie has carried a copy of the clipping from the Chicago Tribune ever since.

It was at Edgewater that Chick Evans got his start as a 9-year-old caddie under George, who often wonders what would have become of Evans if a coin he tossed in 1899 hadn't come up heads.

"You could see right away Evans had tremendous natural ability," said George. "But he and another caddie by the name of Joe Moheiser were always getting into fistfights. Moheiser was every bit as good as Chick as a golfer.

"I warned them one day and said the next time it happened, one of them would have to go. A few days later, they were at it again.

"I broke 'em up and then told them I'd toss a coin and let them call it. I said the loser would have to leave for good. Chick called heads and heads it was. Moheiser left the course and I never heard from him again."

Evans went on to win the U.S. amateur and Open championships in 1916. He repeated as amateur king in 1920 and was runner-up three times.

It was in the winter of 1901–02 while teaching in Pasadena that Turpie listed among his pupils John D. Rockefeller Sr., richest man in the world.

"Rockefeller would take a half-hour lesson, and then we'd play nine holes," he recalled. "He would have his valet along with a pail of ice and a towel. John D. would dip the towel in the ice water and soothe his bald head.

"He'd paid the exact fee—$1 for a lesson and $2 for the nine-hole instruction, and he'd tip his caddie a dime."

Turpie remembered crowds of three to four hundred gathering outside the hotel where Rockefeller stayed to watch him eat with his family and friends.

"The man loved golf and played it until he was well up in his 90s. He never scored well, but he enjoyed getting out in the sun, and I'm sure this contributed to his long life."

In 1919, Turpie was the referee for the most famous tournament in New Orleans up to that time. Bobby Jones was in the Crescent City as a boy wonder of 17 seeking to retain his Southern championship.

Turpie has never forgotten his first impression of Bobby.

"I caddied for Vardon and most of the great ones," he said, "but there was something special. He had tremendous rhythm and touch even then. I remember his hands were extremely sore before the tournament, and I taped his clubs so he wouldn't have to close them so tightly.

"When a callous came off his left hand in the first round, his mother wanted him to withdraw, but Bobby refused."

It was in the qualifying round that Jones hit his famous "shoe shot."

"Bobby's shot off the first tee bounded off the right side of the green and ran into the discarded shoe of a workman. They called me over for a ruling, and when I saw he wasn't entitled to lift under the rules then in force, I told Bobby he would have to play the ball—and the shoe.

"I'll never forget it. He took out his niblick and pitched both shoe and ball onto the green. The ball rolled out and, although Bobby wound up with a bogey, the shot was all anyone talked about."

Jones bowed to local pride Nelson Whitney in the semifinals, and Whitney went on to trounce Lou Jacoby, 12 and 11, in the 36-hole final.

"Whitney may have beaten Jones even if Bobby's hands were okay," said Turpie. "But anyone could see the young man had it. I told the writers that in 10 years, he would be the best in the world. Jones was a gift from heaven."

The power golf of today, and the spectacular achievements of marksmen like Arnold Palmer, have failed to cool Turpie toward the old-time giants.

"Vardon, Jones and Hagan—these men were craftsmen," says Turpie. "They played with no more than nine clubs, crude implements compared to the matched set of today.

"The only irons were the mid-iron, mashie, niblick and mashie-niblick. You didn't have nine irons to zero in on the target. You had to improvise with different wrist movements depending on what club you were using. The old timers were masters at it.

"I know most people will think I'm an old fogey, but the players today are more robots than craftsmen. They play every week and get to be mechanical. In the old days, you had only three and four tournaments a year."

George fell in love with New Orleans when he paid a brief visit in 1899 to assist his brother here. He dropped anchor permanently in 1915 after aiding in the planning of the New Orleans Country Club course.

"It's been a good life," he says. "Seven years ago I lost my wife, and it took me quite a while to get over it, but I've been blessed with a fine family, many friends and a million memories."

Pat's Cheerful Darkness
April 27, 1971

Lead-in:
Pat Browne once told me after he lost his sight, he would attend golf tournaments as a spectator and position himself near the first tee.

And then he would wait . . . and listen.

From the sound of the club hitting the ball, Browne could tell instantly if the golfer had made solid contact.

Speaking to Browne and fellow blind golfer Charlie Boswell over the years, I came away with a profound appreciation for the gifts they showered on others. You think you've got troubles? Watching people like Pat Browne and Charlie Boswell was a tonic that had a lasting effect.

• • •

"The Lord never gives anyone more than he can handle."

Pat Browne Jr. can't remember who said it, but he has lived—and will live—by that simple creed, through five years of darkness and the darkness that lies ahead.

Because he has, images change, one of the angular basketball stars at Jesuit and Tulane who arched up those soft one-handers dissolving to a smooth-swinging golfer of 38 who is, at once, blind, cheerful and undaunted.

In tomorrow's GNOO Pro-Am at Lakewood, Pat will join Masters champion Charles Coody in an afternoon foursome he is confident will be beneficial.

"I played with Lionel Hebert in the pro-am at Greensboro and I can't tell you how much he helped," he was saying yesterday while getting in some practice wallops at a Jefferson driving range.

"Lionel couldn't have been nicer. I was playing badly and he went out of his way, telling me how to get more body turn into my shots and how to take the club back."

Browne, of course, repaid the favor simply by playing, leaving Hebert, as he will Coody tomorrow, with an inspiring lesson of perseverance and courage—a word, incidentally, Pat does not buy.

"I don't consider myself courageous," he says. "I consider myself lucky. I could have been a cab driver or a doctor. If I had, the transition would have been awfully tough. But I was a lawyer, a job in which hearing and speech is more important than sight."

Pat left his sight on Airline Highway in February of 1966 from injuries in a head-on smashup. Seven months later, he was back practicing law, losing a $130,000 judgment.

Laughs Pat today, "That was some comeback."

He picked up the golfing pieces just as easily.

Shortly after entering Tulane (where he captained the basketball and golf teams), Pat won the city junior tournament in 1952 and once got his handicap as low as four.

So, it wasn't too difficult for Bobby Monsted, who, like Pat, lettered in basketball and golf at Tulane, to rekindle Browne's interest in the game. Soon Pat became a frequent fixture on the practice tee.

"I owe everything to great friends—my dad, of course, and people like Henry Sarpy and Don Doyle," says Pat. "My job is easy. Henry and Don have the patience and they have to do all the bending and stooping."

A low-80s shooter, Sarpy has been Pat's coach since the accident, while Doyle, a longtime friend just back from a Vietnam tour in the Marines, takes over when Sarpy isn't available.

"They do everything," says Pat. "Club selection, lining you up on your shots, giving you the lay of the land on your putts. The delicate shots are the toughest, especially those just off the green."

In tournament play, blind golfers abide by all of the rules of golf save one—in a trap, they are allowed to ground their club.

Pat has played in two national events sponsored by the U.S. Blind Golfers Association. He finished seventh in 1969 at Chattanooga and third last year at Greensboro.

At Greensboro, he shot 99–108 to finish behind winner Charlie Boswell, former Alabama football and baseball star, and Joe Lazzaro. Boswell shot 93–107, Lazzaro 100–101.

"My best round was last year at San Diego in a tournament designed to raise money for the handicapped," says Pat. "I played with Dick Martin of Rowan and Martin and shot 83."

Browne will be heading for the same event next month and, come September, he'll be in Houston for the blind nationals.

"They tell me the course is flat, and that's good news," he says. "Those hilly layouts always gave me trouble, even when I could see the hills."

Browne feels any person with his problem has only one choice—to live as close to a normal life as possible.

"What made it easy for me was the abundance of friends and, I guess, the things I learned as an athlete. Things like if you're knocked down, get up. My dad learned the same lessons, and I'm sure they helped him, too."

"Looking back now, I guess the greatest shock I had was when the doctor told me in the hospital—my jaw was broken and I couldn't eat—that I was anemic.

"My weight slipped from 210 pounds to 170, but I went to Tulane and put myself in the hands of good old Bubba Porche. He got me up to 195 and it was the best I ever felt in my life."

Pat does all his "reading" by record. "It's a great deal," he laughs. "All you have to do is put on a book, lie down and listen. Charlie Boswell wrote a great one called 'Now I See.' I recommend it to everyone."

Recommended, too, is Pat Browne's outlook on life—warm, sunny, no trace of bitterness. A vitamin shot for those mad at the world.

Nicklaus' Masters Victory Something like a Fairy Tale
April 14, 1986

In 1986, I was in Augusta along with my son Peter, who was covering the Masters for the *New York Post*. In those days—if you can believe it—there was no live TV coverage of the first eight holes. Masters chairman Clifford Roberts feared broadcasting play on the front nine would water down the Masters' mystique.

So we followed the leaders through the early holes before it was time to head back to the press room to watch the live TV coverage. As we cut across the par-5 eighth fairway, Jack Nicklaus was walking past us to his tee shot. He was walking uphill in more ways than one. He was six shots—hopelessly—behind.

"Look at all those people still following Jack," my son said. "They're crazy." I agreed. Jack was out of it.

What followed were the most memorable 10 holes in golf history. Jack played the final 10 holes in 7-under par to win his sixth green jacket.

Yes, sir.

• • •

AUGUSTA, Ga.—Jack Nicklaus, age 46, shot a 65 on Sunday to win his sixth Masters.

Seve Ballesteros hit it in the water on 15.

With a chance to tie, Tom Kite missed from 12 feet and Greg Norman missed from 16 feet.

Those are the bare-bones facts.

But hardly the whole story.

The whole story is larger than life, almost make-believe, the way the drama unfolded on a golden afternoon, the way it kept building, the way the chorus of sound continued to thunder through the trees at Augusta

National, as golf's Golden Bear, buried but not forgotten, came back from the tomb.

It was quite a picture, father and son, locked in a teary embrace, as they walked off the 18th green after daddy had played the final four holes eagle-birdie-birdie-par to give a vintage field something to shoot at—and his delirious legions something to remember.

"Hey, Dad," said Jackie as they headed for the 14th tee after a birdie at 13, "is this the noise you used to hear?"

His father was misty-eyed. "I had to keep reminding myself I still had some golf to play," said Jack Nicklaus. "I had to get hold of myself. It was pretty wild out there."

And it would get wilder still, when the Bear holed a 12-foot eagle putt on 15, when he birdied No. 16 from three feet, when he stood on the 17th and "heard a strange sound."

At first, he didn't know what it was. Then he found out. Ballesteros, who had electrified his gallery, and seized this tournament by the throat with a pair of eagles, had found the water on the 500-yard 15th.

Suddenly, washed-up Jack Nicklaus, winless the last two years, was tied for the Masters lead.

So what do you do at a time like this?

On this day, if you're Jack Nicklaus, you birdie the 17th hole with a devilish putt of 11 feet, make a clutch par on the final hole, then watch the young men give it a go.

As Kite's try for a tying bird slid by, Jack squirmed in his chair as he watched it on TV in the Bobby Jones cabin. When Norman came to 18 with another chance to force a playoff, he stood up. "I couldn't stand it any more sitting down," he said.

The man who had seen Lee Trevino chip in to snatch away a British Open, who had seen Tom Watson chip in at Pebble Beach to steal a U.S. Open, finally got a break over something no golfer can control—another man's shot.

It's safe to say only next of kin were pulling for those putts of Kite and Norman to drop. Galleries that had witnessed a record 63 on Saturday were now witnessing the 20th major championship by the greatest golfer of all time.

"Are you the greatest?" Jack was asked afterward.

"I'm not answering that. All I want to do is keep playing as long as I enjoy it. I know I'm not the golfer I used to be, I know I'm past my prime, but I still feel I'm good enough to win every now and then."

This "now" was special.

On Sunday, Jack Nicklaus trailed a vintage field—Ballesteros, Tom Watson, Kite, Norman, Bernhard Langer—and he beat them all, the "oldest" Master winning on a young man's course.

For someone who was winning his 71st tournament as a professional, there was no greater moment.

"I can't tell you how great it was having Jackie out there carrying my bag," said Nicklaus, once again with tears welling in his eyes. "He kept saying, 'Come on, Dad, you can do it.' This made it very special."

Jackie Nicklaus was not yet 2 years old when his dad won his first Masters in 1963, when his winning score was 286.

Now that he is the oldest Masters champion at 46, with a winning score of 279, what did this mean?

"It means I'll shoot 272 when I'm 56 and win again," said the guy in the green coat, size 44-long.

Barbara Nicklaus was shedding tears of her own.

She missed her husband's first victory here because she was busy giving birth to their second son—Steve.

"This definitely is the best of all," said Barbara. "Better than the first, better, than the fifth. Better than anything."

The only problem, said Barbara, is to decide where the sixth Masters trophy goes—to the trophy case at Jack's Muirfield course in Ohio or to the family home in North Palm Beach.

"It's a nice decision to have," said Mrs. Golden Bear.

Spirits High as Usual as Italian Open Turns 25
March 4, 1997

I'm left-handed in just about everything, except my handwriting. The Teresian Sisters who staffed St. Louis Cathedral School in the French Quarter made sure of that.

Being educated in a Catholic elementary school in the 1930s meant you did what the nuns told you. When they saw me drawing and then forming letters with my left hand, they said that wouldn't do—they didn't want my left hand smearing the still-wet ink as I moved across the page—so they "encouraged" me to write with my right hand.

Why is all this important? When I picked up golf, I could play only one way—left-handed.

I never took golf too seriously. I'd play once or twice a year, and I had a "set" of clubs that looked like hickory shafts. Actually, the steel shafts were covered with a yellow plastic that made them look like wooden shafts.

Walter Hagen would have approved.

Bill Bumgarner, who worked with me at the *States-Item*, never let me forget it when I played with him, Nat Belloni, and Ron Brocato in an Italian Open foursome. I think I had five mismatched clubs in my bag, including a "spoon" and a "mashie."

Bill was driving the golf cart when we got to my ball about 150 yards away from the green. Bill assessed the shot and then went around to the back of the cart to look at my bag.

"Well, Pete," Bill said, "it's either a hard 9-iron or a soft 3-iron."

• • •

"Look at it this way," said Butch van Breda Kolff, coach of the New Orleans Jazz, "the wine will take care of the wind, and the wind will take care of the wine."

It was 1976. Butch was preparing to challenge the elements, not to mention the spirits, at City Park, and he was speaking for everyone who teed it up in an Italian Open: Let the tee shots fly and the good times roll.

The Italian Open turns 25 on Monday, marking the silver anniversary of the city's first major charity golf tournament, one that has pumped more than a half-million dollars into a variety of causes, from St. Michael's Special School to the Opera Guild to Cabrini Day Care.

Past fields have included an assortment of celebrities, from Joe DiMaggio to Phil Rizzuto, from Louie Prima to Pete Fountain, from Eddie Arcaro to Dizzy Dean, from Chi Chi Rodriguez to the late Joe Gemelli.

Gemelli was one of the event's founding fathers, a promoter famous for his list of celebrities "who have been invited and, as yet, have not declined."

Over the years, Gemelli's list would include the likes of Frank Sinatra, Mario Andretti, Liza Minnelli, Robert De Niro, Marcello Mastroianni,

Al Pacino and Sophia Loren. "I just spoke with Sophia's agent," Gemelli would inform the media. "The agent said, if she finishes her movie in time, she'd love to come."

Of course, Sophia didn't make it. But you can't have everything. "Maybe next year," said Gemelli.

A celebrity who did make it, regularly, was the late Fair Grounds handicapper Allen "Black Cat" Lacombe. After a round in one of the early Italian Opens, one in which the Black Cat hit at least 20 balls out of bounds (and, on one hole, watched his tee shot strike a horse in the City Park Riding Stables), the Cat reported his score to playing partner Bob Roesler as "three over par."

Asked to explain, the Cat said he used a scoring method made famous by Egypt's King Farouk. During World War II, the paths of the Cat, who was in charge of a U.S. boxing team, and the Egyptian ruler crossed. One day Farouk, a boxing fan and avid golfer, invited G.I. Lacombe to play a round at the Cleopatra Country Club. When it was over, and the king had announced his score, an excellent one, to a puzzled Cat, Farouk explained: "I only count the shots I like."

Which sort of speaks for most Italian Open participants, where a glass of chianti and a muffuletta are always within arm's reach. There have been tournaments at City Park where a golfer drove his cart into a lagoon. But there is no record of anyone—it happened one year in an Italian Open—driving his golf cart from City Park to Fat City.

All in the name of charity.

With the North and West courses in play on Monday, tournament chairman Louis Capagnano said, among other things, there will be a drawing on the 19th hole in which contributions of $6,000 ($3,000 for each course) will be donated in the name of two golfers to a designated local charity.

"We'll also announce the winner of the 'Podnuh Award,' named in memory of the late Dizzy Dean," said Capagnano.

No one enjoyed the Italian Open's blue-collar ambience more than the Hall of Fame pitcher, who came out of the Ozarks and exploded on the major leagues with a good fastball and bad grammar.

Dizzy, who never met a stranger, would play 18 holes, then sit around and spin yarns of his days as a member of the Gashouse Gang, the world champion St. Louis Cardinals of 1934.

"The trouble with them boys today," Diz liked to say of the modern-day players, "is they ain't got enough spart."

Asked to explain the Ozark inflection, Dizzy replied: "Spart is the same as fight or pep or gumption. Like the Spart of St. Louis, that plane Lindbergh flowed to Europe in."

Just one of many Italian Open memories.

Tiger's Will Crushes Challengers' Psyches
April 9, 2001

Let's put it this way: Two of the greatest performances in the history of golf's four majors—a 12-shot victory in the 1997 Masters and a 15-stroke triumph in the 2000 U.S. Open at Pebble Beach—both were accomplished by Tiger Woods.

What made both of those performances other-worldly—almost like Secretariat lapping the field in the 1973 Belmont by 31 lengths—is that no other golfer, not Jack, not Ben, not Arnie, ever put together four rounds in a major to humiliate a field as did Tiger.

And, he did it twice.

Despite Tiger's embarrassing personal fall from grace and his recent physical, mental, and swing woes, he will be remembered for his 2000 and 2001 run in which he captured four consecutive majors, pounding foes into submission with his length, his nerves, and his unbridled swagger.

Is that package gone forever?

That is the maddening mystery of golf.

• • •

AUGUSTA, Ga.—It's not the eye of the Tiger.

It's more the will of the Tiger.

At sundown Sunday, you could look into the eyes of David Duval and Phil Mickelson and see what Tiger's will can do.

From Duval, a vacant stare, some mumbling answers, an observation about "the man's invincible feeling."

From Mickelson, it was more of a mind-numbing look, an admission of mental lapses, the half-hearted accolade of "he does what's required to win."

That's what Tiger Woods does. He keeps damaging the psyche of anyone getting in the way, sometimes with a crushing 15-shot victory, as was the case in the 2000 U.S. Open; sometimes in overtime, as was the case in the 2000 PGA Championship; and sometimes by defeating the second- and third-best golfers in the world in a test of nerve and verve, as was the case Sunday at Augusta National.

There was the memory of poor Bob May, in the wake of his playoff loss in the PGA last August, shrugging his shoulders and lamenting, "I shot three 66s, and he still beat me."

When the green curtain descended on another Masters, Tiger had beaten Duval by two shots, Mickelson by three.

This was a day when eight Duval birdies were not enough. This was a tournament where Mickelson came within a whisker of becoming the first man to shoot four Masters rounds in the 60s, and that would not be enough.

Why?

Well, because it was a day when Woods would shoot a 68 that helped define, one more time, why the 25-year-old kid is truly a gift from the golfing gods.

Under the Georgia sun, in breezy conditions, there were many moments when a scorchingly hot Duval and grimly determined Mickelson hit the kind of golf shots to force the other guy into some major mistakes.

In golf, it usually works that way. But not when you have Woods in the equation.

In a way, Tiger's mistakes came down to two putts he failed to make. Tiger missed a six-footer to save par on the 12th. And he missed a three-footer for a birdie at the 15th.

Let's say, in view of the crunching pressure eating at someone in search of a fourth straight major championship, those misses proved Tiger really is human.

But let's see why he belongs in a class of one.

With Duval charging, with Mickelson hanging tough, Tiger arrived at the seventh hole at even par for the day. He knocked his approach to eight feet on the seventh and made birdie. He saved par on the ninth with a tricky six-footer. He saved par on the 10th with a 10-footer, "my biggest putt of the day." And he became one of only three golfers to birdie the 455-yard 11th, almost holing his 149-yard approach.

After bogeying the 12th, he hit what he called "my best shot of the day, a high-sweeper that I've been practicing," leading to a tap-in birdie on the 485-yard par-5 13th.

This war wasn't over. It was Duval and Mickelson who cracked with bogeys on the 170-yard 16th—Duval with a 7-iron that wound up over the green ("It was my best tee shot of the day"), Mickelson with a tee shot that wound up in no-no land, on a shelf that led to three putts.

Meanwhile, Tiger ("I know where the trouble is") Woods was keeping his tee shot on the 16th below the hole, setting up a routine par.

After Duval missed a five-foot birdie try at the 18th that could have tied Tiger, at least for the moment, Woods showed up moments later and rolled one in from 15 feet to send him into a second green jacket with a 272 score that was only two shots shy of the record he set four years ago.

Watching Tiger go about his business, you had to figure if Duval had birdied 18, so would Tiger.

The thought of winning his sixth major, winning four in a row, did not leave him trembling in anticipation.

"You're not going to believe this," he said, "but I felt relaxed all week. I never looked at the major streak. Subconsciously, it made me more at ease. That's why I'm as relaxed as I am right now, just because of my mindset all week."

That's the scary part. Tiger knows how good he is. And, what's even scarier, he keeps proving it.

The only thing he's chasing now is the ghost of Jack Nicklaus and those 18 professional major championships won by the Golden Bear. By age 25, Jack had won five majors. With three majors to go before he turns 26, Tiger has won six.

There was a question put to Tiger on Saturday about having a chance to do something—win four straight majors—that we may never get to see in our lifetime.

What about it, Tiger?

"Well," said Mr. Woods, smiling, "I hope you live a little longer."

In the saga of Tiger Woods, many chapters remain to be written.

With Faithful in Tow, Palmer Says Goodbye
April 10, 2004

When Arnold Palmer showed up at Augusta for the first time, as a rookie pro in 1955, he and Winnie made the trip in a second-hand trailer they anchored in a trailer park that charged an $11 hookup fee. He left town with a $695 check for finishing 10th. But still no guarantees.

In 1958, the year the New Orleans Open started up again, tournament committeeman Garic Schoen recounted, Palmer asked that his $400 tournament check be cashed before he left town. A 2-year-old daughter and a wife pregnant with a second child were waiting to hit the road.

A month later, the hand-to-mouth existence came to an end when Palmer won his first Masters. He won his fourth the same year—1964—Cassius Clay won the heavyweight title.

Before Palmer began attacking the flag with the slashing style of a buccaneer, there were no gallery ropes. This was no country club product making birdies and eagles. This was a guy from Pennsylvania steel country who gave the sport the kind of blue-collar appeal it had not known.

• • •

AUGUSTA, Ga.—Everyone has a story about the man, real or imagined. Mine was a simple answer to a simple question.

"What kind of golfer was President Eisenhower?" I asked Arnold Palmer during one of his visits to the New Orleans Open.

There was a pause followed by a chuckle.

"Let's just say," came the reply, "he swung the club a little like I do."

It was vintage Palmer, a golfing legend with the sort of off-balance slash that endeared him to millions of weekend duffers.

This would especially apply to a retired general who counted himself a proud member of Arnie's Army, who insisted Arnie call him Ike, whose obsession with the game helped form a lifelong bond at a time when a hero of World War II was riding into the sunset determined, perhaps more than anything in later life, to shave a shot off a dreadful handicap that remained top secret.

You wonder what Ike would be saying about his friend's ride into a special sunset of his own here Friday, Arnold Palmer's final competitive round at Augusta National in his 50th Masters, a tournament that shaped the legend, a tournament Arnold Palmer burned into the national consciousness, taking the game of golf along for the ride.

Never have a pair of 84s been greeted with standing ovations at every hole, two rounds without a birdie, two farewell rounds that were painful to watch, that is, if you remember the man who won the tournament four times, attacking the flag with a gambler's instinct, like some swashbuckling pirate with a sword in his hands.

Remembering those days, when the roar of the crowd enveloped the Pennsylvania strong boy with dashing looks and wavy hair, it was sad to see Arnold Palmer play his final hole, a 465-yard par-4, with a driver off the tee and a driver off the fairway that still left him short of the green.

Thirty-eight-year-old Bob Estes had out-driven his 74-year-old playing partner by 125 yards on a hole a younger Palmer would eat up with a drive and a six-iron on his march to green jackets.

So, yes, it was time a pirate took his leave, realizing his time had come.

"I'm through, done, cooked, washed up, finished," he said as he reluctantly bid goodbye. "I'm not happy about it, but it's time. I know one thing. I can never separate myself from Augusta National."

He never will. It was Palmer who brought the gallery ropes to professional golf, arriving when the stars were aligned for a perfect marriage: the coming of color television, giving us the picture of the blue-collar kid with broad shoulders, walking the Augusta National hills, standing in the fairway, puffing on a cigarette, flipping it to the ground, grabbing a club, hitching his pants and knocking the little white ball on the green.

Then there was the sight of a knock-kneed putting stance, a swipe, and a ball rolling, sometimes 30 feet into the cup, sometimes falling after a curling journey of six feet, which is what happened when Arnold Palmer birdied the final two holes to win his second Masters in 1960.

"You could always tell the roar for a Palmer birdie or a Palmer eagle," Gary Player said Friday. "It was different. Arnie was the king here."

Player should know. Palmer handed his friend the green jacket in 1961 when he took a double-bogey six on the 18th. The following year, with Player two shots ahead with two holes to go, Palmer sank an "impossible" 45-foot chip for a birdie, followed it with a 20-foot birdie putt on the 18th, then won the next day in a three-way 18-hole playoff, making up three shots on Player on the back nine.

"I think the only people pulling for me that day," said Player, "were my caddie and my wife."

From the late '50s into the '60s, such was life among the flowers and pines at Augusta National, when Palmer was winning the first and last of his seven major championships, when the Yankees were on a historic roll, when the Baltimore Colts were beating the New York Giants in overtime, when Palmer was every bit as large on the sporting stage as a Mickey Mantle and Johnny Unitas.

Arnold Palmer's enduring popularity can be measured in his marketing success: At age 74, he still commands $20 million per year in endorsements.

"In one way or another," said Palmer, "I hope to remain part of the Masters. I look forward to watching, seeing the winners come around as they do each year, seeing their struggles. As for me, I plan on playing a little golf here and there. I'm sure not planning to roll over and die, that is, unless I can't help it."

CHAPTER 7

HORSE RACING

Not a Horse Race, a Horse
June 10, 1973

On the first Saturday of May in 1973, Secretariat served notice he was a special horse. Just how special we would find out in five weeks.

In the Kentucky Derby, which started it all, both Secretariat and Sham ran to Derby records—Secretariat to a stunning 1:59 2-5s for the classic 10-furlong distance, Sham to an unofficial 1:59 4-5s. Both smashed the two-minutes-flat hung up by Northern Dancer in 1964.

Secretariat shattered for all time the notion that sons of Bold Ruler could not win at a mile and a quarter. The wonder horse was only beginning to show off, and the world soon would find out what kind of stamina he had over a mile and a half.

• • •

ELMONT, N.Y.—In Baton Rouge, you had Rod Milburn winning under a powder blue sweat band, Steve Prefontaine behind a rakish mustache and Dave Wottle under a golf hat, but the weekend—maybe the year, maybe this generation—belonged to the animal wearing the blue-and-white-checked headpiece in New York.

The Belmont wasn't a horse race. It was a horse, one of those once-in-a-lifetime superstars whose greatness perhaps was best reflected in the way jaded New Yorkers lost their composure and acted like little kids as Secretariat came screaming to Triple Crown glory.

Here was an athlete scaling the heights. When you measure his new American record for a mile and a half (2:24) against the old one (2:26 3-5s), it means Secretariat beat the ghost of Gallant Man by 13 lengths and, on the way, beat his Kentucky Derby record for a mile-and-a-quarter by two lengths (1:59 flat compared to 1:59 2-5s).

All done without much urging from Ron Turcotte, whose winner-circle smile suggested the look of a man who had an elephant removed from his shoulders.

It brought back a casual meeting with Turcotte and trainer Lucien Laurin late in the day on the first Saturday in May. Jockey and trainer were on their way out of Churchill Downs, having come from a victory party honoring Mrs. Penny Tweedy. They accepted congratulations from some straggling reporters, but it was obvious, even though the Derby was behind them, the pressure was still there.

It was there until Saturday, there until Secretariat, who does pretty much as he wishes, seemed to congratulate Sham in the backstretch for giving it one more try. Then the son of Bold Ruler set off for a date with thoroughbred legend.

Before the race, Laffit Pincay, Sham's rider, was not radiating optimism. Understandably, "that other horse" had already done enough to Sham at Churchill and Pimlico to evoke some sort of reverence from an opposing rider.

Saturday Sham tested his adversary early but simply could not keep up. Without the Derby and Preakness bridesmaid, there would have been little pre-Belmont speculation, or drama for the first half-mile, as the two made a match race out of it.

As Sham faded to finish an incredible 45½ lengths behind a horse he was within three lengths of his last two times out, you had to wonder what Saturday's whipping might do to Sham's future. It could be the classic broken-heart story of all time.

Meanwhile, Secretariat looks ahead to some rest and a likely date with older horses at Saratoga in August, before beginning his life as a stallion in Kentucky.

As he takes his leisure, and eats his oats, you'll be hearing the usual comparisons of greatness, which can never be proven. Names like Man O'War, Count Fleet, Citation will come galloping out of the past.

Veterans who saw these runners are still calling Secretariat "an incredible specimen of the thoroughbred," "the perfect horse," "an equine Adonis."

What Secretariat is is big—and fast. Lucien Laurin once recalled he was skeptical about how well Secretariat might run as a 2-year-old because, as the trainer explained, "he couldn't be as good as he looked."

Charles Hatton of the Racing Form, an early admirer, says Secretariat "is less lengthy and light of middle than Man O'War, less long-backed and coachy than Citation, less lacking in substance than Count Fleet."

But, as the late trainer Jim Fitzsimmons once said, it's the things one cannot see that matter most in judging a thoroughbred.

Obviously, Secretariat has proven he has heart as well as speed.

Will he be as prolific as his dad at stud? That's another question. The credentials are impressive.

Mrs. Tweedy can now look back on the $6,080,000 syndication and wonder how much her colt would command today. Some observers put it close to $12 million. But that's so many dollars under the bridge.

Today people are talking not of dollars, but of beauty and power in motion Saturday in New York, a blend that recalled the thoughts of William Faulkner who, after watching Swaps beat Nashua in 1955, observed:

"Unlike the other animals which man has domesticated, the horse is economically obsolete. Yet it still endures and probably will continue to as long as man himself does, long after the cows and sheep and hogs and chickens, and the dogs which control and protect them, are extinct.

"Because the other beasts and their guardians merely supply man with food, and someday science will feed him by means of synthetic gases and so eliminate the economic need which they fill. While what the horse supplies to man is something deep and profound in his emotional nature and need. It will endure and survive until man's own nature changes."

How High Will This Star Rise?
June 12, 1988

Louie Roussel III and Ronnie Lamarque might have been the original Odd Couple. Louie was the fastidious worrier, Ronnie the free-spirited lounge singer. Both hit it big on Risen Star, son of Secretariat, who finished third as a result of a bad trip in the 1988 Kentucky Derby but went on to win the Preakness and the Belmont.

In Roussel's memory, nothing was any better than the mural Risen Star painted in the Belmont. Second to the pace-setting Winning Colors after six furlongs, the son of Secretariat blew past the Kentucky Derby winner, pulling away to a lead of six lengths after a mile and a quarter, a lead that stretched to more than 14 at the finish.

After the huge Belmont victory, Lamarque serenaded a national TV audience with his ditty "Risen Star Salutes New York."

"Sure, there've been greater horses than Risen Star," said Roussel, taking note of Citation, Secretariat, Seattle Slew, and Affirmed. "But no horse was asked to overcome more. Star had to overcome Ronnie's singing."

• • •

ELMONT, N.Y.—He blew 'em away.

He handled the field like a Mike Tyson, emphatically, chillingly, in the fashion of some awesome animal going about his business with surgical precision.

No longer is the question: Just how good a colt is Risen Star?

The question today is: How great a thoroughbred may Risen Star become?

As you assessed the knockout scored by this 3-year-old in Saturday's Belmont Stakes, you began tripping over some Hall of Fame names.

Risen Star ran the second-fastest 1½-mile Belmont ever—after his daddy, Secretariat—and he ran a tick faster than Gallant Man.

Risen Star's winning margin—14¾ lengths—was the fourth-biggest in the history of this "test of champions," beaten only by Secretariat, Count Fleet and Man O'War.

How's that for classy company?

For Eddie Delahoussaye, it had to be the easiest $130,000 he ever had earned in 20 years as a jockey, especially for a trip that lasted two minutes, 26⅖ seconds.

"I never touched him," said the little man from New Iberia, La., who picked up 10 percent of the $1 million Triple Crown bonus and 10 percent of the winning purse of $303,720. "When I ran past the filly, my horse was just galloping. I never, never hit him. I never asked him to run. All I did was show him the whip."

It may turn out that Risen Star broke a lady's heart. Winning Colors, looking to be the first filly to win the Belmont in 83 years, struggled home 41¾ lengths behind the winner, carrying a resigned Gary Stevens, who realized his dream had ended after six furlongs.

"When he went by me," Stevens said, "I knew he was the winner."

Two hours earlier, back at Barn 8, Louie Roussel III had continued to agonize, as he had done all week, over his colt's tender leg.

When Roussel arrived at the track at 6:30, Dr. Ken Reed informed him there was still slight swelling in the right front leg two inches above the ankle. "Horses have run, and won, with a lot worse," Reed explained. Roussel pronounced him 90 percent fit.

"If he wins," Roussel said, "they'll say I was playing games. If we lose, they'll say I shouldn't have run the horse or because he worked too fast (three furlongs in 33⅗) on Friday."

Then the trainer offered his pre-race sentiments. "The Star will either win by 10 or be off the board."

Once the six-horse field left the gate, and Roussel saw his colt break cleanly, his confidence skyrocketed. "I told Eddie not to let the filly dictate the race and he didn't," he said. "When he was able to lay so close running as easy as he was, I felt we had it."

On the track, Risen Star was pulling Delahoussaye out of his saddle, as he had done to exercise rider Jimmy Nichols on Friday.

"I got a strained right shoulder that tells me how much this horse wants to run," said Nichols, who was aboard last week when Risen Star took off during a gallop and, Roussel said, kicked himself in the ankle.

"Everybody thought Friday's work was too fast. But they didn't realize that this is a great horse. Great horses can work fast with no problem. If Custer had Risen Star at Little Big Horn, the Indians never would have caught up with him."

In the mind of co-owner Ronnie Lamarque, the outcome was never in doubt. "As we say in the auto business," Lamarque was saying as they saddled Risen Star, "this is a done deal."

When it was history, Lamarque talked of the expected speed duel between the winner and Winning Colors. "I said if the filly goes six furlongs in 1:13 or better, we'll be laying three or four lengths back. If she goes any slower, we'll be in front. At the mile marker, we'll be taking her name and address and setting up a breeding season."

An hour after the race, on the roof of the Belmont track, Lamarque was singing—for one radio station after another—"Risen Star Salutes New York."

Earlier, the largest Ford dealer in Louisiana had had his picture taken behind the million-dollar bonus courtesy of Chrysler.

This followed Chrysler's presentation of a LeBaron to the winner trainer. As cameras clicked, Edwin Edwards, onetime governor, shouted: "Ronnie, are you going to get Louie to put that Chrysler on your used car lot?"

Lamarque smiled. At the moment, he was tossing an idea around.

"You know, there's probably a movie to be made about all this. Maybe they could call it 'A Tale of Three Stars.' The horse would play himself. Martin Sheen would play Louie."

And who would play Lamarque? "Robert De Niro," Lamarque said. "But he'd have to take some singing lessons first."

Rooney Still on the Track

May 25, 1990

A few years before writing this column, I had met Mickey Rooney at the 1988 Belmont Stakes, which Risen Star, owned by New Orleans' own Louie Roussel III and Ronnie Lamarque, would go on to win. Before the post positions were announced, Mickey, eight times married, offered a rollicking 10-minute, stand-up routine about his love affair—imagine that—with the Sport of Kings.

"I have all kinds of systems for betting the horses, but inside information is absolutely the best," Mickey said.

So Mickey told a story on himself. In Puerto Rico, he got a tip on the No. 5 horse, at 40–1 odds, in the second race. He bet $100 on No. 5 to win, and, sure enough, the longshot won by 10 lengths.

Ecstatic, Mickey galloped to the betting window to cash in. The mutuel clerk looked at Mickey's ticket and shook his head, sadly.

"Sorry," the mutuel clerk said, "he not supposed to win."

• • •

"Azucar," said Mickey Rooney. "Does the name ring a bell?"

It didn't.

But then I'm not as old as one of Hollywood's classic survivors, not old enough to tell you Azucar, a 7-year-old colt ridden by George Woolf, won the inaugural Santa Anita Handicap in 1935.

"Shucks," winked Rooney, "I'm old enough to remember Tijuana when it was Agua Caliente. It was like an American Monte Carlo. It attracted the movie crowd that wanted to get away. I went to Caliente when I was 8, and two things happened: I fell in love with Mexican food, and I fell in love with thoroughbred racing. It's one love affair that's still going strong."

Age-wise, Rooney is in the home stretch, at the eighth-pole, closing in on the big 7–0, but the onetime Andy Hardy, now in town starring in Neil Simon's "The Sunshine Boys," the story of two aging vaudevillians, gives no evidence of wearing out.

Like Kelso and John Henry, those four-legged millionaires who raced into their ninth year, Rooney seems indestructible.

With him, there's always been another show and, apparently, another race.

"Skidoo," Rooney is telling you, "is scheduled to run Saturday at Hollywood Park. Good horse. He's 3. Ran him at Santa Anita this year. Paid $28 to win."

Over the years, the joke was Rooney, who has been to the wedding post eight times, was a victim of fast women and slow horses.

"I like to say I started out losing $2 and spent $2 million trying to get it back. But I josh. I was never a plunger at the racetrack. And I never spent big money on fashionably bred horses."

At the moment, Rooney owns 15, six of them in training, running under the banner of North Ranch Stables.

It was Louis B. Mayer, the czar of MGM in the glamour days of the studio, who got Rooney going.

"He promised me a Kentucky-bred foal," said Rooney. "The worst thing about it was the wait, about a year and a half."

When it arrived, Rooney named it Inintime. Johnny Longden rode the colt in his 2-year-old debut at Hollywood Park.

Because he was riding for the Hollywood cameras, Rooney was far better known than one of the winningest jockeys of all time.

In '37, Rooney was playing a crooked jockey in "Thoroughbreds Don't Cry," which happened to be his first film with Judy Garland.

226 • THE BEST OF PETER FINNEY, LEGENDARY NEW ORLEANS SPORTSWRITER

A year later, in the tear-jerker "Stablemates," he was riding for a trainer played by Wallace Berry.

Six years later, he's a trainer, watching Elizabeth Taylor win the Grand National in "National Velvet."

"I'm guessing I made about 10 movies involving horse racing," said Rooney. "I gotta laugh. In the early '30s, there was one called 'The Information Kid.' Maureen O'Sullivan was 19, I guess. Tom Brown played a jockey, and he must've weighed 145 pounds."

The diminutive Rooney fit the jockey mold perfectly. In the late '30s, at 114 pounds, he was climbing aboard such Santa Anita Handicap winners as Kayak II and Seabiscuit for morning gallops.

"In those days, you didn't need a license to do that. I've always admired jockeys. I remember Willie Shoemaker when he first came up. He probably rode 25 winners for me. Talk about a survivor. Then you look at someone like Laffit Pincay. He's got the strength of nine men 7 feet tall."

Sort of like Mickey Rooney.

Next month he's off to Vancouver to film the "The Black Stallion." Twenty shows there, then off to France for eight more. Next year, there are 52 "Stallion" episodes in the planning stage for cable TV.

"You can say I've spent a lot of time around horses," this from someone whose movie credits include "Francis in the Haunted House," the story on the talking mule.

Down the line, for a possible closer, Rooney would like to write a handicapping book for which he already has a title.

"I'm going to call it 'Systems.' I tried most of 'em. Some of them worked sometimes."

When you ask him if his eighth marriage, now going on 16 years, is for keeps, he asks a question: "What's for keeps? That's like asking, 'Are you going to live to be 95?'"

Don't bet against Rooney making it. Come September, he'll only have 25 years to go. For him, that's like a six-furlong sprint.

CHAPTER 8

THE OLYMPICS

Summer of '36, 36 Years Later

March 25, 1972

A few months before the 1972 Olympics in Munich, Jesse Owens stopped by the *States-Item* to promote a documentary film, *The Black Athlete,* for Teacher's Scotch. We got so absorbed in our conversation that he lost track of time.

"Man, I've got to get to the airport or I'm going to miss my plane," Jesse told me.

"No problem, I'll drive you," I told him.

On the way to Moisant, Jesse reflected on his four gold medals in the 1936 Berlin Olympics, which rebutted Hitler's argument regarding the superiority of the Aryan race.

As I dropped off Jesse at the airport, he reached into his bag and handed me a bottle of scotch. Jim Mora never did that.

One sober postscript: Jesse talked glowingly about the ability of the Olympics to spread global sunshine. Instead, dark evil was unleashed in Munich. A Palestinian terrorist group called Black September took 11 Israeli athletes hostage and killed them all.

• • •

Go back 36 years, to the summer of 1936, and you had an Olympics called "the most ominous pagan spectacle of modern times," the Adolf

Hitler invitational, a track meet held to the echoes of the goose-step and under clouds darkened by threats of a worldwide conflict.

At the time, the propaganda arm of the Nazi party was beating the drums for Aryan supremacy. In June of '36, it got a boost from the right hand of Max Schmeling, who chilled a heavyweight pretender from Lafayette, Ala., in 12 rounds.

While Joe Louis, son of a cotton field laborer, nursed his bruised pride until his day of vengeance in 1938, along came another Alabama native, son of a sharecropper—from the city of Danville—who, like Louis, had migrated North.

In six days, in one of the most remarkable feats in Olympic history, Jesse Owens left the swastika at half-mast, evoking shouts of "Yes-sa Ov-ens" from the German fans in flag-bedecked Berlin, who set aside ideological differences to applaud athletic brilliance.

All the while, Hitler watched coldly.

When the Star-Spangled Banner was played, he looked the other way; when Jesse won his fourth gold medal, he left the stadium.

What did Owens think of Hitler's snub? Was he swept up by the one-on-one talk of the time—Fascism vs. Democracy, Germany vs. the World, White vs. Black, Adolf vs. Jesse?

"Man, I had no time to think about Hitler," Jesse was saying yesterday. "I was too worried about those cats out there on the track. I didn't give politics one thought. With me, it was the start, the body lean, the knee action. I was so worried over what I had to do, my weight went from 163 to 149 in six days. To me, Hitler was just a name."

Today Jesse Owens is still a name. The years have been kind to the man voted "the greatest track athlete of the half century (1900–1950). He is 59 ("and holding," says Jesse), with thinning hair and an eager look, and only about 30 pounds over his running and jumping weight.

Owens is in town for Teacher's Scotch, which has put together a 38-minute documentary—*The Black Athlete*—that will be premiered tonight at the Rivergate.

"It's not preachy," says Jesse. "It simply tries to tell the contributions the black athlete has made, all the way from Jack Johnson to Joe Frazier."

Jesse is looking forward to the '72 games at Munich, where he will be honored during the opening-day ceremonies.

"I think we're getting away from the country vs. country idea and drifting more toward man vs. man. This is good. It's what sports is all about. Not black vs. white or white vs. yellow. But man vs. man.

"What we're doing is getting back to Greece, to the B.C. days. Competition is getting keener and keener. You have small countries with outstanding athletes.

"As I see it, this should help eliminate some of the political overtones. Athletics belongs to the young. At Munich, you'll have 12,000 athletes living together, and out of this will come friendships that will endure."

It's a tribute to Owen's formidable talents that his feats endured longer than most.

More remarkable than what happened in Berlin was what took place in Ann Arbor, Mich., in 1935. Only a sophomore at Ohio State, Jesse Owens wasn't sure he'd be competing in the first Big Ten meet of the season.

He had a job running an elevator from four till midnight to pay his way through school. He lived in a fraternity house that had the usual share of short-sheeting and water fights.

It was a water fight that sent Owens down a flight of stairs a week before the meet in Ann Arbor.

"Two days after I fell, my back stiffened on me," says Jesse. "So the heating pad and the red pepper rub became a routine. The day of the meet, I couldn't even warm up my back hurt so bad. Coach wanted to scratch me in the 100. But I figured I'd give it a shot."

What happened next was triumph of mind over matter.

At 3:15, Jesse ran 9.4 to equal the world record of Frank Wycoff in the 100. At 3:25, he took his first and only broad jump of the day, leaping to a new world record of 26-8¼. At 3:35, he was knocking three-tenths of a second off the 220 world mark, running it in 20.3. And at 4 o'clock, he was skipping over the 220-yard low hurdles in 22.6, four-tenths better than the world record set 11 years earlier.

So what you had was a sophomore with an aching back breaking three world records and tying another in 45 minutes, setting a record in the broad jump that would endure for 25 years.

"After it was over," says Jesse, "and the adrenalin stopped pumping, the pain in the back returned. I remember driving back to Cleveland in the backseat of a sportswriter's car. That night I had to sleep on a board.

Later, I found out I had a disc problem that wasn't really corrected until back surgery about six years ago."

Out of Ann Arbor and Berlin, Jesse Owens became an idol to thousands of his race. "You know," he said, "I had an idol too. When I was 13, Charley Paddock came by my school to give a talk. He was called 'the world's fastest human.' From that time on, I wanted to be just like him. I began right there thinking of the Olympics."

Jesse refuses to become pessimistic over today's society. "All we need to do is return to some of the things in the Bible," he says. "To realize what a privilege it is to be living on God's earth.

"As long as people walk and talk together, you'll be narrowing the gap of misunderstanding. You can't expect a perfect world. But you can expect a better one. What athletics does is let in a little bit of sunshine."

Angolan Team Just Happy to Be in Olympics
July 25, 1992

One of my favorite sports moments took place in 1992 at the Barcelona Olympics. Chastened by the failure of a team of U.S. collegians to win the basketball gold medal at the 1988 Olympics in Seoul, the U.S. Olympic Committee set out to assemble "the greatest collection of basketball talent on the planet"—forever known as "The Dream Team."

With an All-Star NBA roster that included Michael Jordan, Magic Johnson, Larry Bird, Patrick Ewing, Charles Barkley, Chris Mullin, David Robinson, and John Stockton, U.S. coach Chuck Daly—the head coach of the Detroit Pistons—made and kept one vow.

He never called a single time-out in eight games, which the U.S. won by an average of 44 points.

The Dream Team's Olympic debut came against Angola.

Barkley had been conspicuously passed over by Indiana coach Bob Knight for the 1984 Olympic team even though he was the most dominant player in practice sessions. He had waited for this moment for a long time, and he summed up succinctly the fate awaiting Angola.

"I don't know anything about Angola," Barkley said, "but Angola's in trouble."

They were. The U.S. outscored Angola 46–1 in one stretch, with the only point coming on a free throw after Barkley was called for flagrantly throwing an elbow. The U.S. won 116–48.

• • •

BARCELONA, Spain—Sunday's game plan is no secret.

Actually, as the coach of Angola's Olympic basketball team broke it down, it's quite simple: "Press on the ball," Victorino Cunha said. "Overplay the passing lanes. Fly to the rebound."

Most of the 10 million citizens in a country on the west coast of Africa will be watching Sunday, huddled around TVs in homes, barrooms and shops, as their heroes go to war against America's Dream Team in a first-round game.

Cunha, a short, bearded, bowlegged fellow, will be watching from the bench. Expecting, maybe, the biggest upset of all time?

"No, no," Cunha excitedly said. "I'm not crazy coach. It's impossible for us to win. We have no chance. Our goal is to keep the score (margin) below 45 points.

"We have no pressure, because we know we're going to lose. We are a small team—our tallest man is 6-foot-7—but we will play hard. You'll see."

Cunha's champions of Africa had just completed a two-hour session in the Olympic basketball arena, an hour on the main court, where he worked his ragtag outfit two-on-two and three-on-three, followed by a one-hour scrimmage on a practice court.

He surprised his audience by announcing his team would not be falling back into a zone against what he said "was the best team since the game was invented in 1891."

"Zone?" Cunha said incredulously. "No, no. Never, never Angolan team play zone. Never, never, never."

He pointed to 6-2 Paulo Mercado, who was wearing a maroon top. "He will take Michael Jordan," Cunha said. Then to 6-6 Jose Guimaraes, dressed in white. "He will play Magic Johnson."

Did Cunha think Mercado, who makes about $30,000 a year playing in Europe professionally, could handle Jordan? Cunha smiled.

"You're asking that when no one in the NBA can guard him?"

Angola's best player was not at Thursday's practice. Jean-Jacques Conceicao was at Olympic stadium practicing for today's opening ceremonies.

"Jean-Jacques will carry the Angola flag," Cunha said. It figures to be an easier job than what he'll be asked to do Sunday: guard Patrick Ewing. But what is basketball anyway?

Nothing more than a toy store, especially for men who watched their country destroyed in a civil war (to win independence from Portugal) that began in 1975 and didn't end until last year.

Conceicao lost a brother and an uncle.

"The war devastated our country," Cunha declared. "We lost schools, hospitals, everything. Gunfire and bombs make you forget all about sports."

When it comes to basketball, Cunha spoke with obvious pride of Angola's long road back. Angola has won the African championship two of the last three years.

"Portugal used to beat us 40 points," he said. "Now we beat them."

When his team won its way into the Olympics, it returned home, to the Angolan capital of Luanda, for a victory parade.

"The parade took five hours," Cunha said. "A half-million people came out to see us."

While half of Angola's 12-man team earns between $30,000 and $80,000 playing professionally, the other half holds down jobs. Some drive trucks. Some work in civil service. One is an electronics engineer. None makes more than $5,000.

As the Dream Team relaxes in hotel suites costing up to $500 a day, Cunha's players are happy to be in the Olympic Village, looking for ways to spend their pocket money.

In Barcelona, their $20 per diem does not go a long way. It is the memories that make them rich.

"We had a great time touring the U.S.," said Cunha of a recent visit. "We won five games, lost four, and we made enough money to buy new basketball shoes and a 30-second clock. Now we get to play against a great NBA team."

A nice way to live a fantasy, Jose Guimaraes said.

"Before we play," said Guimaraes, "let's take many, many pictures. When I am 60, I put on my tape. I see this is me. I played against these guys, the best in the world. I am happy."

CHAPTER 9

LAGNIAPPE

"Just Call Me Gorgeous"
September 7, 1960

Before Hulk Hogan, The Undertaker, Stone Cold Steve Austin, and Ric Flair, there was "Gorgeous George" Wagner, the Arnold Palmer of pro wrestling.

I forget who set me up with Gorgeous in 1961, but I do remember walking away from the interview with a story that simply wrote itself.

Sometimes, if you're very lucky, that happens, and usually it's because the person tells a story in such a compelling way that all you have to do is pay attention and write it down.

Gorgeous may have perfumed his body with a variation of Chanel No. 5, but in the gimmick department, he was No. 1.

• • •

"You'll have to excuse my appearance," said the fellow whose well-scarred dome was flanked by two cauliflower ears and topped with wavy, white locks. "Today is Sunday and all the beauty parlors are closed."

I had caught Gorgeous George with his hair down.

Rather than express outrage at such misfortune (Gorgeous also needed a manicure and his orchid shirt was a bit rumpled), he was all charm and candor.

In the course of an hour, you learned that the man who a decade ago built wrestling into a $36-million-a-year bonanza was part showman, businessman, historian and athlete.

Showmanship definitely takes preference.

The act he stages tomorrow night at the Municipal Auditorium blends cleanliness and color and, because it coincided with the advent of television, it launched the wrestling boom.

It begins when his valet, in cutaway, striped pants and derby, enters the ring carrying a silver tray on which rests a huge spray gun. A bath mat is draped around his arm.

After he sprays the ring, ropes and neighboring areas, George ("just call me Gorgeous") enters in a robe that stretches from his neck to the floor. His hair is in ringlets. As he walks, he inspects his manicure and sometimes tosses a golden bobby pin into an audience that is a mixture of cheers and catcalls.

The match begins, and always Gorgeous' curls become involved. The result is of no particular significance: sometimes he loses, most of the time he wins.

"Are all wrestling matches fixed?" I wanted to know.

"Well, you'd just as soon ask me if I beat my wife or lie on my income tax return," said Gorgeous.

"We're all entertainers, but don't you believe all the boys making top money can't wrestle. They've got scars to prove it. You look them over closely. I say they're athletes."

Financially, the top attractions are in the class with people like Williams, Musial, Mantle and Mays.

"I'll put it to you this way," says Gorgeous. "If I could have made the money I made and paid taxes like they used to back in the '30s, I'd be a multi-millionaire."

Wrestling revenue has bought Gorgeous a turkey ranch and three homes (all painted orchid) in California.

"I've been on all kinds of TV shows and I'm the only wrestler ever featured in a movie—*Alias The Champ*. The next project is a book on my life."

Gorgeous makes like a historian when he explains he is not the first long-haired wrestler to wander on the scene.

"We had four presidents—Washington, Lincoln, Buchanan and Teddy Roosevelt—who were wrestlers. Lincoln was a pro. He wrestled a guy named Jim Anderson here in New Orleans for $10. At least that's what Robert Reep says in his book, *Lincoln at New Salem*. Check me on it."

It was Washington's picture on the dollar bill that started Gorgeous on his curly locks trail.

It took the 43-year-old, 210-pound native of Seward, Neb., a long time, however, before he could make his buffoonery pay dividends.

He quit school at an early age and took odd jobs—packing strawberries, grinding oil well bits, repairing typewriters and chopping cotton.

He left home at 19, to wrestle for peanuts.

"Your hands were your breadwinners," he said. "Many a night I'd lay in a cheap hotel, hungry and broke, wishing I were home."

His rise began in 1941 in Eugene, Ore., when he decided to get a pair of royal blue trunks with sequins and a $250 robe purchased with his winnings. Both were startling departures from the customary sweat-stained garb of the day.

Some fans grabbed his neatly folded robe off his chair and tossed it all around the auditorium. By the time he got it back, it was in shreds, Gorgeous was so mad he challenged the whole house.

The fans raised a rumpus and suddenly George was in demand. It was at Eugene, too, that George heard a lady fan remark: "My, isn't he gorgeous?"

A bell rang—George Wagner had a first name.

The spray gun gimmick first appeared in Columbus, Ohio, because a doctor warned Gorgeous about a severe mat burn on his knee.

"It got so much attention when we were doing it merely to disinfect the ring as a safety measure that we decided to dress it up," George said. "Hence the valet."

Next step came one day in Honolulu when Gorgeous, bothered by his long hair getting in his eyes, decided to get a permanent. Three hundred people soon gathered outside the salon, and that night he was a sensation.

"Every 10 days," he says, "I need a touch-up job. I'm in every day for a wave, and that's $6 or $7 a crack, so I've got my overhead. Funny, huh?"

George the athlete, who idolizes Strangler Lewis, says he has mastered 90 holds—his favorite being the flying mare. In this one, he'll get a headlock, twist his legs and then jump in the air while spinning. This jerks his opponent off the ground—he falls—and Gorgeous falls on top.

It isn't always that simple. One night, Leo Nomellini, the former all-American tackle, threw a flying tackle at Gorgeous and rendered him unconscious.

"They carried me from the ring on a stretcher and, as I was moving through the crowd, all those irate husbands started kicking me—they're my biggest enemies."

Few are faster on the gimmick-uptake than Gorgeous. Awhile back he was a guest on the Jack Paar show and swore Paar into his fan club, making the comedian promise he would never mistake a "Georgie pin" for a common bobby pin.

The next night Paar walked off the show and headed for Hong Kong.

"Was it your perfume that drove him to the Orient?"

"No, never," he replied. "I use Chanel No. 10, you know. Why be half safe?"

Mental Violence in Iceland
July 12, 1972

Before the Civil War—long before there was a Bobby Fischer or a Boris Spassky—there was Paul Morphy of New Orleans.

The son of a Louisiana Supreme Court justice, Morphy learned chess as a child by watching his father and uncle play. By age 9, he was considered a prodigy. Three years later, he defeated a visiting Hungarian master.

Morphy was just 20 when he earned his law degree—he had the ability to recite the Civil Code of Louisiana by heart—but he still was too young to practice law. He traveled to New York and later to Europe in 1857, vanquishing all comers, and was acclaimed the greatest player in the world.

At 21, Morphy retired from competitive chess to concentrate on his law practice, but he struggled over the next two decades and was so haunted by delusions that his family tried to have him institutionalized. He died in his bathtub in 1884 at age 47.

• • •

You are reading words written by a fifth-rate Chinese checker player but one who cannot help but be fascinated by that Super Bowl of chess finally off the launching pad in Reykjavik, Iceland.

It's fascinating if only because of a comparison with that last man-to-man battle of sorts in New York—Joe Frazier vs. Muhammad Ali—a match in which physical violence was the idea.

As world champion Boris Spassky sits across those magical 64 squares from challenger Bobby Fischer in Iceland, the idea is to inflict mental violence, and who's to say the loser will not be more permanently scarred than, for example, the Quarry brothers were the other day.

When Spassky, a 35-year-old Russian of Armenian descent, arrived in Iceland he was accompanied by an entourage that included two grandmasters, one international master—and a psychologist. The latter may be vital.

Fischer arrived later by himself, one reason being he's difficult to live with and impossible to fathom, as many geniuses are. Last year, in a match against a former world champion, the 29-year-old high school dropout put his opponent in the hospital from sheer mental exhaustion.

Brent Larsen, a grandmaster who doesn't hide his personal dislike for Brooklyn Bobby, calls Fischer "an arrogant young man who likes to see his opponents squirm." Once asked who he thought was the world's greatest player, Fischer replied: "It would be nice to be modest but it would be stupid if I did not tell the truth. I am."

So there you have one side of Bobby Fischer, 6-2, 185, whose build is not unlike some quarterbacks. While much has been made over the mental capacity of quarterbacks, how much they have to absorb, how many variations they are required to store away, alongside the mental file of folks like Fischer and Spassky, Joe Namath's most complicated game plan would look like something out of ding-dong school.

In the average game of chess, there are, count 'em, 1,000,000,000,000,000,000,000,000,000,000,000,000,000,000,000,000 possible moves. So it's no wonder Boris took a psychologist along, or why some feel Bobby Fischer is one pawn away from the head shrinker.

Fischer has walked out on tournaments before. He has complained of lighting—too bright, or not bright enough. One time, in South America for a match, he changed hotel rooms three times in three days. From Iceland came word that Bobby, owing to religious beliefs, did not want to engage in any tournament activity from sundown Friday to sundown Saturday. Problem is, in Iceland, the sun never goes down entirely. There was talk of calling in a rabbi (even though Fischer is not a practicing Jew) to determine the time of sundown. But Iceland has no rabbis.

And you think Duane Thomas was a problem?

Spassky had some hangups of his own. For one thing, he asked for a room temperature (the match will be played in an auditorium seating 3,000—at $5 per ticket) of 21 degrees centigrade (about 70 degrees Fahrenheit) while Fischer was demanding 24 degrees centigrade. As a way out, Boris suggested: "We could add 24 and 21 and divide by two."

There's no doubt Spassky has more at stake. In Russia, home of the world champion since the 1940s, chess is more than the national pastime. It's the national soul. If there's one irony to the current showdown, it's that Americans may hold a deeper admiration for the Russian (because of Fischer's behavior and demand for more money), the Russians a deeper admiration for the American.

Fischer is the most popular American in the Soviet Union since Van Cliburn, a popularity based on his aggressive game, his ability to get into an apparent jam and then pull out victory with Byzantine twists only Bobby foresees. Many Russians are impatient with the conservative play of many Soviet grandmasters.

Hereabouts the local chess colony anxiously awaits their own version of Ali-Frazier, Pirates-Orioles, Oklahoma-Nebraska, Cowboys-Dolphins.

"I look for Spassky to spar in the opening games, sort of like a boxer in the early rounds," says Clay Shaw, amateur chessman but one who follows the sport closely. "Fischer seems to be more of an attacker. Nothing can approach the mental strain of chess on this level. These two men have done a lot of meditating, they've walked lonely roads, shut themselves up like monks, to get into the proper frame of mind."

United States champion at age 14 and a grandmaster at 15, Fischer last visited New Orleans eight years ago where, at the YMCA, he took on 75 opponents simultaneously, winning 70 matches, losing three and drawing two.

His comments on Paul Morphy, an Orleanian who conquered the chess world in the mid-1800s, were generous. "In a set match," said Fischer, "Morphy could beat anyone alive today."

Of Boris Spassky, then a contender for the world title, Bobby said: "He can blunder away a piece and you are never sure whether it's a blunder or a fantastically deep sacrifice."

So now the battle of wits is underway with a $250,000 jackpot, plus TV and movie rights, up for grabs. If all 24 games are played (three a week), the brain-bubbling match could last two months.

Yesterday, before the match began, I was able to reach Fischer by ham radio for an exclusive interview. "I thought there was nothing more complicated than chess," said Bobby, "until I heard Walter Cronkite trying to explain the California delegate situation."

Your move, Boris.

L.A. Times' Murray Was a Great Journalist, Greater Man
August 19, 1998

Trying to be funny and incisive in print, five days a week, can lead to ulcers, but the *L. A. Times'* Jim Murray had the talent—the ultimate antidote—to pull it off. Reading Jim Murray could be joyful and painful at the same time.

The soaring pleasure came hidden in reading his sparse sentence structure, which typically allowed for a punchline that was delivered in exactly the right place with exactly the right image.

The pain came from wishing you had thought of it first.

Jim Murray was a brilliant, dignified, humble man.

I often think about what Jim's take might be on the current treadmill style of sports reporting, where writers are expected to tweet 50 times during a game and still try to cover it. They often are not even "there" because they are looking down at their laptops, tweeting out another 140 characters: "Anthony Davis just sneezed ... rubbed his nose ... more, later."

Would Twitter have detracted from Jim's mission of a good story well told? Let's just say, I'd take his tweets over your tweets, thumbs down.

Jim could have won the Pulitzer for best sentence, but Twitter would have banned him for trying to link too many good ones together.

• • •

To say Jim Murray was a better person than sports columnist is sort of amazing because, when it came to entertaining a reading audience, there was none better at the job than this gentle legend, none better at mixing wit and insight, humor and pathos, all the while, it seemed, with the roar of the crowd as background music.

Jim Murray was special, an awesome talent totally without ego, someone who squirmed in the face of praise, who overcame a life of tragedy—loss of one eye, near loss of another, loss of a wife to cancer, loss of a son to a drug overdose—and wrote, on and on, with unique brilliance, filing his final column on Saturday from Del Mar racetrack, the day before he died at his Los Angeles home at age 78.

Unless pressed for a story by a colleague, at a championship fight, in the barn area at Churchill Downs, at a Super Bowl or a World Series, you never heard Jim drop a name, when he could have talked of many things: the time Ronald Reagan showed up at a Jim Murray testimonial and did a 10-minute standup routine; the time Murray was covering a Texas-Arkansas football game and was being held against a fence as a suspicious character by a member of the Secret Service, this taking place as President Nixon walked by and said, "Hi, Jim"; the time he shared a cocktail with a dying Humphrey Bogart; the time he couldn't make an awards dinner and asked Bob Hope to sub for him; the time he escorted Marilyn Monroe to a Hollywood restaurant, and she asked if it would be OK if she left with a friend, Joe DiMaggio; the letters he received for columns in the Los Angeles Times, from the likes of Jack Benny, Bing Crosby and Groucho Marx.

Jim covered the Hollywood scene for Time magazine and was part of the original staff at Sports Illustrated, before moving to the L.A. Times in 1961, after which he began showing up on Public Enemy posters in the mayor's office of various cities. He would leave many Chambers of Commerce grumbling.

Cincinnati: They still haven't finished the freeway outside the ball park. It's Kentucky's turn to use the cement mixer.

St. Louis: The city had a bond issue recently, and the local papers campaigned for it on a slogan, "Progress or Decay." Decay won in a landslide.

Baltimore: A guy just standing on the corner with no place to go with rain dripping off his hat. Baltimore's a great place if you're a crab.

Detroit: Should be left on the doorstep for the Salvation Army.

Los Angeles: Underpoliced and oversexed.

If you knew Jim Murray, you knew it wasn't mean-spirited, it was all part of a 700-word laugh.

Jim told me once, "In this business, all you've got to do is keep fooling the reader."

He did it, day after day, with some Hall of Fame one-liners.

The Indy 500: "Gentlemen, start your coffins. It was the run for the lilies."

Jim said of Floyd Patterson, the much-knocked-down heavyweight: "He's been on more canvases than a Canadian sunset."

Of Merlin Olsen, defensive lineman of the L.A. Rams, he observed: "Went swimming in Loch Ness—and the monster got out."

His assessment of Conrad Dobler, who had a reputation as the dirtiest player in football: "To say Dobler plays football is like saying the Gestapo played 20 Questions."

When Casey Stengel died, Jim began his tribute: "Well, God is getting an earful today."

On the death of Dizzy Dean: "Dizzy Dean died the other day at the age of 11 or 12. The little boy in all of us died with him."

It was different, and touching, when his first wife died 14 years ago, after 38 years of marriage. On that sad day, Jim did something he rarely did. He got personal.

"She never told a lie in her life," he said of Geraldine. "And she didn't think anyone else did. Deceit puzzled her. Dishonesty dismayed her. She thought people were good. Around her, surprisingly, they were."

When he won a long-overdue Pulitzer Prize in 1990, he remained in character. "I always thought Pulitzers were for overturning a government or exposing a stock market scandal, not for correctly quoting Tommy Lasorda."

I last talked to Jim in January during Super Bowl week. We talked of Clark Shaughnessy, inventor of the modern T-formation, and why he should be in the NFL Hall of Fame. Murray was chipper. He had covered every Super Bowl except one, number XIV in Miami, the time he went blind on Saturday and spent Super Bowl Sunday undergoing a five-hour operation for a detached retina, the start of his troubles. He was enjoying the San Diego weather, enjoying seeing old friends, even if it had to be with one blue eye.

For anyone inquiring about sports columnizing, and there were always some, his advice was the same: Just keep fooling your readers.

Jim Murray was quite a guy.

INDEX